WRITING WOMEN IN KOREA

Writing Women in Korea

Translation and Feminism
in the Colonial Period

Theresa Hyun

University of Hawai'i Press | Honolulu

09 08 07 06 05 04   6 5 4 3 2 1

Library of Congress Cataloging-in-Publication Data

Hyun, Theresa.

Writing women in Korea: translation and feminism in
the colonial period / Theresa Hyun.

   p. cm.

Includes bibliographical references and index.

ISBN 0-8248-2677-9

1. Women translators—Korea—History.

2. Translating and interpreting—Korea.   3. Korean
language—Translating.   4. Korean literature—
Women authors—History and criticism.   I. Title.

P306.8.K6 H98 2003

418'.02'08209519—dc21   2003009995

University of Hawai'i Press books are printed on acid-
free paper and meet the guidelines for permanence
and durability of the Council on Library Resources.

Designed by April Leidig-Higgins

Printed by The Maple-Vail Book Manufacturing Group

To my parents, John and Katherine Margadonna,

and my husband, Professor Chong-Min Hyun

contents

This book has come out of research projects on translation and cultural change in Korea in which I have been engaged since the mid-1980s. I began with an examination of the correlations of translations of foreign literary works and cultural changes in Korea in the late nineteenth and early twentieth centuries. These explorations were further pursued in several international conferences where scholars discussed translation as an aspect of cultural change in various contexts.[1] I came to realize that one of the most fruitful approaches is to consider the links between translation and writing by and for women as an indication of more general cultural changes. Korea provides us with a particularly cogent case study since during both the Chosŏn period and the early twentieth century translation offers a key to understanding shifts in gender and class relations.

The findings of this book have implications that can prove useful for collaborative research projects. I have chosen to focus on the period from the turn of the twentieth century to the late 1930s, when Korea was under Japanese colonial domination. One of the salient features of Korea's recent history is the fact that Koreans began to develop a national consciousness at the moment when their sovereignty was being threatened by foreign powers. The predicament of the colonized country that had to adapt to the culture of the colonizer while at the same time maintaining its own traditions was repeated in many places during the nineteenth and early twentieth centuries.² In many such cases translations played an essential role in encouraging women to become modernized without deserting their place at the center of traditional family life.

I would like to acknowledge the grants given by the Daesan Foundation and the Faculty of Arts of York University that enabled me to begin the research for this book. I would not have been able to write this book without the advice and guidance of a number of Korean scholars, including Yi Hye-Sun, Cho Dong-Il, Shim Jae-Ryong, Sŏ Jŏng-Ja, Chŏng Ha-Yŏng, Kim Yu-Sŏn, Kim Mi-Hyŏn, Ch'oe Hye-Sil, Song Yŏng-Sun, and Lee Bann. Yoon Ho-Byeong and Kim Soon-Sik gave generously of their time in reading the manuscript. Kim Jae-Hong has helped me to understand the richness of modern Korean poetry. My colleagues at York University, Doug Freake and Gisela Argyle, provided useful suggestions and much needed encouragement. I owe a great deal to the Ewha Archives and the Ewha Museum for allowing me to gather materials and obtain photographs. My thanks go to Patricia Crosby and Ann Ludeman for their excellent editorial advice and to Bojana Ristich for her superb copyediting. Finally, Park Ae-Ran, Kim Hye-Kyŏng, Lisa Wood, Christina Sanchez-Soto, and Jaspreet Gill have all demonstrated patience and efficiency in preparing the manuscript.

introduction

This book focuses on the correlations between translation of foreign works into Korean from the early 1900s to the late 1930s and new forms of writing by and about women. The central thesis underlying this research is that at certain times in Korea, when there have been both changes in writing systems and increases in translation activities, there have also been corresponding changes in representations of women in the written works of the period, and these new representations have political and social implications. In order to explore the connections among translation, new forms of writing, and the new representations of women, the study examines the following types of materials and translation activities: (1) shifts in the way translators handled material pertaining to women; (2) the work of women translators of the 1920s and 1930s; and (3) the relationship between translation and the original works of Korean women writers of the period.

The book is divided into chapters that consider phases and aspects of the process of creating feminine ideals through translation. Chapter 1 outlines the cultural background of the Chosŏn period (1392–1910), when a vernacular writing system was invented that made it possible to translate texts into Korean.[1] During the Chosŏn period the translation of Chinese writings aimed at the education of women reinforced the official ideals of feminine behavior that were considered essential for political and social stability. In Chapter 2 I examine legends about the lives of European heroines translated into Korean at the beginning of the twentieth century. These works presented new images of patriotic women that encouraged Korean women to support essentially male-centered goals. Chapter 3 considers the New Woman ideal, which related to educated women of the 1920s and 1930s, some of whom had studied overseas.

One of the important ways of fostering the New Woman ideal was through the translation of foreign literary works. I examine the newspapers and magazines of the 1920s and 1930s that published translations of the works of foreign women authors, as well as those of male authors, such as Ibsen, who presented a new image of emancipated women. Chapter 4 explores the role of women translators, such as Kim Myŏng-Sun, who began to be active in the 1920s. I consider the scope of their work and the constraints they faced as translators. Finally, Chapter 5 deals with new forms of writing by three Korean women writers—Kim Myŏng-Sun, Pak Hwa-Sŏng, and Mo Yun-Suk—whose work was closely related to new trends imported into Korea through translation. I argue that these women writers and translators deserve recognition for their contributions to Korea's emerging sense of itself as a modern and independent nation, as well as for their creation of new forms of writing.

This work has several aims: to emphasize the importance of women translators and writers in early twentieth-century Korea, to place Korean literary and cultural activities in the wider perspective of feminist and cross-cultural studies, and to contribute to an understanding of the central role of translation in creating new gender and national identities.

Scholars of Korean literature have written on the development of literary translation in the twentieth century.[2] In addition, women's studies scholars have begun to take an interest in the Korean women writers of the 1920s and 1930s.[3] However, to date very little has been written about the place of women translators in the Korean literary world. This study attempts to provide insight into the essential connection between the work of women translators and writers and literary/cultural developments in Korea in the 1920s and 1930s.

In recent years interest has been increasing in the connections between nationalist and feminist movements in many societies around the world. Lois West's collection, *Feminist Nationalism* (1997); Partha Chatterjee's *The Nation and Its Fragments: Colonial and Postcolonial Histories* (1993); and Kumari Jayawardena's *Feminism and Nationalism in the Third World* (1986) are but a few examples of a growing trend of studies that "examine how academic discourse constructs nationalism as a male enterprise, frequently unconsciously gendered, and how feminists are struggling to put women at the center of analysis."[4] Alice Yun Chai is one of the scholars who has commented on the role of modern education at the end of the nineteenth and beginning of the twentieth centuries in introducing women to literacy, as well as to ideas about freedom and democracy.[5]

The nationalist movement began to develop in Korea in the late nineteenth century, when Korean sovereignty was being threatened by foreign aggression. The struggle for independence continued during the period of Japanese colonial domination from 1910 to 1945.[6] As in many other colonized societies, the raising of the status of women in Korea was seen as an essential step toward modernization. Women were encouraged to become educated in order to contribute to national development, while at the same time fulfilling their traditional roles within the family. Women's political participation in early twentieth-century Korea grew out of the nationalist movement. The new voices of Korean women writers and translators give testimony to the struggles of a people.

However, conspicuously absent from these studies of nationalism is a consideration of the crucial importance of translation in bringing about the cultural confrontations necessary to change views about women and reorganize societies. Since the 1970s certain translation studies scholars have been developing "an approach to literary translation which is descriptive, target-oriented, functional, and systemic; and an interest in the norms and constraints that govern the production and reception of translations, in the relation between translation and other types of text processing, and in the place and role of translations both within a given literature and in the interaction between literatures."[7] Consideration has been given to the connections between gender issues and translation theory and practice by Sherry Simon and Luise von Flotow.[8] According to this approach, discussions of translation theory are complemented by examinations of specific corpuses of translations. Both the macro level of overall trends and the micro level of close readings of individual translations are required to develop the discipline of translation studies. Therefore this book considers the work of the Korean translators of the early twentieth century in the light of centuries of cultural change through translation.

I have found it extremely useful to organize my research on translation in Korea according to the principles of the so-called descriptive-explanatory school of translation studies. Considering translation as an essential part of the process of cultural change enables us to take account of a wide range of phenomena that occurred during the early twentieth century in Korea. For many centuries Korean literary activities were carried out on two levels:

"formal" culture, which was promoted through writing in Chinese, was mostly the province of upper-class males, while "informal" culture, which utilized writing in the vernacular script, was considered appropriate for the lower classes and women. During the Chosŏn period translation was pivotal in maintaining gender and class divisions, and in the early twentieth century Korean translators provided one of the keys to modernization. Thus Korea offers us a particularly interesting case for the study of translation as a force in changing gender and national identity.

This book attempts to come a step closer to providing answers to such far-reaching questions as the following: How have women translators contributed to literary and cultural change? How do writing on women and women's writing relate to changes in national identity? In the process I hope to provide insights into Korea's place on the map of world literatures and cultures.

chapter one

Cultural Background

In order to understand the significance of the upheavals that took place in Korea in the early twentieth century, it is necessary to have an overview of cultural traditions. This chapter focuses on those aspects of traditional culture that directly relate to the main concerns of this book—namely, the ways in which translations and representations of women in written works relate to social and political changes.

The term "writing system" is used in two principal ways in this book: on the one hand, it refers to scripts, and on the other, it covers styles of writing. Literary and cultural life in traditional Korea operated on two levels since the means that Koreans employed for written communication, Chinese writing, known as *hanmun* in Korean, differed significantly from their native tongue. In order to remedy the difficulties stemming from such a two-tiered linguistic system, the native phonetic script was invented in the fifteenth century. I refer to this script both by its original designation of *hunmin chŏngŭm* (correct sounds for instructing the people) and by its modern name, *han'gŭl*. However, the invention of the new script resulted in another split (as indicated in the introduction): *hanmun* became the exclusive province of the male-dominated ruling class, while *hunmin chŏngŭm* was considered appropriate for women and other marginalized groups who were denied access to training in *hanmun*. The vernacular script became a vehicle for translating materials aimed at educating women to fulfill their prescribed roles within a Neo-Confucian society, as well as the medium for most writing by women. In this chapter I explore the social and political implications of the connections between translations and writing by and for women in traditional Korea.

This chapter is divided into two main sections: the first deals with the traditional period up through the end of the Chosŏn dynasty (1392–1910), and the second treats the transitional period at the end of the nineteenth and beginning of the twentieth centuries. In each of these main sections I consider the development and usage of writing systems, translation, and representations of women in written texts.

Traditional Background

Writing Systems before the Invention of the Vernacular Script

Writing in *Hanmun*

Hanmun was the script employed in traditional Korea, and even after the invention of *hunmin chŏngŭm,* it remained the official form of writing for many centuries. There are no indications that there was an indigenous form of writing, and there is general agreement among scholars that *hanmun* was the earliest form of writing on the Korean peninsula.[1] *Hanmun* refers to the system of writing of the Han Chinese; although we cannot be sure of the exact date, there is some evidence that it was first used on the Korean peninsula during the first century B.C.E.[2] In 109 B.C.E. Han China established four commanderies on the Korean peninsula, and certain segments of the population were exposed to the usage of Chinese characters. Among the oldest records in *hanmun* are stone monuments, such as the one commemorating Kwanggaet'o, a Koguryŏ (37 B.C.E.–668 C.E.) king of the late fourth and early fifth centuries. These monuments give an indication of the high degree of proficiency that had been reached in the use of *hanmun*.[3]

Various documents from the fourth through the sixth centuries testify to the development of *hanmun* on the Korean peninsula. There is evidence that even in the late third century people from the kingdom of Paekche (18 B.C.E.–660 C.E.) were transmitting documents in *hanmun* to Japan.[4] After the official recognition of Buddhism in Koguryŏ in 372 C.E., Buddhist scriptures in Chinese translation began to be imported, and their interpretation required a deep knowledge of *hanmun*. Historical records from late fourth-century Paekche and sixth-century Silla (57 B.C.E.–935 C.E.) give evidence that *hanmun* was taking root. Therefore by the time the Unified Silla period began in the seventh century, the usage of *hanmun* was already well established. In Unified Silla the importation of Confucian texts increased, and by the mid-eighth century place names and official government positions were designated in Chinese characters. In the Koryŏ period (918–1392) Chinese culture and writing became an important part of everyday life.[5]

Methods of Modifying *Hanmun*

Before the invention of *hunmin chŏngŭm* there were two basic modes of writing on the Korean peninsula: (1) pure *hanmun,* and (2) systems of modifying *hanmun* to suit the requirements of the Korean language—for example, *kugyŏl, hyangch'al,* and *idu.* Chinese is referred to as a positional language in which words stand independently, and their grammatical function relates to their position in the sentence. In contrast, Korean is an agglutinative language in which grammatical function is manifested by suffixes.[6] Therefore *hanmun* does not fit the structure of Korean, and attempts were made to overcome this gap.

Kugyŏl was a system of reading Chinese texts that used Chinese characters in fixed ways to express Korean grammatical functions. It was mostly used as a system of textual explication. *Hyangch'al* used certain Chinese characters for their sound and others for their meaning to come as close as possible to Korean usage. *Hyangga* were Silla poems that used this system. Although this was an effective system for adapting Chinese characters to Korean usage, it had fallen into disuse by mid-Koryŏ, when *hanmun* culture was becoming stronger. *Idu,* which used certain Chinese characters to express syntactical relations, was employed mostly in official documents.[7]

Literary Images of Women before the Invention of the Vernacular Script

Literary images of women before the invention of *hunmin chŏngŭm* varied greatly according to such factors as time period, location, and genre. In this subsection I briefly consider a few of the important themes that appeared before the Chosŏn period. This concise review is not intended to present a comprehensive survey but rather to indicate some of the feminine images that tended to reappear in later eras.[8] I focus on four main themes: the self-sacrificing daughter, the faithful wife, the fervent believer, and the devoted lover.

Many scholars believe that the oldest songs on the Korean peninsula were shamanist chants.[9] Although these belong to the domain of orally transmitted songs, they present basic themes that were transformed throughout the ages. From ancient times women acted as shamans and mediums and took part in ritual chants and dances. Many of the shamanist narrative songs (*sŏsa muga*) center around the themes of female sacrifice and suffering. One good example is *Princess Pari (Pari kongju),* with the following plot: a couple with seven daughters abandons the youngest; the parents become sick and can be cured only by a rare medicine; the other daughters refuse to search for the medicine; the abandoned daughter undergoes various trials and obtains the medicine; she is welcomed back into the family as a result of her virtuous actions. The daughter's willingness to sacrifice herself for her parents stems from her filial devotion. Korean literature continued to develop the image of women who were fearless in the face of death because of their spirit of self-sacrifice. The filial daughter who undergoes great hardships for the sake of her parents is a recurring motif in Korean literature and can be seen in late Chosŏn works like *The Tale of Sim Ch'ŏng (Sim Ch'ŏng chŏn).*[10]

Chinese poems *(hansi)* were written on the Korean peninsula before the Unified Silla period, and some present distinctive feminine images. "My Love, Do Not Cross the Water" ("Kongmudoha ka"), which some scholars think dates from the first century B.C.E., is the lament of a woman whose husband has drowned in a river. Overcome by grief, she drowns herself in an attempt to follow him since she cannot go on living in a meaningless world without her beloved. This poem illustrates the sanctity of the marriage bond, which was of primary importance for women throughout the traditional period. The self-sacrificing woman of the shamanist songs takes on religious significance in some of the Silla *hyangga*. "Prayer for Rebirth in Paradise" ("Wŏnwangsaeng ka"), a late seventh-century work, is related to the legend of two friends, Ŏmjang and Kwangdŏk, who make a pact that whoever leaves the world first should come back to inform the other. Kwangdŏk marries and lives with his wife as a devoted Buddhist, while Ŏmjang works as a farmer. When Ŏmjang hears Kwangdŏk's voice outside his window telling him that he has already departed this world, Ŏmjang goes immediately to Kwangdŏk's house, where they are holding the funeral. He arranges to live with Kwangdŏk's wife, but she refuses to sleep with him, explaining that in ten years of marriage she never had intimate relations with Kwangdŏk. Through her virtuous conduct the wife enables both men to be reborn in paradise. In "Hymn to the Thousand-Eyed Goddess" ("Do ch'ŏnsudaebi ka"), a mid-eighth-century work, a mother implores the goddess to restore sight to her blind child. As Buddhist culture was assimilated in Silla, shamanist images of women were blended with the ideal of the supplicant who prays for the welfare of her family.[11]

Although Buddhism continued to take root in Koryŏ, there were many other complex factors affecting literary production at this time. Foreign invasions, military insurrections, and despotic governments created chaotic conditions and resulted in the separation of many families. During the period of the Mongol invasions in the thirteenth century, many women were sent to the Yuan court as tribute, and therefore many songs and poems dealt with separation and longing for loved ones. Koryŏ produced many sexually explicit songs that were expurgated by the stern Neo-Confucianists of early Chosŏn. "The Turkish Bakery" ("Ssanghwa chŏm") hints of erotic adventures in the context of social corruption, and "Will You Go?" ("Kasiri") conveys both the sorrow of parting and the endurance of love in separation. Many Koryŏ songs focus on pessimistic themes such as the pain of women who have been abandoned by their lovers.[12]

Vernacular Writing, Translation, and Images of Women in the Chosŏn Period

Invention of the Vernacular Script and Writing Systems

Hunmin chŏngŭm was invented during the reign of King Sejong, who directed a group of scholars from the Royal Research Institute (Chiphyŏnchŏn) to devise a writing system in accord with the spoken language. The first literary work to employ the new alphabet was *Songs of Flying Dragons (Yongbi ŏch'ŏn ka)* (1445), which celebrated the founding of the Chosŏn dynasty. When *hunmin chŏngŭm* was officially promulgated in 1446, Sejong stated in his preface to the explication of the alphabet that Chinese characters were difficult to learn and most of the common people could not express themselves in writing; therefore: "Thinking of these, my people, with compassion, We have newly devised a script of twenty-eight letters, only that it become possible for anyone to readily learn it and use it to advantage in his everyday life."[13] In spite of the objections of certain members of the scholarly elite to the new script, it provided a medium for the translation of Buddhist scriptures and Chinese texts, and therefore new avenues of obtaining knowledge were opened for women and other groups who had been excluded from education in the Chinese classics.[14] After the invention of *hun-*

min chŏngŭm, writing systems were aligned according to the gender and class divisions of Chosŏn society: the vernacular script was mostly used by the lower classes and women, while *hanmun* was mostly used by upper-class men and served as one of the means by which they maintained their hold on power. In this subsection I consider, first, the uses of *hunmin chŏngŭm* for translating Buddhist scriptures, Chinese classics, and Chinese fictional narratives, and, second, the development of *hanmun* in Chosŏn. Uses of the vernacular script by women for correspondence, personal narratives, and literary works will be treated in the subsection on women writers and representations of women.

Annotation style *(ŏnhaech'e),* one of the most important vernacular writing styles in Chosŏn, was a way of translating Chinese texts using vernacular explanations.[15] The distinction between Chinese writing and vernacular writing reflects *sadae chuŭi,* the attitude of reverence that Chosŏn aristocrats held for Chinese culture.[16] In order to understand the concepts underlying the annotation *(ŏnhae)* process, we need to consider the reasons for the invention of *hunmin chŏngŭm.* Since the upper classes claimed a monopoly on the use of Chinese writing as one of their distinguishing features, it was not in their interest to promote a script that could be used by both upper and lower classes. When Sejong promulgated the vernacular script, he started a project to teach proper pronunciation of Chinese characters.[17] Thus it would seem that in addition to his stated aim of providing a means of expression for the common people, Sejong intended the new script as an aid to correct pronunciation of Chinese characters for members of the upper classes. When a text was processed according to the *ŏnhae* principles, extreme care was exerted to follow the source as closely and literally as possible.

The first text to be translated in this way was the introductory explanation to the *hunmin chŏngŭm* itself. When the new alphabet was promulgated in 1446, an explanation of its usage appeared in *hanmun,* along with *Ŏnhae hunmin chŏngŭm,* a vernacular annotation of the explanation.[18] When Queen Sohŏn died in 1446, a text on the life of Sakyamuni, *Sŏkkabo,* was prepared in *hanmun* as an offering for the repose of her soul, and an *ŏnhae* version, *A Detailed Life of Sakyamuni (Sŏkbo sangjŏl),* appeared in 1447.[19] Sejong died four years after the promulgation of *hunmin chŏngŭm,* and his work was continued by his successor, King Seijo, who promoted the translation of Buddhist scriptures. Kankyŏngdokam, the government translation bureau established in 1457, produced many translations of Buddhist scriptures that contributed to the spread of *hunmin chŏngŭm* and constitute an important source of information for research on the development of vernacular writing.[20] The correlation of the translation of Buddhist scriptures and the development of writing systems has ancient roots. Buddhist scriptures, originally written in Sanskrit or Pali, were translated into Chinese when the religion spread to China and contributed to the expression of abstract concepts in Chinese. In turn, the translation of the Chinese versions of Buddhist scriptures into *hunmin chŏngŭm* expanded the Korean philosophical vocabulary. However, when Buddhist scriptures were first being translated into Korean, Buddhism had already been somewhat discredited by the early Chosŏn Neo-Confucianists, thus limiting the effectiveness of the translations.

After the Kankyŏngdokam was closed in 1471, the focus of translation activities shifted from Buddhist scriptures to Chinese classics and various other texts, including those dealing with literature and medicine. Here I consider the translation of Chinese classics and literary works; I treat the translation of educational texts aimed at women in the section on educational texts, women, and translation activities. From the late fifteenth to the late sixteenth centuries translation activities focused on Chinese classics, works dealing with Neo-Confucian ethics, literary works, and texts on medicine and agriculture.[21] The works of the Tang poet Tu Fu (712–770) were widely read in the original during the Koryŏ period, and the early Chosŏn scholar elite took an interest in his works as representations of ethical principles. The *ŏnhae* version of Tu Fu's works, which appeared in 1481, was a very literal rendering that did not follow Korean syntactical order.[22] The fact that another translation of Tu Fu's works appeared in 1632 indicates the continuing interest that Chosŏn scholars had in the Tang poet. Translation norms of the time are illustrated by versions of *Lesser Learning* (K. *Sohak;* Ch. *Xyaoxue*), a collection of moral lessons that were originally compiled by disciples of the Song dynasty scholar, Chu Hsi (1130–1200). The first *ŏnhae* version of 1517 was considered too free, and therefore another version appeared in 1586 that followed the source text more closely.[23] A project to translate the Chinese classics, involving many scholars, began in the late fifteenth century and continued until the late sixteenth century. The early Chosŏn kings aimed to create an ideal Confucian state, so the translation of these works was considered a necessity. Since the translations were rendered in a literal way so as to preserve as much as possible of the source texts, the result was somewhat stilted in Korean.[24] Throughout the Chosŏn period Chinese classics and Confucian works continued to be translated using the *ŏnhae* method.

Translation activities in Chosŏn changed significantly after the Hideyoshi invasions of the late sixteenth century.[25] At this time many Chinese fictional works began to be imported, and the translation of these works got under way in the seventeenth century. The translations tended to be free, and many were so far from the source texts that they could be considered adaptations. The translators aimed to please readers who did not distinguish between an original and a translated work.[26] Since fictional narratives were not considered on the same level as Confucian classics or traditional poetic works, the norm of following the original as closely as possible was replaced by one of attempting to achieve acceptability with the target audience.[27] The following are some of the most widely read Chinese fictional narratives to be translated in late Chosŏn. *Tales of Prosperous Times* (K. *T'aep'yŏng kwanggi;* Ch. *Taiping guangji*), a tenth-century collection of ancient legends that was imported during Koryŏ and widely read in the original, had been translated into Korean by the seventeenth century. *The Romance of the Three Kingdoms* (K. *Samguk chiyŏnŭi;* Ch. *San-kuo-chih yen-yi*), originally written in the early Ming dynasty and attributed to Lo Kuan-Chung (c. 1330–c. 1400) but later extensively revised, portrays the demise of the Han empire and the rise of the three warring kingdoms. Translations of this work into Korean tended to be abridgements that focused on episodes of interest to Korean readers.[28] *Water Margin* (K. *Suho chŏn;* Ch. *Shui-hu chuan*), one of the earliest Chinese vernacular fictional narratives, is thought to have been written in the fourteenth century and has been attributed to Shih Nai-An and Lo Kuan-Chung. This work deals with the exploits of a group of daring bandits who roam the countryside robbing the wealthy and evading government troops. Hŏ Kyun (1569–1618) is said to have had this work in mind when he wrote the satirical narrative *The Tale of Hong Kil-Tong (Hong Kil-Tong chŏn)* in Korean. *The Journey to the West* (K. *Sŏyugi;* Ch. *Xiyouji*) is a comic tale attributed to Wu Ch'eng-En (c. 1506–1582) and is based on the pilgrimage of monk Hsuan-Tsang (596–664) to India to obtain Buddhist scriptures and bring them back to China. *The Gold Vase Plum* (K. *Kŭm pyŏng mae;* Ch. *Chin p'ing mei*) is an anonymous work of the late sixteenth century considered to be one of China's greatest pornographic masterpieces. In spite of the fact that it was banned because of its pornographic content, it was recognized as a work of literary value in Chosŏn. There are many studies that explore the impact of Chinese fictional narratives on Korean works of late Chosŏn.[29]

During the Chosŏn period while various usages of the vernacular script were developing, *hanmun* continued to occupy a dominant position. Writers of *hanmun* in Korea frequently followed trends in China. In early Chosŏn many writers imitated well-known Tang and Song stylists, but by mid-Chosŏn scholars were returning to ancient classical styles. The fact that *hanmun* was not static was demonstrated by the controversy over usage that developed during the reign of King Chŏngjo at the end of the eighteenth century. At this time Pak Ji-Wŏn (1737–1805) developed an original *hanmun* style that he employed in his work, *Yŏlha Diary (Yŏlha ilgi)*. In this work Pak recounted his travels to Ching China, employing an innovative and lively style. This new kind of writing met with the disapproval of King Chŏngjo, whose policy was to make a clear distinction between classical *hanmun* and newer styles, with only the former receiving official recognition. Chŏngjo used the power of the kingship to stop the spread of writing from late Ming and early Ching, to forbid the importation of European writings, and to block the development of new narrative forms that were considered subversive to the established order.[30]

Position of Women in Chosŏn

Before we consider writing by and for women in Chosŏn, it will be helpful to briefly review the social status of women during this period. Although the situation of women varied depending on the political and social conditions of each era, throughout the Chosŏn period women's lives were limited by the regulations of a patriarchal and hierarchical society. As Martina Deuchler has pointed out, when the Chosŏn dynasty was founded in 1392, "it ushered in a period during which Korean society underwent major changes— changes that have continued to influence the lives of Korean women to the present day."[31] The founders of Chosŏn were guided by the model of the ideal society set forth in the Chinese classics, as well as by the metaphysics of the twelfth- and thirteenth-century Song Neo-Confucianists. According to the latter, universal harmony results from the complementarity of all things: heaven and earth, light and dark, male and female. In early Chosŏn there was an attempt to overcome the supposed laxness of late Koryŏ morals by strictly applying Confucian ethics, which required separate functions for men and women. The strict suppression of women, which characterized later Chosŏn, took several generations to enforce, and during this time the rules concerning the separation of the sexes began to be applied. Some of the newly promulgated laws concerned adopting sons to carry on the male line, discouraging the remarriage of widows, discriminating against the sons of concubines, and favoring other provisions designed to regulate family life.[32] For the system to work, it was necessary that the authority of the male household head be unquestioned and that women know their place as keepers of order within the patriarchal family.

Underlying the changes in the legal system was the Confucian concept of the strictly hierarchical nature of all human relations, which was summarized by the three most basic ones: loyalty between ruler and subject, filial responsibility between father and son, and separation of functions between husband and wife. The rules of feminine behavior included the three obediences, according to which a woman was supposed to obey her father when young, her husband when married, and her son when widowed. Failure to follow the rules incurred severe penalties, as illustrated by the seven faults for which a woman might be divorced: disobedience to parents-in-law, failure to produce a son, adultery, carrying a hereditary disease, larceny, jealousy, and garrulousness. In late Chosŏn an increasing emphasis on chastity for women was related to social changes. At this time the *yangban*, or aristocratic elite, tried to maintain their hold on power by limiting the number of men who had access to official government positions. As the size of the upper classes grew, the *yangban* attempted to limit power struggles among competing factions by strictly controlling patrilineal descent. As time went on, the increasingly oppressive treatment of women, whose main function was to produce male heirs, was not restricted to the upper classes but spread to the lower classes, who were encouraged to emulate the Confucian model of feminine behavior. Monuments were erected to honor those who adhered to exemplary feminine virtue, such as widows who committed suicide, regardless of their age, or preferred to remain in dire poverty for their entire lives rather than remarrying. Late Chosŏn society placed such a strong emphasis on chastity that in some extreme cases widows preferred dying of starvation to remarrying.[33]

Educational Texts, Women, and Translation Activities

Throughout the Chosŏn period there was great emphasis on training women to fulfill their roles within the patriarchal family, and many works aimed at the education of women were translated from Chinese or written in the vernacular. Martina Deuchler writes: "The social precepts of the Confucianists were laid down in the Chinese classics, but few women learned enough Chinese to read them. Their key to the classics was the vernacular versions the kings of the early Yi dynasty propagated for the instruction of women."[34] Girls were excluded from the schools where boys learned the Chinese classics, and therefore upper-class families educated their daughters privately in their homes. Even in the families of scholar officials women were not supposed to acquire the knowledge of Chinese classics that was required of men who functioned in high government positions. Nevertheless, there were many upper-class women who attained great proficiency in reading and writing *hanmun*.

The attitude toward the education of women in Chosŏn was typified by King Sejong, who attributed the downfall of Chinese dynasties to the meddling of overeducated women and boasted that the ignorance of Chosŏn women kept them from interfering in government affairs!³⁵ Throughout the Chosŏn period educational texts were produced to indoctrinate women and discourage them from going beyond their proper functions. One of the earliest was *The Proper Application of the Three Social Principles (Samgang haengsildo)*, an illustrated collection of stories teaching the three social relationships: loyal subject, filial son, dutiful wife. The work was originally written in *hanmun* in 1431, and the vernacular translation appeared in the late fifteenth century. Another important early work was *Instructions for Women (Naehun)*, compiled in 1475 by Queen Sohye, the mother of King Sŏngjong. This work gathered excerpts from Chinese didactic works and translated them into the vernacular in order to provide examples of virtuous behavior for the women of Chosŏn. King Sŏngjong established a clear-cut educational policy that owed much to *Naehun*, the first work to be translated for women in Chosŏn. Among the Chinese works used in Chosŏn was *Lesser Learning*, which covered such topics as decorum, good conduct, and proper speech. *Four Works for Women* (K. *Yŏsasŏ*; Ch. *Nusishu*), a Chinese educational work of the early seventeenth century that compiled some earlier works, was translated into the vernacular in 1736 and again in 1907 by Pak Man-Hwan. In mid-Chosŏn many male scholars began to write works on the education of women. One of the representative works, *Essential Points for Women (Kyujung yoram)*, was written in the vernacular by the sixteenth-century scholar Yi T'oe-Gye, who took examples from the lives of exemplary women to illustrate the principles of virtuous conduct. According to Yi, it was useful for upper-class women to read excerpts from the Chinese classics and to know a few basic facts about the history of their country, but writing poetry was appropriate only for courtesans. *Master Uam's Rules for Women (Uam sŏnsaeng kyenyŏsŏ)*, written in the vernacular by the seventeenth-century scholar Uam Song Si-Yŏl for his daughter before her marriage, became one of the most widely imitated of the educational texts in Chosŏn. The eighteenth-century Practical Learning (Sirhak) scholar Yi Dŏk-Mu compiled *A Scholar's Notes (Sasojŏl)*, which treated the education of women in a detailed manner.³⁶ This work was originally written in *hanmun* and translated into Korean in the nineteenth century. The author pointed out that Chinese works written hundreds of years earlier were not appropriate for the women of Chosŏn, and therefore he emphasized aspects of contemporary behavior: how to fulfill the roles of daughter, wife, and mother and the importance of remaining faithful even in widowhood. This work stated that if women attended to their domestic tasks assiduously, they would hardly have time to read even vernacular works, let alone Chinese classics.³⁷

During the Chosŏn period, educational works for women, whether translations or originals, aimed to instill certain forms of conduct such as obedience, frugality, diligence, and patience. At this time educational policy did not attempt to develop individual talents but rather stressed that women existed for the benefit of the patriarchal family and the state. In spite of this restrictive atmosphere, there were a number of women who were noted for their learning, even though their activities were limited to the family. One of these was the mother of the sixteenth-century official Yi Jun-Kyŏng, who taught her son the Confucian classics. Sin Saimdang, mother of the sixteenth-century scholar Yulgok, was revered as a model of erudition and wisdom. Many of the women in the royal palace were skilled in both *hanmun* and vernacular writing. Even in the face of the rigid restrictions of Chosŏn society, many of these learned women must certainly have produced translations.

In addition to educational texts and Confucian classics, another area in which women were involved was the translation of Buddhist scriptures. As we have already seen, in the mid-fifteenth century, during the reign of King Seijo, a major project to translate Buddhist scriptures was carried out. The enthusiastic support that this work received from Queen Chŏng-Hŭi and many upper-class women indicates that such translations had a wide readership among women. The support of women readers in high places assured the translation and publication of Buddhist works in spite of the opposition of many members of the male scholarly elite. The establishment of the Kankyŏngdokam also owed much to the support of Queen Chŏng-Hŭi. After King Seijo's death, the scholar elite denounced Buddhism and promoted Neo-Confucianism, with the result that the Kankyŏngdokam was closed. At this time Queen Chŏng-Hŭi and Queen Sohye continued to promote the translation of Buddhist scriptures. In the late fifteenth century King Sŏngjong published revised editions of some of the Buddhist scriptures in honor of his grandmother, Queen Chŏng-Hŭi. In early Chosŏn the translation of Buddhist scriptures preceded that of the Confucian texts and benefited greatly from the support of the women of the royal family.[38]

Another activity that involved women in later Chosŏn was the translation of Chinese fictional narratives, which, as I mentioned above, began to develop in the seventeenth century. Many women readers became interested in these works, which provided a diversion from the dry educational texts. Frequently such narratives focused on the traditional virtues of loyalty, filial duty, and chastity, and they taught moral lessons, as we will see in the next section. The translated Chinese works were closely related to the development of original narratives in Korean, most of which were anonymous.[39] It is quite possible that many of these works were translated by women. The work of women translators in Chosŏn is an unexplored area for future research that will yield rich insights into the development of writing systems, as well as many other aspects of cultural change.

Women Writers and Representations of Women

As we have seen, upper-class women in Chosŏn led extremely restricted lives and were discouraged from pursuing the kind of knowledge of the Chinese classics that was required for men of the elite ruling group. The writing of upper-class women was never supposed to go beyond the limits of the family, and the only women whose works were freely circulated were *kisaeng*, courtesans who were considered social outcasts. Even within these constraints some women managed to leave behind writings, mostly in the form of letters, poetry, diaries, and memoirs. In this section I briefly consider, first, the main kinds of writing styles used by women; next, the work of a few of the important women writers; and finally, the feminine images in fictional works of late Chosŏn.

Vernacular writing styles in late Chosŏn can be divided into at least two main categories: *naeganch'e* and *kasach'e. Naeganch'e* refers to correspondence and was related to other types of prose writing by women. Although letters written in Chinese, known as *sŏ*, were more highly regarded than *ŏngan* or *naegan*, vernacular correspondence played a significant role in Chosŏn.[40] *Naeganch'e* began to develop in the late fifteenth and early sixteenth centuries and was the style of vernacular correspondence between members of the royal family and upper-class families. One example is King Sŏnjo's late sixteenth-century letter assuring his daughter of the safety of the country after the Japanese invasions had been repulsed. Vernacular letter writing also provided opportunities for upper-class women to express themselves concerning everyday matters, experiences, and emotions.[41] This style combined colloquial elements with some *hanmun* influence, reflecting the lifestyle and social situation of upper-class women, and allowed everyday events to be described with elegance and precision. This truly Korean writing style was related to personal narratives written by women, including diaries, travel accounts, and memoirs. Some examples include *The Memoirs of Lady Hyegyŏng (Hanjung nok),* in which the author tells of events in the royal palace in the eighteenth century, and *The Diary of Ŭiyudang's Journey to the North (Ŭiyudang kwanbuk yuram ilgi),* which is Lady Ŭiyudang's account of her early nineteenth-century voyage to the northern part of the country.[42]

Kasach'e developed as a lively and rich style to express the sorrows and joys of the lives of women in the inner rooms of Chosŏn households.[43] *Kyubang kasa* are long narrative poems, written mostly by upper-class women, that deal with the daily experiences of women in traditional households.

Women were expected to leave their parents' homes to live in the households of their in-laws, where they would serve as wives, mothers, and daughters-in-law. Since there were no educational institutions for women, one of the easiest ways for mothers to educate their daughters was to have them memorize *kasa* verses, which were rhythmically divided into groups of four syllables.

While the writings of upper-class women were supposed to remain within the confines of their homes, courtesans were allowed a certain freedom of expression. Although they were a marginalized group, they were trained in poetry and music in order to provide entertainment at gatherings of upper-class men and government officials. Some of the talented *kisaeng* made important contributions to Korean literary and artistic traditions. One of the most well-known *kisaeng* poets was Hwang Jin-I (c. 1506–1544), who was noted for her *sijo,* a concise native Korean poetic form. Although only a handful of her works remain, they are considered masterpieces that skillfully combine evocations of the loneliness of separation with a playful, satirical quality. Yi Mae-Ch'ang (1513–1550) was another *kisaeng* who left behind some works noted for their originality, including *hansi* and *sijo.*[44]

Yi Ok-Bong (c. 1550–1600) was the daughter of a concubine who also became a concubine, an extremely precarious position in aristocratic households. The existence of a separate literary genre, literature by concubines *(sosil munhak),* indicates that many of these women left behind literary works. Yi Ok-Bong wrote several poems that were published in China, but there was no separate edition of her works in Chosŏn.[45] One of her representative works, "Sorrow of Parting" ("Pyŏl han"), centers around the separations that characterized the lives of women in upper-class households.

Hŏ Nansŏlhŏn (1563–1589) was an extremely promising writer whose works not only became known in her own country, but were also published in China in 1606 and in Japan in 1711. She was born into a prominent aristocratic family; her brother was Hŏ Kyun, the author of *The Tale of Hong Kil-Tong.* She became proficient in *hanmun* and appreciated the works of the Tang poet Tu Fu. Although she died at the age of twenty-seven, she left behind many *hansi* that were published posthumously. Her will stipulated that her works be burned after her death, but her brother collected and edited the works stored in her maternal home. Hŏ Nansŏlhŏn's works present images of sorrow and sacrifice and convey the pressures and restrictions on women's lives.[46]

Fictional narratives in late Chosŏn present distinctive feminine images. Although most of these works are anonymous, it seems quite likely that some of the authors must have been women since many of the readers were women. These works can be divided into the following categories: heroic narratives, family narratives, moral tales, and love stories. In heroic narratives most of the main characters are men, but in some cases a female character takes on a male role as general or leader. We can imagine that upper-class wives, suffering from the oppression of the patriarchal family, sought release in stories that depicted women in a fantastic light. Family narratives depicted women in the typical female roles of daughter, wife, and mother. These works came closest to representing the experiences of women in late Chosŏn and attracted readers from all social classes. Many of these narratives deal with conflicts between wife and concubine or daughter-in-law and mother-in-law. Kim Man-Jung's seventeenth-century work, *Lady Sa Travels to the South (Sassi namjŏnggi),* was written first in the vernacular and later translated into *hanmun.* The work deals with the conflicts between wives and concubines and was meant to deliver a moral lesson to women.[47] Late Chosŏn witnessed the rising popularity of moral tales such as *The Tale of Sim Ch'ŏng,* which emphasizes the ideal of the filial daughter. *The Tale of Ch'un-Hyang (Ch'un-Hyang chŏn)* is the popular story of the daughter of a courtesan who falls in love with the son of an aristocrat. This tale depicts the overcoming of class boundaries and criticizes the inequalities of Chosŏn society.

Although women writers as a group did not receive recognition in Chosŏn, the works of a few exceptional women survived. The dominant view prescribed that women should learn only what was necessary for their functions within the family and should never publish their writings. The heritage of some of the women writers of Chosŏn has been preserved through the efforts of their descendants or other people who admired their works.

Cultural Change in the Late Nineteenth and Early Twentieth Centuries

The period from the early 1870s to around 1910, known in Korean as the Kaehwa (enlightenment or opening), was a time when all aspects of Korean society were fundamentally changing. After centuries of isolation under the dominant influence of Chinese culture, Chosŏn was compelled to open its ports to trade and to enter into diplomatic relations with Japan and Western nations. This was a time of rapid modernization and of confrontation with foreign civilizations. In this section I consider changes in the situation of women, developments in writing systems, and translation activities.

Changing Situation of Women

Legal Status

One of the important works that made suggestions about changing the status of women in late nineteenth-century Korea was Pak Yŏng-Hyo's *Letter on Enlightenment (Kaehwa sangsŏ)* (1885). Pak, a member of the Progressive Party, took part in the 1884 uprising against the Chosŏn government and sought refuge in Japan, where he wrote petitions urging King Kojong to reform the government.[48] Among the suggestions in Pak's petitions were several concerning women: recognition of women's human rights, abolition of the slavery and abusive treatment of women, establishment of equal education for males and females over the age of six, abolition of child marriage and concubinage, and removal of obstacles to the remarriage of widows. These proposals concerned fundamental changes to the Chosŏn social system and were ten years in advance of the reform of 1894.[49]

The reform of 1894 covered various aspects of Korean life, including the legal system, education, and the military. Among the provisions that directly affected women were those forbidding marriage for men under twenty and women under sixteen and allowing remarriage for widows. Although the reforms of 1894 were significant, they did not basically change the lives of women during the transitional period from traditional Chosŏn to modern Korea. For instance, the system of concubinage was not officially abolished until 1915, when a concubine could no longer be listed on her patron's family record. At this time divorce laws were modified, making divorce less severe for women. In spite of these changes, the great majority of women were unable to go beyond their traditional role within the patriarchal family, and women's rights were not really guaranteed until the constitution that was promulgated after World War II.[50]

Education

Christian schools played a crucial role in promoting modern education for women in Korea during the transitional period. One of the first modern educational institutions, the Ewha Girls' School (Ewha Yŏhakkyo), was founded in 1886 by an American Methodist missionary in order to educate young Korean women to become good wives and mothers, as well as faithful Christians. Owing to the reluctance of Korean parents to send their daughters to school, Ewha was started with seven orphans. Since Koreans were still influenced by the concept of *"Namhak yŏmaeng"* (Men are learned; women are ignorant), the founding of the first girls' school posed a challenge to the values of traditional society, which was based on gender and class discrimination. Upper-class women were supposed to remain secluded in their homes, and therefore recruiting students was one of the most serious obstacles to establishing educational institutions for women at the time. The prevailing mistrust of foreigners was a further obstacle to the promotion of missionary schools. In 1890 there were still only a handful of students from marginal backgrounds at Ewha, but when Progressive Party member Pak Yŏng-Hyo sent his daughter to the school, a few upper-class families followed suit.

Although the reform of 1894 recommended equal education for boys and girls between the ages of seven and fifteen, it was difficult to put this new educational policy into practice. During the first decade of the twentieth century many private girls' schools were established, but the fact that even in 1908, twenty-two years after its founding, only five students graduated from Ewha Girls' School indicates the difficulty of promoting education for women at the time.[51]

The first private school for girls founded by Koreans was Sunsŏng Girls' School (Sunsŏng Yŏhakkyo), established in 1898 by the members of a women's organization, the Ch'anyanghoe (see below).[52] Although the founders of this school were determined to educate women for the modern world, they faced severe financial difficulties. From 1905 to 1910 ninety-six private girls' schools were founded, but they continued to be plagued by a lack of funds.[53] In 1908 the government founded Hansŏng Girls' High School (Hansŏng Yŏja Kodŭng Hakkyo), but the school had great difficulty recruiting students. The Japanese also began to establish girls' schools that aimed to train young women to be submissive wives and dutiful citizens of the Japanese empire.[54]

Religion

The first foreign religion to challenge the hegemony of the Confucian worldview was Catholicism, which reached Chosŏn in the seventeenth century through contacts with missionaries residing in Ming China. At this time scholars became interested in Sŏhak (Western learning), primarily as a new form of knowledge rather than as a source of religion. Certain Catholic dogmas negated the basis of the Chosŏn class structure, such as the idea that all people are equal in the eyes of God. Catholicism's focus on the worship of a transcendent God undermined the centrality of the Neo-Confucian bonds between subject and ruler, father and son, and wife and husband. This religion began to gain converts in eighteenth- and nineteenth-century Chosŏn, giving women a new status. Kwŏn Yuhandang was a Catholic woman whose book, *A Record of Words and Deeds (Ŏnhaengrok)*, demonstrated a modern consciousness of the status of women and emphasized that the dignity of women came from God.[55]

Another religion that challenged the late Chosŏn class and gender distinctions was Tonghak (Eastern Learning), founded by Ch'oe Jae-U, a descendant of an impoverished aristocratic family. The basis of this religion, *innaech'ŏn,* the idea that heaven is within each person's heart, became a means of protesting the hierarchical structure of Chosŏn society, which entailed the oppression of the common people. Although Tonghak recognized women's basic human rights, its female adherants were still expected to follow their husbands. In 1901 Kang Il-Sun, a Tonghak believer, formed his own religion, Chŭngsankyo, which expanded women's rights. This religion is based on the principle of *chŏngŭm chŏngyang,* or balancing the forces of yin and yang to bring peace to the world. Chŭngsankyo teaches that if the traditional debasement of women ends, then a brighter society can be created.[56]

Economic and Social Activities

In the 1880s and 1890s intellectuals began to challenge Korean traditions, and a small percentage of women started to become educated. In 1898 a women's movement began to develop, and the establishment of women's organizations gave women their first opportunity to function in society at large in order to improve their status. In 1898 the Ch'anyanghoe, the first women's association in Korea, was formed. It had the aim of establishing a girls' school, and it focused on improving women's educational and social opportunities.

The decade from 1900 to 1910 saw the formation of many women's organizations. In 1907 women participated in the movement to repay the national debt, and this was one of the first opportunities for them to take part in political activities. By the early twentieth century Koreans were becoming increasingly financially indebted to the Japanese, and many women believed that financial and political independence were linked. The focus of women's groups shifted from education to anti-Japanese resistance.

After the Japanese takeover, Korean women began to play a more active role in the Independence Movement. The Songjuk Secret Association (Songjuk Pimil Kyŏlsadan) was a women's organization formed in 1913 to promote independence. On the surface this was a consumer group, but its real purpose was to send funds to independence groups in Shanghai and Beijing. The association contributed to the Independence Movement and supported women's participation in nationalist activities until the end of the Japanese colonial period in 1945.

Many women actively participated in the March 1, 1919, demonstrations and were arrested and sent to prison. Through such participation women went beyond the restrictions of traditional society and began to expand their sphere of influence. After March 1919 various anti-Japanese women's organizations were formed with the aim of collecting funds to send to the Korean Provisional Government in Shanghai. Many of their leaders were arrested by the Japanese military police.

In the 1920s the Japanese colonial government instituted a cultural policy in an attempt to shift attention away from the increasing political repression. As part of this policy, women's organizations, such as the Chosŏn Women's Educational Association (Chosŏn Yŏja Kyoyukhoe), were encouraged to concentrate on education, as they had at the beginning of the twentieth century. Many women believed that national independence could not be achieved without economic development, so they formed such groups as the Women's Association for the Promotion of Native Products (T'osan Aeyong Puinhoe). While the Christian and socialist women's organizations began separately, in the late 1920s the Kŭnu Association (Kŭnuhoe) united women of various ideological beliefs into a nationalist front. This group sent a team to investigate the Kwangju student demonstrations and actively participated in political affairs.[57]

Changes in Writing Systems

As we stated above, the language used for writing, *hanmun,* was quite different from the spoken language, and methods were devised to modify *hanmun* to suit the needs of the Korean language. We also saw how the invention of *han'gŭl* altered literary life in Chosŏn. In the late nineteenth century the predominance of *hanmun* finally came to an end. In 1894, at the moment that the independent kingdom of Korea was declared, King Kojong proclaimed that henceforth official documents were to be written in either *han'gŭl* or a mixed Sino-Korean script. At this time three basic writing systems were being used: pure *hanmun,* pure *han'gŭl,* and mixed Sino-Korean scripts.[58] Mixed scripts began to develop in the 1890s and came to be widely used in textbooks, newspapers, and many other kinds of works. However, mixed scripts employing many Chinese characters tended to be used by intellectuals and were somewhat at odds with the attempts to bring about agreement of the written and spoken language in a vernacular style suited for average people. Two works that indicate the diversity of writing styles at the time were Yu Gil-Jun's *Observations on a Journey to the West (Sŏyu kyŏnmun)* and *The Independent (Tongnip sinmun). Observations on a Journey to the West* was published in 1895 and deals with the author's opinions about Western civilization. This work employed a mixed script that relied heavily on Chinese characters. Yu felt that it would be difficult to express himself in pure *han'gŭl,* so he wrote in a style similar to the *ŏnhaech'e* style used to translate Chinese classics. *The Independent* (1896–1898) was remarkable as the first Korean newspaper to be printed in pure *han'gŭl.* This publication also developed a system of spacing between words that made it easier to read a text in *han'gŭl.* Within the first few decades of the twentieth century *han'gŭl* came to be widely used in literary works, newspapers, and textbooks, as well as official documents. The two publications noted represent the ends of the spectrum in terms of writing systems at the time: the intellectuals preferred a mixed script using many Chinese characters, while pure *han'gŭl* was promoted in publications aimed at a broader audience.[59]

Translation

Translation in late nineteenth- and early twentieth-century Korea contributed to the development of writing in *han'gŭl,* as well as to the creation of new feminine images, as we will see in the next chapter. In this section I consider two types of translations that were related to new forms of writing: Bible translations and translations of literary works.

Bible Translations

Translation of the Christian Bible into Korean was part of the movement to import foreign civilization and contributed to the promulgation of vernacular writing. One of the early projects to translate the Bible into Korean was initiated in 1876 by John Ross and John MacIntyre, missionaries in Manchuria who worked in collaboration with native Koreans such as Yi Ŭng-Ch'an, Paek Hŭng-Jun, and Kim Jin-Ki. Their translations of the Gospels of John and Luke appeared in 1882, followed by the Gospels of Matthew and Mark, the Acts of the Apostles in 1883, and finally the entire New Testament in 1887. This version, known as the Ross translation, formed the basis for some of the subsequent translations of the Bible and marked a turning point in *han'gŭl* usage by contributing to the development of modern prose style.[60] The Gospels of Mark and Luke were also translated into Korean in 1884 by Yi Su-Jŏng, who was residing in Japan, and were brought into Korea in 1885 by two missionaries. Finally in 1910 the *han'gŭl* translation of both the Old and New Testaments appeared.[61]

The translation of the Bible was influential during this transitional period in Korea on at least two levels. As noted above, the Bible introduced new concepts that undermined the class and gender structure of Chosŏn society and negated some of the basic principles of Neo-Confucianism. In addition, *han'gŭl* versions of the Bible contributed to the movement to bring about agreement of the written and spoken language and helped to promote the spread of literacy.[62] Ross and many of the other missionaries realized that the most effective way of transmitting the message of Christianity to large numbers of Koreans was by translating the Bible into *han'gŭl.*

Translations of Literary Works

The new literary forms, such as *sinch'esi* (new poems) and *sin sosŏl* (new novels), which appeared around the turn of the century, were related to the importation of foreign literature in translation. Ch'oe Nam-Sŏn was one of the first to experiment with new poetic forms that differed significantly from traditional ones.[63] He is also one of the earliest translators of Western poetry into Korean, and his original poem, "From the Sea to the Boys" ("Hae egesŏ sonyŏn ege"), is similar to a section of Byron's *Childe Harold's Pilgrimage.*[64] One of Ch'oe's important contributions was as editor of the journals *Boy (Sonyŏn)* and *Youth (Ch'ŏngch'un),* which were among the first to publish translations of literary works. *Boy* (1908–1911) was a magazine for young people that aimed to instill patriotism and to encourage young men to build a strong, independent nation. This journal published abridged translations of the works of authors such as Tolstoy, Hugo, Byron, and Tennyson, as well as historical materials, with the aim of educating young people about the world outside the narrow confines of their own country. *Youth* (1914–1918), which continued the project of translating foreign works in order to educate young people, included selections from Tagore, Hugo, Maupassant, Tolstoy, Milton, and Cervantes. (Another journal called *Youth [Ch'ŏngnyŏn]* appeared in the 1920s and aimed to introduce Western literature and culture.) Ch'oe Nam-Sŏn holds an important place in the cultural history of early twentieth-century Korea as one of the first modern translators to systematically introduce foreign literary works into the country.[65]

If we attempt to classify translations at the turn of the century according to the source country, we see that the largest number of works came from Great Britain, followed by Russia, France, Germany, the United States, Greece, and Italy. Most of these translations were adaptations, abridgements, or summaries, and very few were complete works. In the early twentieth century Japan played the role of intermediary in the reception of foreign culture, and over 50 percent of translations into Korean were based on Japanese intermediate translations. Since most of the Japanese translations were summaries, abridgements, or adaptations, the indirect Korean translations followed suit. While Korean translators at the turn of the century tended to translate historical materials for didactic purposes, in the 1910s there was a growing tendency to translate a variety of literary works.[66]

The next chapter considers how, at the beginning of the twentieth century, an original work and two translations of historical legends promoted the ideal of the patriotic woman as part of the attempt to protect national interests.

chapter two

European Heroines in Translation: The Search for New Models

Paik Nak-Chung writes: "When the notion of a national literature first emerged in the waning days of the Chosŏn dynasty . . . it was no doubt a direct response to the impact of the opening of the kingdom to the modern world-economy in 1876, and mainly took the form of trying to duplicate the achievements of European national bourgeoisies."[1] At the turn of the twentieth century in Korea translation was an essential part of the process of importing foreign culture, and the translation of foreign literature into Korean contributed to the creation of a national literature. This chapter offers a preliminary exploration of the complex relationships among translation, emerging nationalism, and changing representations of women at the turn of the twentieth century in Korea. In the first part I review the international pressures and internal upheavals that marked the entry of Chosŏn into the international system at the end of the nineteenth and the beginning of the twentieth centuries. Next I consider the feminine images in certain types of late Chosŏn fictional narratives as prototypes of early twentieth-century heroines, and then I give an overview of the translation of historical texts into Korean at the turn of the twentieth century. The main part of the chapter consists of an examination of two translations into Korean and one original Korean work. I argue that the two translations function as transitional works from traditional to modern narrative and that they do this by employing the narrative technique of the intervention of the narrator in such a way as to present a new feminine ideal. The original work demonstrates how Korean authors at the time were exploiting this new way of representing women for political purposes.

International Pressures and Internal Upheavals in Late Chosŏn

During the first decade of the twentieth century Japan moved to make Korea a colony, and Koreans lost control of their government and society. The threat of aggression from abroad was one of the important factors that encouraged Korean translators to turn to texts dealing with the lives of patriotic heroes from other countries. A brief review of events leading to the final downfall of the Chosŏn dynasty will be helpful in understanding the context of translation in Korea at the turn of the twentieth century.

Japan was victorious in the Sino-Japanese War of 1894–1895, which was fought on Korean territory. This marked the end of Chinese domination of Korean affairs and opened the way for Japan to realize its own ambitions on the Korean peninsula. As a result of agreements signed between Japan and Korea in 1904, important Korean governmental matters, both domestic and international, were in the hands of the Japanese. According to the terms of the Taft-Katsura Agreement of 1905, the United States recognized Japan's domination of Korea in return for Japan's recognition of American control of the Philippines. In the same year England renegotiated the Anglo-Japanese Alliance and recognized Japan's right to control Korean affairs. The 1905 Treaty of Portsmouth ended the Russo-Japanese War, in which Japan had been victorious, and eliminated Russia as the final obstacle to Japan's colonization of Korea.

After having obtained the tacit approval of the international powers, Japan formed the Society for Advancement (Ilchinhoe), a front organization to promote the establishment of a protectorate over Korea. In response Koreans formed the Society for the Study of Constitutional Government (Hŏnjŏng Yŏnguhoe) in protest against Japan's encroachments on their national sovereignty. In spite of this opposition, the 1905 Protectorate Treaty made it mandatory for Korea to consult Japan before making any agreements with foreign countries, thereby depriving Korea of its sovereign rights on the international level. The wrath of the Korean people was aroused, and the Japanese censors failed to suppress bitter criticism of the treaty in the Korean newspapers. Opposition to the treaty was also expressed through speeches, petitions, demonstrations, and suicides by a number of Korean government officials, including Min Yŏng-Hwan, an aide to the king who left a letter to the people before taking his own life in protest. This strong opposition did not deter the Japanese, who were only waiting for a convenient moment to complete their takeover of Korea. The Protectorate Treaty was counter to the wishes of King Kojong, who sent several men on a secret mission to explain the unjust treatment that Korea was suffering and to appeal for help at the Second Hague Peace Conference, which opened in June 1906. There was cruel irony in the fact that the Koreans were not permitted to take part in the conference since Korea was a protectorate of Japan and lacked the sovereign rights of an independent nation. One of the emissaries, Yi Chun, was overcome with grief and died in The Hague. Although the Koreans attracted quite a bit of international attention, the Japanese were undaunted and proceeded to dissolve the Korean army in 1907, depriving Korea of all military strength.

In May 1910 General Terauchi Masatake was appointed resident-general with the mission of carrying out the annexation of Korea. He suspended the publication of Korean newspapers, and on August 22, 1910, the prime minister signed the annexation treaty. King Kojong had been forced to abdicate in 1907; his son Sunjong was also forced to abdicate on August 29, 1910, and to yield his country to the Japanese. The resident-general ruled Korea with an iron hand, instituting a Japanese gendarmerie that brutally suppressed any opposition. The resistance to Japanese domination took several forms. The king and the upper classes supported the mission to The Hague and tried to enlist the aid of Russia against the Japanese. These strategies proved ineffective since Japan was already in control of important segments of the government. At the same time guerrilla units known as the Righteous Armies (ŭibyŏng) fought fearlessly against the Japanese and were supported by the local populace. Although lacking the strength necessary to drive out the Japanese, the Righteous Armies represented the patriotic aspirations of the people.[2]

Late Chosŏn Fictional Narratives

In order to properly evaluate the work of Korean translators at the beginning of the twentieth century, it is necessary to consider the tradition of

Chosŏn fictional narratives.³ In this section I briefly review, first, heroic feminine images and then narrative techniques that were modified by the writers and translators at the turn of the twentieth century.

Heroic Feminine Images

The period of the late sixteenth and early seventeenth centuries was one of upheavals in Chosŏn. A series of invasions, by the Japanese in the 1590s and the Manchurians in the 1630s, devastated the countryside and brought about cultural changes. These events also affected literary production since the importation of Chinese fictional narratives increased and the experiences of war were described in various types of works.⁴ Certain heroic tales recounted the deeds of those who distinguished themselves in the struggles against foreign invaders.⁵ Among the most widespread types of narratives were those that focused on the adventures of Korean folk heroes (such as *The Tale of Hong Kil-Tong*) and those that featured aristocratic heroes against a Chinese background.⁶ As noted in chapter 1, female protagonists were the focus of many traditional works, including shamanist narrative songs such as *Princess Pari*. An example of a work that features a female protagonist who receives supernatural aid is *The Story of Suk-Hyang (Sukhyang chŏn)*. This is the story of two lovers, Suk-Hyang and I-Sŏn, who transcend class boundaries to become husband and wife. The existence of versions in both Chinese and the vernacular indicates that the work enjoyed a wide readership. *The Story of Chŏng Su-Jŏng (Chŏng Su-Jŏng chŏn)* belongs to a group of stories about female commanders *(yŏjanggun chŏn)*. Chŏng Su-Jŏng is an only child who becomes an orphan after her father dies and her mother is captured by pirates. She dresses as a man, goes to a mountain temple where she learns the magical arts from a priest, pursues a military career, and displays great courage in leading attacks against foreign invaders. This work follows the plan of military narratives that focus on male protagonists.⁷

The Story of the White Crane Fan (Paekhaksŏn chŏn) tells of a young man and woman who pledge eternal devotion and take a fan with a white crane design as the symbol of their love. However, their families force them to become engaged to other people, and the woman leaves home to join the military, where she fights foreign invaders. After she rescues her lover from an enemy prison camp, all ends well. This work combines elements of love stories and tales of military exploits.⁸ The stories featuring female military commanders follow a basic plot: the heroine encounters an obstacle, she dons men's clothing, becomes a leader, fights valiantly against the enemy, but in the end returns to fulfill the traditional female role. In Chosŏn an upper-class woman married the man chosen by her parents and spent her life confined to the inner quarters of the house and serving her in-laws. We can imagine that tales of daring heroines provided entertainment for these restricted women.[9]

Techniques of Chosŏn and Early Twentieth-Century Narratives

Many of the early twentieth-century Korean narratives employ the techniques of Chosŏn fictional narratives. Song Min-Ho has identified Four characteristics of Chosŏn fictional narratives. First, they tend to be divided into sections, and conventional expressions are used to introduce the beginning of the work *(hwasŏl)* and the changes of scene *(kaksŏl, ch'asŏl).* Second, they tend to employ literary style *(munŏch'e),* and there are cases of Chosŏn fictional narratives in verse. Third, they tend to follow a chronological order based on the events in the protagonist's life. Fourth, many are divided into chapters, following the Chinese model.[10] The Korean nationalist narratives of the early twentieth century, whether translated or original, tend to display these features. The two translations that I consider in this chapter, *The Story of a Patriotic Lady* (Joan of Arc; *Aeguk puin chŏn*) and *The Story of Madame Roland (Raran puin chŏn)*—to which I will refer as *Joan* and *Roland*—and other works dealing with the life of an exemplary person employ the methods found in heroic narratives of the Chosŏn period. For instance, *Joan* includes an introduction that outlines the life and background of the protagonist, each change of scene is accompanied by the conventional expressions of traditional narrative, and the characters are described in stereotypical terms. The speeches that Joan makes to the people and her dialogues with King Charles also resemble the style of Chosŏn military narratives.[11]

Another feature of Chosŏn fictional narratives that was used by writers and translators in the early twentieth century was that of the omniscient narrator, who intervenes with comments and explanations. Many Chosŏn fictional works focused on the events in the life of an idealized character. Except for folk opera *(p'ansori),* the voice in Chosŏn narratives was unified, and there was an alternation between explanation and dialogue.[12] With the exception of folk opera, the voice in most Chosŏn narratives was purely explanatory. In the literary style narratives the impression is somewhat static, rather like a series of slides with comments.[13]

Traditionally in Korea upper-class males considered heroic tales and other popular stories to be pernicious, and women were the main consumers of such works. However, at the turn of the twentieth century, nationalist intellectuals began to realize the efficacy of fiction works as a means of communication. Therefore, while writers and translators employed some features of traditional works, they strengthened the evaluative role of the narrator so as to transmit a message of crucial importance. The prologue and epilogue of *Roland* and the comments inserted between the scenes of *Joan* clearly bring out the narrator's opinions and emotions.

Translation of Historical Texts

When studying Korean literature of the early twentieth century, scholars have tended to focus on the New Novels (*sin sosŏl;* discussed below) rather than the historical and biographical narratives (*yŏksa chŏngi sosŏl*). While the New Novels tended not to deal directly with contemporary events, the historical narratives conveyed the spirit of nationalism and in a few cases presented new feminine images while at the same time retaining some traditional techniques.[14] Since the three works that I analyze in the main part of this chapter can be considered part of this latter group, in this section I consider the characteristics of historical narratives and then the links between the work of the Chinese reformer Liang Chi-Chao and Korean literary production at the time.

Characteristics of Historical Narratives

After the Japanese compelled Chosŏn to open its ports to trade in the 1870s, Koreans began to undertake various nationalist activities, as discussed above.[15] Historical narratives, in sharp contrast to the New Novels, emphasized the necessity of remaining vigilant and protecting national interests.[16] Most of the historical works that appeared during the first decade of the twentieth century aimed to arouse patriotic sentiments. At this time intellectuals were facing two challenges: one was to counter Japanese aggression, and the other was to go beyond the feudal system in their own country and build a modern nation. The historical narratives contributed to this nationalist and modernizing movement.[17]

Historical narratives were written or translated from the late 1890s to around 1910, when Korea was increasingly threatened by Japanese aggression, and therefore these works reflect the concerns of nationalist intellectuals. Three of the important writers of historical narratives at this time were Pak Ŭn-Sik (1859–1925), Chang Ji-Yŏn (1884–1921), and Shin Ch'ae-Ho (1880–1936), who were all active in the nationalist movement, as well as being historians and journalists.[18] When the newspaper *Capital Gazette (Hwangsŏng sinmun)* was founded in 1898, Chang Ji-Yŏn and Pak Ŭn-Sik took on editorial roles, and in 1905 Shin Ch'ae-Ho also began to contribute as a columnist promoting reformist thinking. After the Japanese annexation of Korea in 1910, Pak Ŭn-Sik and Shin Ch'ae-Ho went into exile in China, where they continued to work for the Independence Movement. The historical narratives that these men wrote or translated were closely connected with their work as nationalists and journalists.

The following are among the historical works that were translated into Korean around the turn of the century: *A New History of the West (T'aesŏ sinsŏ)*, 1897; *A Concise History of Russia (Aguk Yaksa)*, 1898; *The History of American Independence (Miguk tongnipsa)*, 1899; *The History of Poland (P'aran malnyŏn chŏnsa)*, 1899; *The History of the French Revolution (Pŏpguk hyŏksin chŏnsa)*, 1900; *The History of Modern Egypt (Aegŭp kŭnsesa)*, 1905; *The History of the Fall of Vietnam (Wŏlnam mangguksa)*, 1906; and *The History of the Philippines War (Piyulpin chŏnsa)*, 1907. *The History of Modern Egypt* deals with the global colonial expansion of the great powers. Chang Ji-Yŏn translated this work, which was published by the *Capital Gazette* and had an introduction by Pak Ŭn-Sik. This work was read as presenting a situation similar to the one Korea was facing at the time. Egypt was an ancient and distinguished civilization, but because of economic considerations, the people were trapped into servitude. *The History of the Fall of Vietnam* was translated into Korean a couple of times during this period. This was a work by the Vietnamese nationalist leader Phan Boi-Chau, with comments added by Liang Chi-Chao, who had interviewed Phan. The work appeared in China in 1905 and was soon translated for Koreans, who avidly read it until the Japanese banned it in 1909. Liang's comments alluded to countries that were falling victims to colonialism, including Chosŏn.[19]

A number of biographies of well-known historical figures were written or translated into Korean between 1905 and 1910. In addition to *Joan* (translated by Chang Ji-Yŏn) and *Roland,* both 1907, translations of this type include the following: *The Story of Bismarck (Pisamaek chŏn)*, 1907; Shin Ch'ae-Ho's *The Story of Three Heroes of Italian Unification (It'aeri kŏnguk samgŏl chŏn)*, 1907; and Pak Ŭn-Sik's *The Story of the Founding of Switzerland (Sŏsa kŏngukji)*, 1907. Some original biographies in Korean also appeared: Shin Ch'ae-Ho's *The Story of Ŭljimundŏk (Ŭljimundŏk)*, 1908, and Pak Ŭn-Sik's *The Story of Yŏn Kaesomun (Yŏn Kaesomun chŏn)*, 1911. These works extolled the accomplishments of traditional heroes and emphasized the need to regain sovereignty. Among the translations, one of the most notable was *The Story of Three Heroes of Italian Unification,* which deals with the period from 1848 to 1860, when Mazzini, Cavour, and Garibaldi led the struggle for Italian unification. This work, which portrays the spirit of patriotic sacrifice, was also translated by Chu Si-Kyŏng and was widely read and discussed.[20] *The Story of the Founding of Switzerland* recounts how William Tell led the Swiss to independence. This work, divided into ten parts, employs traditional narrative techniques and stereotypical expressions. In the introduction to his translation Pak Ŭn-Sik explains that the story is inspiring, and instead of writing an original version, he translated this one to educate people on the importance of maintaining national independence.

Liang Chi-Chao's Ideas and Korean Writers

Korean nationalists, writers, and translators of the early twentieth century owe a debt to the work of the late Ching scholar Liang Chi-Chao (1873–1929), who lived at a time of upheavals, and contributed to the transformation of Chinese society. This was a time when China was undergoing the collapse of the feudal system, the introduction of constitutional democracy, and far-reaching cultural changes. At the time of Liang's birth the Chinese government was being weakened by clashes with Western powers competing for trade rights with it; when Liang died, China was involved in a civil war. While still in his teens, Liang visited Beijing, where he met many famous scholars and was exposed to new trends in the intellectual world; from this point on he devoted himself to nationalistic renewal. These early experiences helped him to formulate the aim of his educational, historical, and literary writing, which was to build a strong, new nation by educating the people and developing their capacities. For Liang, literature was subsumed under the greater goal of nationalist renewal, and therefore the value of literature stemmed from its power to revitalize a people. He felt that it was useless to write only for the sake of esthetic pleasure, and he emphasized the effectiveness of literary works in helping to reform national politics and awakening the people.[21]

Liang Chi-Chao's literary innovations mainly focused on three genres: poetry, prose, and fiction. His poetic innovations aimed at renewing poetry and borrowing trends from Europe since he felt that modern poetry should be differentiated from traditional poetry in terms of form and content. However, he also felt that even new poems should maintain certain aspects of traditional poetics. Liang contributed to new prose styles by eliminating empty phrases, expressing himself freely in a clearly understandable manner, endeavoring to make terminology more precise, and emphasizing grammar and logic, which were both weak in traditional writing. Along with many of the other reformers, Liang believed that fiction works were more effective than scholarly ones in reforming society. In 1902, while living in exile in Japan, he wrote stories that aimed to awaken people to the need for government reform. In an article published at this time, "The Relationship between Fiction and Power Structures," he criticized the tendency of traditional fiction to promote immoral behavior and stated that the best way to reform morals, religion, and education was to reform fiction writing since it possessed great power over people's minds. In another article, "The Translation of Political Fiction," Liang criticized the image of women in traditional Chinese fiction, such as *The Dream of the Red Chamber,* which depicted illicit love affairs, and he suggested two methods of overcoming the decadent tendencies of fictional narratives. First, biographies of exemplary people of both Asia and Europe should be translated for didactic purposes. Liang himself translated some works dealing with foreign nationalist heroes. Second, political reforms could be encouraged by portraying such programs in fictional works. In his work as a reformer Liang particularly emphasized the importance of literature in educating people and contributing to social change. By the late 1910s Chinese writers were going beyond traditional forms and producing works in a colloquial style dealing with themes suggested by foreign literature. Liang can be considered one of the seminal figures of the transitional period who paved the way for the creation of modern literary forms in China as well as Korea.[22]

Liang Chi-Chao's work relates to Korean writing in the early twentieth century in at least three ways. First, his works were not simply quoted in a superficial way, but many Korean intellectuals employed his approach in attempts to solve the problems of building a modern nation. Second, many Korean writers adopted Liang's theory on the social utility of literature. Third, many Korean translators followed Liang's advice on translating foreign works dealing with the lives of patriotic heroes in order to inspire the people.[23]

The basis of nationalist thought in late nineteenth- and early twentieth-century Korea can be found in the works of writers like Pak Ŭn-Sik and Chang Ji-Yŏn, who were interested in bringing about social reforms, as well as in the works of An Ch'ang-Ho and Yang Ki-T'ak, who attempted to combine Confucian culture and Christian concepts.[24] In their efforts to develop reformist thinking, Korean intellectuals were greatly aided by Liang Chi-Chao's assimilation of certain aspects of European thought that were considered beneficial to the creation of a new morality for modern society. Liang's ideas reached Korea through translations of his works by Pak Ŭn-Sik, Chang Ji-Yŏn, Shin Ch'ae-Ho, Chu Si-Kyŏng, and others.[25] At this time many foreign historical narratives and biographies were translated into Chinese or Japanese and then into Korean. Two of these, *The Story of Three Heroes of Italian Unification* and *Roland,* were first translated into Chinese by Liang Chi-Chao. In addition to these works, many others by Liang were introduced, and they facilitated the reception of foreign culture in Korea and the development of nationalism among Korean intellectuals. The *Capital Gazette* and other Korean newspapers published articles about Liang's ideas, and two of his works, *The History of the Fall of Chosŏn (Chosŏn Mangguksa)* and *Japan's Chosŏn (Ilbon ŭi Chosŏn),* attracted wide attention among Korean readers.[26]

Liang's ideas on the education of women and the role of women in national reform were reflected in the Korean work *Freedom Bell (Chayu chong)* and reached many women readers (see below). In his essay, "The Relationship between History and Patriotism" ("Yŏksa wa aeguksim kwa ŭi kwangye"), Shin Ch'ae-Ho emphasizes the need to educate women about history, and he points out that if women are patriotic like Madame Roland, then they will perform as loyal citizens. Liang's thought was not only prevalent among the male reformers who were recommending new educational programs, but it was also echoed by women intellectuals. *Directions for Women (Yŏja chinam)* (started in 1908), is an example of a women's magazine that published articles about Liang's thought written by women who stressed that patriotic duties should be shared by both sexes. According to this way of thinking, women were the foundation of national strength, and Korean women were encouraged to model themselves on the patriotic heroines of Europe.[27]

Translation and New Feminine Images

As we have seen, in texts and translations of the Chosŏn period women were represented as dutiful daughters, faithful wives, devoted mothers, and sometimes even warriors who ultimately return to fulfill traditional roles. Of course there were other ways of representing women—love poetry by courtesans, for instance—but these alternative views were never in competition with the officially sanctioned models of feminine behavior rooted in Confucian teachings.[28] Traditional narratives depict conflicts between those who uphold the Confucian ideals and those who obstruct them. The role of women in these struggles based on cosmic principles is essential: if women desert their place as guardians of traditional values, the whole edifice of the elite class crumbles. Chosŏn society gives us a clear example of what some feminist scholars refer to as the gendered phenomenon of constructing the nation.[29] The translations of the stories of Joan of Arc and Madame Roland appeared in Korea at the moment when historical texts were being imported to buttress a sense of national pride and independence. These translations function on two levels: on the one hand, they continue the tradition of promoting feminine ideals according to which "the home in its essence must remain unaffected by the profane activities of the material world—and woman is its representation."[30] On the other hand, by proposing an alternative model, they open the way for the creation of new narratives.

The Story of a Patriotic Lady

The Story of a Patriotic Lady, which deals with the life of Joan of Arc, was published in Korean in 1907. Neither the original source nor the intermediate translation have been identified.[31] Translations of the lives of European heroines such as Joan of Arc and Madame Roland were available in Japanese and Chinese at the turn of the century in Tokyo. These translations were printed in magazines and had a wide influence among Japanese students and Chinese exchange students in Japan.[32] Although the intermediary text for the Korean translation has not yet been identified, it seems quite likely that it entered Korea by way of exchange students studying in Tokyo, since this was a common method of bringing foreign texts into Korea. The Korean translation might very well have been based on a Chinese translation by Liang Chi-Chao or even one by Lu Xun, the famous Chinese writer who translated many foreign works while studying in Japan. Chang Ji-Yŏn, the Korean translator, was noted for his writing skill in Chinese, and he would have had the linguistic competence to undertake such a translation. Although there is no agreement on the original source for Chang's translation, in general it follows the plan of the *Jeanne d'Arc* by the French historian Jules Michelet that that appeared in 1853. Certainly the heroine of the Korean translation resembles Joan, patriot and nationalist, as she was seen by French writers of the mid- to late nineteenth century.[33]

Like most narratives of the transitional period, *Joan* combines traditional and innovative features. I consider the following aspects of the work: the degree to which it retains traditional techniques, the particular use of interventions by the narrator, and the creation of a hybrid feminine image. *Joan* begins by using the style and terminology that is typical of traditional Korean narratives, including those which dealt with military exploits. The similarities (as noted above) include outlining key points of the story in the introduction, using set expressions to mark the divisions of the story, employing stereotypical phrases, and depicting protagonists who embody the Confucian virtues such as loyalty.[34] Kim Yŏng-Min comments that many historical narratives at the turn of the twentieth century in Korea displayed features of traditional military stories but shifted focus from the deeds of the hero to nationalistic concerns.[35] Chang Ji-Yŏn's translation employs many of the techniques of the military narratives. While some of these works supported the elite and adopted a Chinese background to tell the story of a hero who gained worldly fame and honors, others tended to be more realistic and dealt with the hardships of the common people during war and invasion. *Joan* is more in line with the latter, using dramatic dialogues and speeches to emphasize that loyalty to the sovereign is above honors and riches. Chang Ji-Yŏn avoided exaggeration and pointed out the threat of foreign invasion facing the Korean people.[36]

Interventions of the narrator were a common feature of many narratives of the period since these works had the didactic aim of instilling patriotism in the readers.[37] Interventions in *Joan* consist of three main types: (1) following each section (of which there are ten in *Joan*) the narrator includes a summary with comments; (2) in places the narrator inserts an interjection that conveys his reactions; and (3) at the end there is a long section in which the narrator elaborates on his views. When Joan takes leave of her parents before going off to war, the narrator comments: "Truly, this old man thinks only of protecting his household, while this young woman is filled with the desire to lead the nation." Here he seems to be implying that his own countrymen should worry less about protecting themselves and be willing to sacrifice more for the good of the nation. Another significant intervention occurs just before the attack at Orleans, when the narrator comments: "Truly, when this young woman calls for patriotism, the people are filled with strength to defeat the enemy." This statement could also apply to the Korean people, who, the narrator seems to be implying, needed a strong patriotic spirit to defend their country against the incursions of Japanese colonialism. An example of the narrator's use of interjections occurs when he exclaims about the perilous situation of the French under siege within the walls of Orleans: "Alas! At that moment their position was as risky as meat on a chopping board, stew in a kettle!" Again this exclamation was certainly applicable to the dangers Koreans were facing at the time. At the end of the translation the narrator summarizes the events of Joan's life and adds a concluding comment: "Alas! If only our country had a heroic, patriotic, devoted woman like Joan of Arc!"[38] Finally the narrator has directly stated what he seems to have been implying throughout the translation with his interventions. When we consider the significance of these interventions, it is helpful to keep in mind that Chang Ji-Yŏn was a journalist who was well known for his anti-Japanese editorials. Some of the phrases in his editorials closely resemble passages from his translation.[39]

On one level *Joan* deals with the struggles of the French to drive the English from their territory, but on the other, it warns of the Japanese incursions on the sovereignty of Chosŏn and of the need to encourage resistance and patriotism. We can summarize the ways in which *Joan* promotes nationalist sentiments as follows. First, the Korean title itself, which can be translated as *The Story of a Patriotic Lady,* reveals the didactic aims. Second, from beginning to end the work emphasizes resistance and includes interventions that point out the necessity of repelling foreign invasions. Third, Joan's speeches, like the one just before the battle of Orleans, focus on protecting the kingdom. Finally, even the cover design of the Korean translation portrays a woman struggling for freedom, independence, and the rights of the people.

The translation presents us with a complex model of feminine behavior, setting forth a new image of the heroine while at the same time preserving some traditional elements. On the eve of the heavy fighting at Orleans, Joan makes a speech on the importance of saving the nation, that fosters a new image of women who can actively participate in society. Through her passionate pleas for the defense of the nation, Joan promotes a new ideal of feminine behavior for Korean women, who were still living with the restrictions of feudal society. Discretion in speech was one of the virtues emphasized for women in Confucian texts, and it was highly unacceptable for women to express their views publicly during the Chosŏn period. Thus the translation presents us with a striking new image of women who boldly express themselves in public—even if these opinions concern not the condition of women, but the good of the nation in general terms.

In spite of the novelty of this view of women, the translation still exhibits signs of traditional thinking. The translator describes Joan as if she were a character from a traditional narrative, remarking that she possesses "a lovely face and a graceful carriage" and that she is "one of the country's noted beauties."[40] The Korean Joan expresses her filial devotion to her parents when she takes leave of King Charles after battle; she explains that her old parents have no other children and no one to take care of them, and therefore they eagerly await her return. In spite of these traditional elements, the translation's lasting impact is attested to by the fact that Yu Kwan-Sun, the sixteen-year-old freedom fighter of the 1919 Independence Movement, was widely acclaimed as "Korea's Joan of Arc."[41]

The Story of Madame Roland

Roland deals with the life of Marie-Jeanne Phlipon, a heroine of the French Revolution who married a government minister, became very active politically, and was executed during the Reign of Terror in 1793 by the radical enemies of her husband. She wrote a volume of memoirs while she was incarcerated and waiting to be sent to the guillotine. The Korean translation, which is anonymous and which was serialized in a newspaper in 1907 and then published as a separate volume, was not based directly on a French text, but like the Korean story of Joan of Arc was based on an intermediary text. Although we do not know who the Korean translator was, we do know that the Korean version was based on a Chinese translation done in 1902 by Liang Chi-Chao, who, in turn, was working from a Japanese translation that had appeared in 1886.[42] As I mentioned above, Liang felt that China should draw on all its people, including women, to build leaders. Chinese intellectuals continued to link the improvement of the status of women with nationalist movements: "The issue of women's emancipation was closely intertwined with the entire course of the National Revolution which unfolded in China between 1924 and 1927."[43]

Like the translations of the life of Joan of Arc, those dealing with Madame Roland were influential at the time in East Asian countries. In 1886 a Korean newspaper, the *Capital Weekly (Hansŏng chubo)*, printed a report about a Japanese woman who referred to herself as the "Madame Roland of Japan." She became involved in politics, made public speeches, became embroiled in a conflict, and was finally executed. Madame Roland's followers in Korea were equally enthusiastic, if somewhat less controversial. In 1907 the Korean newspaper that published the translation, the *Taehan Daily News (Taehan maeil sinmun)*, printed a letter from a woman reader who was inspired with patriotism when she read the story of Madame Roland and decided to become involved with the movement to repay the national debt.

As with the Korean story of Joan of Arc, the narrator's interventions are particularly noteworthy. They take three forms: (1) at the beginning and end of the work the narrator directly expresses his voice; (2) the narrator's interjections are included in the body of the work; and (3) the narrator includes explanations of obscure points. As we have seen, at the turn of the century in Korea many historical narratives began and ended with a clear statement of the author/translator's opinions. An example of this type of intervention comes in the prologue, where the Korean text is a fairly literal translation of Liang Chi-Chao's Chinese text. Both translations begin with

Madame Roland's famous words, which she reputedly uttered before the Statue of Liberty in the Place de la Révolution as she was being taken to the guillotine: "O liberty! What crimes are committed in your name!"[44] The narrator goes on to assert that Madame Roland lived and died for freedom, that freedom-loving people of Europe call her their mother, and that she was the mother of the French Revolution. At the beginning of the work there is a doubling of the narrative voices of the Korean and Chinese texts, which are both proposing Madame Roland as the exemplary patriotic woman.

At the end of both the Japanese and Korean versions, the narrator again voices an opinion. The Japanese translation emphasizes that the French Revolution was the most important event of European history and that never before anywhere in the world had such an event taken place. Dictatorship was eliminated, and the free political system was born. The Korean translation includes the following comments: "If we take this woman as our teacher and twenty million Koreans become as one mind and one body, Korea will be equal to the great powers of Europe."[45] Evidently the Korean translator felt it necessary to add this point, not found in the other translations, for the edification of his countrymen.

The translator also uses the kinds of exclamations found in the Korean story of Joan of Arc to arouse an emotional response in the readers. An example is the description of the scene when the Rolands arrive in Paris in 1791 and a group of patriots gather: "Such a pity! Under these difficult circumstances the heroes gather around the stove and rub their hands as they discuss strategy."[46] The translator also intervenes to explain points that were beyond the grasp of the average Korean reader, such as literary expressions based on Chinese characters.

In general these Asian translators present Madame Roland as a courageous heroine who does not flinch when faced with death. Although she is worthy of admiration as a leader in the struggle for freedom, the Korean text still includes some passages that depict her from a traditional point of view. Madame Roland is described in terms worthy of a heroine from a traditional narrative: "Although she is delicate and slender, she can perform a hundred tasks without fail." Madame Roland excuses herself for intruding on the public domain of men when her husband and his friends meet to discuss politics: "I know the proper role of women, so I will not behave inappropriately at the meetings and discussions that daily take place in my surroundings."[47] This picture of the daughter of the Enlightenment observing the Confucian rules of propriety reminds us of scenes from the Korean story of Joan of Arc.

Nationalist Narratives and Changing
Representations of Women: Freedom Bell

As we have seen, the early twentieth century was a period of upheavals in Korea both politically and socially, when new literary forms began to appear. The New Novel movement began with the publication of Yi In-Jik's *Tears of Blood (Hyŏl ŭi nu)* in 1906 and lasted until the late 1910s.[48] The fact that about three hundred New Novels were written in a ten-year period gives us an idea of how popular these works were among Korean readers. The New Novels arose in opposition to traditional narratives, and they introduced new themes, including those relating to the emancipation of women. Yi Hae-Jo's *Freedom Bell* (1910) is sometimes classified with the New Novels, but its use of dialogue makes it somewhat unusual. In *Freedom Bell* there is a direct link between women's issues and the cause of national independence, which mirrors the origins of the women's movement in Korea. "During the Japanese occupation (1910–1945), Korean feminism was entwined with the cause of national liberation. Indeed, the goal of the first organized women's movement under the Japanese protectorship (1905–1910) was to raise funds to pay the debt to Japan that Koreans considered the direct rationale for the protectorship."[49] In the remainder of this chapter I give the background on *Freedom Bell,* relate the work to the translations of the time, and consider the hybrid image of women presented in the work.

Freedom Bell developed the new ways of representing women introduced in the translations from the beginning of the twentieth century. Yi Hae-Jo was one of the most well-known novelists of the period. He grew up in a household where scholarship was stressed, and early in life he showed a talent for classical learning that enabled him to criticize traditional ways of writing. With a prologue and an epilogue providing a frame, *Freedom Bell* is set in 1908 at the birthday party of Yi Mae-Kyŏng, who invites three women friends to engage in discussions on issues of importance for Korean intellectuals; these discussions form almost the entire work.[50] There has been much debate about the genre of this work, but it is generally classified as a dialogue narrative *(t'oronch'e sosŏl).* This was one of the earliest works in Korean to consider the issues of the social position and participation of women in modern society.[51] Although the discussions among the characters cover a broad range of social problems, the question of women's rights is given a considerable amount of space. The discussion topics can be summarized as follows: (1) the importance of equality between men and women; (2) the need for women to take part in social activities; (3) the function of education in overcoming social inequality; (4) the utility of the vernacular script rather than Chinese writing; (5) the importance of raising children to serve national interests; (6) the problem of discrimination against children of concubines; and (7) the hopes for the independence, security, and prosperity of Chosŏn.

Freedom Bell can be related to Liang Chi-Chao's theories on the social utility of literature and his recommendations on the education of women. In fact this work can be compared to a 1905 Chinese novel, Yi Suo's *Huang Xiu Qiu*, which shows the imprint of Liang's work. Although there might not have been direct contact between the authors of these works, they deal with the question of women's rights in a similar way. The female protagonist of the Chinese novel, Huang Xiu Qiu, proclaims that women's liberation can be won if women follow the example of the heroine of the French Revolution, Madame Roland. Huang Xiu Qiu lives in a place called Freedom Village, which reflects the theme of the work. *Huang Xiu Qiu* includes quotations from Liang Chi-Chao's translation of the story of Madame Roland. The heroine of the French Revolution is praised for her sacrifice in the name of liberty, and she provides a model for Huang Xiu Qiu, who also suffers imprisonment and death to bring democracy to her country. After a dream in which Madame Roland gives Huang Xiu Qiu a book of inspiring patriotic legends, the Chinese heroine overcomes the resistance of those who uphold feudalism and establishes Freedom Village.

Freedom Bell reflects a change in attitude toward the education of women based on the realization that the best way to safeguard independence is to promote equality and education among all people. One of the characters, Shin Sŏl-Hŏn, emphasizes the need for educating women in a manner that reflects Liang Chi-Chao's insistence on the importance of education for women in order to maintain national security and prosperity. Shin Sŏl-Hŏn points out that if men and women share the work, it gets done more quickly, and this is the best way to strengthen the nation.

If we compare *Freedom Bell* and *Huang Xiu Qiu* in light of Liang Chi-Chao's thought, we can draw the following conclusions. First, there is a similarity between the title *Freedom Bell* and the Freedom Village where Huang Xiu Qiu lives; since both works are concerned with women's rights, it is possible that Yi Hae-Jo borrowed the word "freedom" for the title of his work.[52] Second, both works make concrete proposals on how education can enable women to achieve equality and go beyond their status as sacrificial victims in a male-dominated society. Third, although they both agree on the social importance of education for women, *Freedom Bell* puts particular emphasis on the link between women's education and national independence. Finally, Yi Hae-Jo, Yi Suo, and Liang Chi-Chao all relate the education of women to the development of a modern economy. In addition to these points, passages of *Freedom Bell* condemn the decadence of traditional Korean narratives in a manner that is reminiscent of Liang's views on the social utility of literature.[53]

Freedom Bell presents a feminine image that is as complex as that found in the translations. An examination of the prologue and epilogue will help in understanding the function of female characters in a work that mostly discusses issues of broad national interest rather than focusing exclusively on the particular situation of women. The prologue is written in a literary style somewhat in contrast with the conversational style of the rest of the work. The work begins with the statement that it is difficult to be born human, but if one loses freedom, one loses the distinguishing human quality. Furthermore, women who are subjugated by men lose their freedom and therefore cannot truly be considered human. At this point the discussions of the four women characters begin. The epilogue introduces a female speaker other than the four whose dialogue constitutes the body of the work. The fifth woman comments that although she is not as well educated as the other four, she shares in their dreams for the prosperity and independence of the nation. The final speaker can be taken to represent the common people, for whose edification the work was written.

The author presents a positive image of women, who openly express their opinions about national affairs in a manner that would not have been acceptable in traditional times. The model of women who struggle for the independence of their country is quite similar to that found in the translations of the lives of European heroines that had appeared a few years earlier. However, if the focus had been only on problems relating to women's rights, *Freedom Bell* would not have had such a wide popular appeal. Although the work begins with a statement about women's rights, it mostly deals with political questions, and women's issues are sometimes even approached in a traditional way. For instance, one of the characters, Kuknan, when searching for solutions to the problem of discrimination against the children of concubines, cites examples that go back hundreds of years. Such reactionary thinking certainly does not harmonize with the image of the enlightened modern woman. In their debates the women cite classical Chinese texts in a contradictory manner, sometimes claiming that the feminine images in these works are beneficial while at other times bitterly criticizing the classics. While this work places great emphasis on education for women, it upholds the traditional view that women's main responsibility is the early training of children. Thus, *Freedom Bell,* like the two translations discussed above, presents a transitional view of women, mixing some traditional elements along with new feminine ideals.

The following chapter considers the next phase of Korean cultural development, when translation was a key element in the introduction of the "New Woman" ideal.

chapter three

Translation and New Feminine
Ideals in the 1920s and 1930s

Due to political and cultural changes in Korea in the 1910s, translators in the 1920s and 1930s concentrated on literary works, as opposed to the emphasis on historical works and biographies at the turn of the twentieth century. The first decade of colonial rule, 1910–1919, is known as the "Dark Period," when all aspects of Korean life came under Japanese domination. Laws restricting the Korean press were so severe that most major newspapers were forced to close down. Political opposition was harshly repressed and many activists were arrested. The colonial education system was organized so as to socialize citizens loyal to the Japanese empire. Accordingly, Japanese was taught as the national language, while Korean was relegated to the status of a second language.[1]

While Korean translators at the turn of the century had introduced works about the lives of patriotic figures from foreign countries in order to encourage a spirit of nationalism, after the Japanese annexation all cultural activities were restricted, and therefore translations could no longer carry an overtly anti-Japanese message. Under these conditions translators turned to literary works that could not be construed as subversive of the colonial regime.

During the 1910s fifteen volumes of literary translations were published, and seventy-four literary translations appeared separately in newspapers and magazines. At this time the following authors were among those whose works were translated into Korean: Jules Verne, Washington Irving, Victor Hugo, Leo Tolstoy, Miguel de Cervantes, Geoffrey Chaucer, Harriet Beecher Stowe, Fyodor Dostoevsky, Ivan Turgenev, and Guy de Maupassant. In most cases translators did not work directly from the originals but consulted Japanese intermediate translations. The appearance of the *Journal of Western Literature and Art (T'aesŏ munye sinbo)* in 1918 greatly promoted literary translation into Korean. In particular Kim Ŏk, many of whose translations appeared in this publication, played a crucial role in emphasizing the need for translating directly from the original and for going beyond the tendency of previous Korean translators to produce abridged works or summaries. Kim Ŏk also stressed the introduction of new esthetic principles through the importation of foreign literary works.[2]

A poem written by Na Hye-Sŏk, one of Korea's early feminist writers, includes the line "Open the door and / Set Nora free" *(Mŭn ŭl yŏlgo / Nora rŭl nohajuge)*. This work, entitled "A Doll's House" ("Inhyŏng ŭi chip"), appeared in the *Daily News (Maeil sinbo)* in 1921, at the moment when the importation of Ibsen's works into Korea was beginning to gain momentum. The fact that at this time well-known Korean writers frequently alluded to characters from Ibsen's plays indicates the extent to which the translation of foreign texts was related to new feminine ideals. In this chapter I examine, first, the debates on the "New Woman" (Sin Yŏsŏng) ideal and the ways in which the social participation of women was increasing. Next I consider the introduction and translation of the works of foreign women writers. Finally, I comment on the new feminine ideals in translated foreign literary works.

Origins of the New Woman Ideal

Women's modernization in Korea was related to the introduction in the late nineteenth century of Protestantism, which influenced ideas on nationalist awakening and female emancipation. The establishment of Ewha, the first modern school for girls in Korea, by Christian missionaries played a decisive role in promoting new education for women. Later the modern education movement and the publication of newspapers and magazines for women helped to eliminate the gap between men and women in terms of cultural and educational backgrounds. Translations of stories about the lives of foreign women and of foreign literary works containing new feminine images contributed to women's self-awareness and spurred them to become active in various fields. The terms for "New Woman," "sin yŏsŏng" and "sin yŏja," were in use in Japan in the 1910s and were frequently used in the 1920s and 1930s in Korea.[3] They referred to women who received a modern, Western-style education; wanted to develop their potential as individuals; and attempted to go beyond the limits of the patriarchal family system.[4]

Debates on the New Woman Ideal in Newspapers and Magazines

In the 1920s two magazines with the title "New Woman"—Sin yŏsŏng and Sin yŏja—promoted women's rights and also helped to make these terms more widespread. At this time in Korea various aspects of the situation of women began to be reexamined, including gender roles and marriage customs. In the inaugural issue of Sin yŏja (March 1920), the editor, Kim Il-Yŏp, emphasized that in order to reform society, the family needed to be reformed, and in order to reform the family, the women in charge of family life needed to be liberated. According to Kim Il-Yŏp, the duty of the New Woman of Korea was to overcome the barriers of repressive traditional customs and reactionary thinking. To enjoy true freedom women needed to attain both self-awareness and economic independence, and in this sense they were not fundamentally different from men. The necessity of overcoming the inertia of the traditional family system so as to safeguard the rights and freedoms of individuals had already been proclaimed in The Independent in the 1890s, but Kim Il-Yŏp was among the first to examine the situation of women in light of these concepts.

Women's World (Yŏja kye) was published between 1917 and 1920 by Korean women exchange students in Japan and focused on the activities of women writers like Kim Myŏng-Sun and Na Hye-Sŏk. It included many articles about the emancipation of women and also published Na Hye-Sŏk's fiction work, "Kyŏng-Hŭi," which deals with a young woman's struggle to become educated and overcome traditional barriers to personal development. Sin yŏsŏng first appeared in 1923 and also focused on women's social participation and emancipation. New Family (Sin kajŏng), which was published by the East Asia Daily (Tonga ilbo) from January 1933 to September 1936, systematically introduced works by foreign women writers. Another important

Korean newspaper, the *Chosŏn Daily (Chosŏn ilbo),* published a monthly, *Woman (Yŏsŏng),* from 1936 to 1940. This was primarily an educational journal that attracted the participation of many well-known women writers before it was forced to close by the Japanese colonial rulers.

In the 1920s the *East Asia Daily* and other Korean newspapers printed many articles that dealt with the New Woman debate. Korean women began to be divided into two categories: those who subscribed to the New Woman ideal and sought to carve out their own place in society, and old-fashioned women who fulfilled traditional roles. Although barely 10 percent of Korean women were literate in the 1930s and the New Woman ideal applied to a small elite, changing expectations for women had far-reaching effects.[5] In the 1920s three women who had studied in Japan and worked as writers were considered to represent the New Woman ideal in Korea: Kim Il-Yŏp (whose work is briefly mentioned above), Na Hye-Sŏk, and Kim Myŏng-Sun. All three actively promoted new roles for women. Na Hye-Sŏk was an exchange student in Tokyo in 1914 when she contributed "Ideal Woman" ("Isangjŏk puin") to *Light of Learning (Hak ji kwang),* another magazine published by Korean students. The article points out that traditional Korean society emphasized virtuous behavior for women as a means of enslaving them and contends that Nora of *A Doll's House* is an ideal woman in the modern sense because of her realistic attitude.[6] As an exchange student in Japan, Kim Myŏng-Sun, whose work will be considered in more detail in chapters 4 and 5, published a story, "A Suspicious Young Girl" ("Ŭisim ŭi sonyŏ"), that was one of the earliest to deal with issues of women's emancipation.

One of the most heated debates centered around the question of new sexual morality *(sin chŏngjo).* At the time female intellectuals like Kim Il-Yŏp and Na Hye-Sŏk promoted a new concept of chastity that rejected the rigid rules of traditional ethics and aimed to provide women with the freedom necessary to live in the modern world. The new view on chastity occupied the attention of both male and female intellectuals and rested on the principle that people should be freed from all oppressive ideologies, including those relating to sexual morality. In an article entitled "My Views on Chastity," ("Na ŭi chŏngjogwan"), which appeared in the *Chosŏn Daily* in 1927, Kim Il-Yŏp explained that for women who followed the traditional rules of behavior love was stale, and therefore chastity should no longer be thought of as a precious jewel to be maintained at all costs, but rather should apply only to those who are in love. In her article "Entering a New Life" ("Sin saenghwal e tŭlmyŏnsŏ"), which appeared in the journal *Three Thousand Li (Samch'ŏlli)* in 1935, Na Hye-Sŏk stated pithily that people should follow their sexual inclinations, much like eating when hungry, and desires should not be repressed. For these women writers of the 1920s and 1930s, women's emancipation started with abolishing the traditional rules governing chastity.

These new ideals of feminine behavior were not without detractors, and there tended to be a gap between men and women concerning the evaluation of the New Woman ideal. In particular, the early Korean feminists' ideas on love and marriage evoked a negative response from some male intellectuals, who bitterly criticized both the outward appearance and the underlying thought patterns of those who adhered to the New Woman ideal. In a 1923 article in *New Woman (Sin yŏsŏng)*, the writer So Ch'un published a scathing critique in which he stated that the term "New Woman" *(sin yŏja)* implied an opposition to "Old-Fashioned Woman" *(kusik yŏja)*. However, the so-called New Women of Korea were far from being more advanced than their traditional sisters. In order to merit the designation, the New Women should go beyond appearance and lifestyle and adopt a new way of thinking. Although So stated that this new way of thinking concerned aspects of behavior far more fundamental than free choice in love and marriage *(chayu yŏnae, chayu kyŏlhon)*, he did not specify precisely what was involved. The issue of free choice in love and marriage developed into a controversy between female and male intellectuals, with the latter tending to focus on the debate over female chastity while ignoring wider questions relating to the emancipation of women. These men tended to associate all followers of the New Woman ideal with a narrow conception of sexually free behavior and to denigrate them as immoral. Some of the critics of the New Woman ideal advocated that women should become emancipated from traditions by devoting themselves to nationalist causes rather than promoting reforms that related to women as a group.

As we have seen, at first the term "New Women" was used to refer to women who had been educated in the new way, but gradually it came to be associated, in the minds of some critics, with women who opposed the traditional sexual mores. In some quarters the New Women were considered little more than high-class prostitutes.[7] The New Woman ideal served a transitional role during the period when traditional ways were being rejected and new values were being formed. At this time the approach to the emancipation of women was not yet fully developed, and there was a tendency to view the New Woman ideal in contrast to traditional expectations. Although thinkers like Kim Myŏng-Sun, Na Hye-Sŏk, and Kim Il-Yŏp pointed out the contradictions in the social expectations for women, they could not formulate their criticisms in a systematic way, and therefore their impact was limited.[8]

Although the new views on women were promoted by a small number of intellectuals, the Korean feminists of this period were striving to overcome the repressive traditions of the patriarchal system in order to emancipate the majority of Korean women from poverty and ignorance. Many articles appeared in *New Woman (Sin yŏsŏng)* about the lives of foreign women, such as "Marriage and American Women Students" ("Miguk yŏ haksaeng dŭl ŭi kyŏlhon" [March 1924]) and "The Interesting Lives of French Women Students" ("Chaemi issnŭn France yŏhaksaeng saenghwal" [April 1924]). In addition, these journals included articles that introduced the experiences of pioneering Korean women who studied overseas, such as Na Hye-Sŏk. Through their travels and studies overseas, these women went beyond the narrow worldview of the traditional Korean woman and gained insights on how to approach women's issues. These publications also dealt with the difficulty that Korean women students faced after graduation. Although in some ways women who became educated were better off socially, their social roles were limited and they faced economic hardships. The view that the followers of the New Woman ideal were sexually promiscuous persisted, and women had to face pressure from parents who felt that traditional marriage was the only possibility for women.

Expansion of Women's Social Activities

In the late nineteenth and early twentieth centuries Korean women began to engage in activities that went beyond those of traditional society. Traditional costumes were among the first things to change, and by about 1910 the hoods and shawls that symbolized the confinement of women were being replaced by parasols that covered the face.[9] While the change in dress represented acceptance of the new culture, in some quarters new fashions were perceived as extravagant luxuries. Shortly after Kim Il-Yŏp published her article on the New Woman in *Sin yŏja* in 1920, *East Asia Daily* published an article by Yi Il-Jŏng, "The Confrontation over Gender Equality," which pointed out that the sexually free behavior of some who called themselves New Women might harm the chances for women to improve themselves. Criticism of Kim Il-Yŏp's version of the New Woman ideal came from various quarters, including working women and those involved in the women's movement. In the 1920s Korean women activists who were concerned about problems resulting from Japanese colonization began to criticize some of the adherents of the New Woman ideal for moral laxness. Unlike Kim Il-Yŏp, who lacked a theoretical foundation for her thinking, some members of nationalist and socialist women's organizations went beyond the question of individual freedom and attempted to link women's issues to larger social problems such as colonialism and class conflicts.[10] This subsection includes an overview of fields where women's activities had begun to develop in Korea around the turn of the twentieth century and were increasing in the 1920s and 1930s, including politics, social and religious activities, and education. The work of women writers will be considered in more detail in chapter 5.

Political Activities

For many centuries Korean women did not take part directly in the political process. Although there were several Silla queens who ruled in their own right, in Chosŏn women of the royal family had only limited and indirect political influence. Since upper-class women traditionally were supposed to remain within their households, taking part in outside activities was out of the question. It was not until the late nineteenth and early twentieth centuries that women in Korea began to realize possibilities for political participation. At that time women began to participate in the Independence Movement and to contribute to patriotic causes. A woman known only by the pseudonym of Ko Dae-Su provides an example of a person of humble origins who played a role in the Enlightenment Movement at the end of the nineteenth century. She was a court lady's maid in Seoul's Chang-Dŏk Palace who became associated with members of the Progressive Party; during a coup attempt in 1884 she passed information to leaders like Kim Ok-Kyun about the secrets of the royal palace. A few days after the coup attempt failed, she was dragged from the palace and stoned to death by a crowd of conservatives and government loyalists.[11]

After the Japanese annexation in 1910 many Korean women took part in anti-Japanese activities. As noted, in 1913 the Songjuk Secret Association was formed. Hwang Ae-Dŏk was the main organizer, and members were carefully chosen. The membership spread all over the country, and members were involved in the March 1919 Independence Movement and other anti-Japanese activities.[12] Women from various social groups actively participated in the Independence Movement, including religious leaders, students, workers, housewives, and courtesans. Many women risked their lives to take part in demonstrations and were sent to prison. Women's involvement in the Independence Movement marked the transition from traditional seclusion to modern political participation. The first women's socialist organization in Korea, the Chosŏn Women's Fellowship Association (Chosŏn Yŏsŏng Tonguhoe), was formed in 1924 with the aim of overcoming the exploitation of women. The founders contended that women's emancipation was based on economic independence, and they established branches in all corners of the country to promote the education of women. This was the first women's organization to promote class emancipation. The Kŭnu Association represented women all over the country and attempted to overcome the division of women's organizations into those with a Christian leaning and those focusing on socialist issues. This organization promoted women's self-awakening and nationalist activities.[13]

Social and Religious Activities

Koreans realized that national independence could not be achieved without economic development, and at this time many people took part in the movement to promote the production and use of native goods. Because of Japanese pressures, the middle classes in the cities were rapidly ruined, and the farmers in the countryside were deprived of their lands. Nationalist leaders promoted economic independence, and women's groups, including the Women's Association for the Promotion of Native Products and the Chosŏn Christian Women's Temperance Society (Chosŏn Kidok Yŏja Chŏljehoe), participated in this movement. The Temperance Society promoted improvements in women's rights and position as well.[14] By 1905 Chosŏn had accumulated an enormous debt toward Japan that threatened national security. Korean women were disturbed by this state of affairs, and a group of them formed the Women's Association to Repay the National Debt (Kukch'ae Posang Puinhoe). Women also contributed money to repay the national debt by selling their jewelry and other valuable items.[15]

In addition to activities that concerned society as a whole, women's organizations also agitated about other matters of concern to women. In 1899 the Ch'anyanghoe launched a campaign to eliminate the system of keeping concubines. In Chosŏn this practice was legal, and jealousy was one of the so-called seven faults for which a wife could be sent away. In this respect the Ch'anyanghoe was a pioneer in promoting the social position of women in Korea. The members of this group marched carrying banners that proclaimed the immorality of men who took two wives, and the president of the association, Chŏng Hyŏng-Suk, demonstrated for a whole week.[16]

Participation in religious activities was also a way for women to go beyond the rigid limitations of traditional society. Kim Kwi-Dong offers an example of the fervor with which Korean women often embraced Christianity. In 1893 as a sixteen-year-old student at Ewha School, she cut off her hair and sold it to raise money for the Chŏngdong Church building fund. At this time her short hair was revolutionary, but she courageously fought against conventional norms in order to uphold her religious beliefs.

Women's religious organizations were active in promoting education for women. In 1922 the Korean YWCA (Chosŏn Kidokkyo Yŏja Ch'ŏngnyŏn-hoe) was founded by Kim Hwal-Ran, Kim P'il-Rye, and Yu Kak-Kyŏng to promote a new lifestyle for women. In 1921 a similar organization, the Ch'ŏn-dokyo Women's Youth Association (Ch'ŏndokyo Yŏja Ch'ŏngnyŏnhoe), was founded to promote hygiene, education, training of rural women, and the eradication of superstition.[17]

Educational Activities

At the end of the nineteenth and beginning of the twentieth centuries, women's education was developing, and some women had the opportunity to study overseas. The following are a few examples of the first women to receive a foreign education. After eight years of studying in Japan, Yun Jŏng-Wŏn visited Europe and America, where she showed promise as a student of music and linguistics.[18] She was recalled by the Korean government and appointed as a teacher in Hansŏng High School. Yun Jŏng-Wŏn's work was motivated by the realization that a country's prosperity required well-educated women who were capable of contributing in their fields. Esther Pak graduated from Ewha Girls' School and in 1890 began to work as an interpreter for foreign doctors. In 1896 she went to the United States and entered medical school in Baltimore. After graduating in 1900, she returned to Korea and became the first Korean woman doctor of Western medicine. Later she established a school for the handicapped and a nursing school.[19] Ha Ran-Sa was admitted to Ewha Girls' School as a married woman, although at the time only unmarried women were allowed to matriculate. In 1896 she left Ewha, studied in Japan for a year, and then went to the United States, where she received a B.A. from Wesleyan University in 1900. After returning to Korea, she contributed to the development of education for women and worked in the Independence Movement.

Introduction of Foreign Women Writers

As we have seen, women's magazines of the 1920s and 1930s, such as *New Family*, *Woman*, and *New Woman (Sin yŏsŏng)*, introduced new feminine images that were related to the development of modern educational methods, the reform of the traditional family system, and the adoption of a modern view of individual freedom, particularly with regard to love and marriage. The translation of foreign texts was crucial in the process of developing these new views.[20] In this section I explain how foreign women writers first came to be translated into Korean; then I consider how foreign women writers were introduced into Korea in groups and as individuals.

During the 1920s translations into Korean of the works of foreign women authors were rare. In 1925 O Ch'ŏn-Sŏk's translations of four Sara Teasdale poems appeared in the literary magazine *Chosŏn Literary World (Chosŏn mundan),* accompanied by a brief introduction. When the inaugural issue of the literary magazine *Foreign Literature (Haeoe munhak)* appeared in 1927, a Sara Teasdale poem was the only work by a foreign woman to be included. In the 1930s women's magazines like *New Family* and *New Woman (Sin yŏsŏng)* published series of articles introducing the women writers of various foreign countries. These articles tended to be limited to general trends, and there were very few detailed analyses of the works of individual authors. At this time newspapers and literary magazines focused on introducing foreign literature, including the works of women poets such as the Englishwomen Christina Rossetti, Elizabeth Browning, and Alice Meynell and the Indian Sarojini Naidu, in addition to Sara Teasdale. Such works were translated as part of a trend toward what the Koreans termed "pure poetic lyricism" *(sunsu sŏjŏng si).* The 1938 *Anthology of Foreign Lyric Poetry (Haeoe sŏjŏng sisŏn),* edited by Ch'oe Jae-Sŏ, includes translations of the works of Christina Rossetti and Elizabeth Browning (among others). In 1939 the poet and translator Pak Yong-Ch'ŏl published *Pak Yong-Ch'ŏl's Collected Works (Pak Yong-Ch'ŏl chŏnjip),* in which he translated twenty-two of Sara Teasdale's poems.

General Trends

Between 1933 and 1935 *New Family* published a series of detailed articles on women writers from various countries, including the United States, USSR, France, and China. One of the articles attempted to give an overview of women writers worldwide. An examination of a few of these articles indicates the policy of Korean critics of the period toward the importation of foreign literary trends in general and women writers in particular. Yu Kyŏng-Sang wrote a fairly detailed article about contemporary American women authors that was intended as a stimulus for Korean women authors. Although the writers Yu mentioned are not well known today, he pointed out how techniques in their works might be useful for the women writers of his own country. Yu cited Zona Gale for the mystical aspects of her writing and Isa Glenn for her perceptiveness and powers of observation as a novelist. Ellen Glasgow was particularly noteworthy for the realism of her character portrayals and her rejection of false sentiments and romanticism.

In his article on modern women authors of the USSR, Ham Dae-Hun asserted that women's literature was weak in every country and writing by women in Russia before the revolution was particularly deficient. Nagrodskaia was the first of three contemporary women writers of the USSR whose works Ham analyzed. According to Ham, her writing had attracted popular attention since it was characterized by the kind of sensationalism that appealed to contemporary audiences. However, apart from superficial sentimentality, Nagrodskaia's works displayed neither psychological depth nor ideological content. The second author Ham treated was Charskaia, whose works he found technically deficient but full of delicate psychological insight. Charskaia's perceptive depictions of characters added a lifelike element to her works. Finally, Ham identified Verbitskaia as an author who promoted women's rights and freedoms.

Four French women authors were introduced in an article by Yi Hŏn-Gu, a graduate of the French literature department of Waseda University who devoted himself to translating French literature into Korean. In his article Yi stated that the French were noted for their love of freedom, reflected in the various forms of literary expression they enjoy as the cultural heritage of their nation. Compared to the people of Chosŏn, who did not know how to express their inner feelings, the French had an innate ability to express themselves fluently and elegantly. Yi explained that Lucie Delarue-Mardrus was noted for the fanciful quality of her works, while Myriam Harry's writing displayed a yearning for the exotic. Gabrielle Colette's writing rivaled that of Anatole France in terms of the perfection of technique and the depiction of emotional states. Rachilde created a literary world where the imagination could take flight.

Chŏng Rae-Dong wrote an article about Chinese women writers in the September 1934 issue of *New Family*. He examined the experience of writing itself, as well as the qualifications of the writers and the kinds of writing being done, since he felt that these issues were instructive for Korean writers. In his summary of the development of the new Chinese literature, Chŏng focused on the themes of women's writing, such as the restrictions of family life, the struggle to achieve independence, and the attempt to participate in social activities. There were a growing number of Chinese women who, like the writer Bai Wei, had graduated from a girls' school, left home, went abroad to Tokyo to discover a new life, and struggled to achieve economic independence.[21] Chŏng explained that both Chinese and Korean women writers resembled Ibsen's Nora to the extent that they disliked household life and did not want to be slaves to men.

Chŏng commented on the writing experiences of some of the prominent Chinese women writers of the period. Lu Yin's approach to creative writing was representative of her era of Chinese women writers, who tended to depict the tragic aspects of their society with warmth and emotional depth. Bing Xin contended that individuality was the essence of creativity, and therefore literature that expressed the self covered the spectrum of pure emotion from tragedy to comedy. Bing Xin's work combined native Chinese literary traditions with foreign influences from authors such as Tolstoy and Tagore. Ding Ling claimed to have embarked on a career as a writer with the dual aim of communicating her inner emotions and improving social conditions.

Individual Writers

The following women writers were among the most frequently introduced into Korea in the 1920s and 1930s: Ellen Key, Alexandra Kollontai, Katherine Mansfield, Sara Teasdale, Christina Rossetti, Elizabeth Barrett Browning, Alice Meynell, and Sarojini Naidu. Two concepts were of crucial importance for the adherents of the New Woman ideal in Korea: those dealing with free choice in love and marriage and those relating to the Swedish feminist Ellen Key's (1849–1926) theories on motherhood and marriage. Key's ideas had been introduced into Japan by the 1910s, and parts of her book, *Love and Marriage,* had been translated by the Japanese feminist Raicho.[22] Therefore Korean exchange students in Japan could easily become familiar with Key's emphasis on women's rights and motherhood. According to Key, men should not have legal advantages, and freedom and equality should be guaranteed for both sexes. Women should be independent from men, and they should not be forced to do work that could interfere with their duties as mothers. In order for women to avoid economic dependency when they become mothers, governments had to institute policies to protect women and children. Since the important thing in marriage was love rather than legal regulations, a loveless marriage was always immoral. In the 1920s and 1930s Key's ideas were more widely discussed than those of Ibsen. The Norwegian dramatist did not suggest what would happen to Nora after she left the house, but Ellen Key's specific proposals on motherhood struck a responsive chord among women.[23] Key's emphasis on love over social customs was reflected in the works of some of the Korean women writers such as Kim Myŏng-Sun, who focused on the ethics of love. In the 1920s and 1930s a number of articles about Ellen Key appeared in Korean newspapers and magazines. In an article that appeared in the literary magazine *Creation (Kaebyŏk)* in 1921, No Ja-Yŏng explained that for Ellen Key the morality of marriage stemmed from love, and the most important thing for parents was to raise their children properly. (Another literary journal also called *Creation [Ch'angjo]* first appeared in 1919.)

The ideas of the socialist feminist Alexandra Kollontai aroused much interest among Korean intellectuals of the period. Kollontai, a member of the Communist Women's International, which was formed in Moscow in July 1920, wrote a fiction work called *Red Love* that was debated in the Korean press and periodicals. The woman translator Kim Ja-Hye published an abridged translation of *Red Love (Pulgŭn sarang)* in *New Family* in 1933. Many people contrasted the female protagonist Vassilissa of *Red Love* with Jeanne of Maupassant's *Une vie*. In 1928 an article in the *Chosŏn Daily* by Sŏ Kwang-Je, "New Love, New Women—A Reading of Kollontai's *Red Love*," claimed that the heroine of Kollontai's work represented women's struggle for freedom and independence.[24] In her 1933 article, "Kollontai's *Red Love*," Chu In-Suk commented that this work represented a socialist view of sexual relations, and she criticized the traditional marriage customs of Chosŏn. In a 1934 article in *New Family* Ha Mun-Ho concluded that Kollontai emphasized work rather than family relations as a means of raising the status of women. Some women readers felt that Kollontai was suggesting possibilities to put male-female relations on a more reasonable and equitable footing.[25]

Ch'ae Jŏng-Kŭn wrote an article in 1936 in *New Family* in which he compared the works of Katherine Mansfield to those of Chekhov. Ch'ae praised her skillful psychological descriptions.[26]

Sara Teasdale was one of the most widely translated women poets in Korea in the 1920s and 1930s. Selections from her works were translated by O Ch'ŏn-Sŏk in 1925 (as noted), Yang Ju-Dong in 1927, Yi Ha-Yun in 1929, and Pak Yong-Ch'ŏl in 1933. O Ch'ŏn-Sŏk included an introduction to Sara Teasdale's works along with his 1925 translations, praising her poems for their conciseness, emotional depth, and melodiousness. He explained that Teasdale was known as a poet of pure lyrical works and that she skillfully infused brief forms with complex meanings. A translator known as Pa Ul introduced Teasdale as the poet of love and commented on the gently flowing melody of her works in a 1925 article.[27] In a 1926 *East Asia Daily* article, O Yŏng compared Sara Teasdale and Sarojini Naidu, remarking on the lyricism and refreshing beauty of their works. While Teasdale could not equal Naidu in terms of depth and religious sentiment, her works were characterized by freshness, restrained emotion, and the lyricism of everyday life. Teasdale continued to gain readers in Korea in the 1930s, and Pak Yong-Ch'ŏl included an article about her work with his 1933 translations. He expressed regret at transmitting only a trace of the delicate beauty of her works in his translations and commented that her poems were appealing because they concisely expressed both the sorrow and cautious happiness of love.

Christina Rossetti's poems were translated by several Koreans, including Yi Ha-Yun, Yagobo, Im Myŏng-Hwa, and Im Hak-Su. P'i Ch'ŏn-Dŭk also translated some of her works and included a commentary in a 1933 *New Family* article. He claimed that an important characteristic of her art was the ability to combine lyricism and religious sentiment. Although death was viewed optimistically, her poems reflected a reluctance to leave the world, which stemmed from a love of life.

Elizabeth Barrett Browning's poems were translated into Korean in the 1930s by Chu Yo-Han, Kim Sang-Yong, Im Hak-Su, and Pak Yong-Ch'ŏl. P'i Ch'ŏn-Dŭk also translated some of her poems and wrote a commentary on her work in a 1933 *New Family* article. He claimed that Browning's attempts to treat philosophical problems led to failure and that she was guilty of carelessness in her longer poems. However, there were many masterpieces among her sonnets and shorter pieces.

Some of the works of Alice Meynell were translated into Korean in 1933 by the woman translator Ch'oe Jŏng-Rim and in 1938 by Ch'oe Jae-Sŏ. Yi Ha-Yun also commented on Meynell's work in a 1930 *East Asia Daily* article. According to Yi, Meynell's poetry differed from the decadent English poetry of the late nineteenth century to the extent that it reflected a delicate feminine sensibility. Her works, whether they dealt with religious sentiments, sexual love, or the appreciation of nature, inspired the reader with a sense of reverence.

Sarojini Naidu's works were first translated into Korean in the 1920s by Kim Ŏk. At this time, next to Tagore, Naidu was the Indian poet whose works were most frequently translated. During the 1920s Korean translators focused on her lyric works, while in the 1930s more of her nationalistic poems were translated.

Feminine Ideals in Translated Literary Works

Translations of the works of Ibsen, Maupassant, Tolstoy, and others contributed greatly to the formation of new feminine ideals in the 1920s and 1930s. In particular, translations of Ibsen and Maupassant provided contrasting models that related to the New Woman ideal.

During the 1920s and 1930s approximately sixty articles about Ibsen's life and work appeared in Korean newspapers and periodicals, and the work of the Norwegian dramatist had a significant influence all over East Asia at the time. Feminists in Japan were accused of being "Japanese Noras," and *A Doll's House* became very popular in China after the translation appeared in 1918. The one hundredth anniversary of Ibsen's birth in 1926 and the thirtieth anniversary of his death in 1936 elicited a number of publications about him. Most of the articles centered around: Ibsen's life and thought; his major works, especially *A Doll's House,* and analyses of Nora's character; and his views on women and the future of the women's movement. Although there were many articles dealing with Ibsen's writing, translations of his works were relatively limited. *A Doll's House* was translated twice in 1922, by Yang Paek-Hwa and Yi Sang-Su, and in 1934 it was translated by Pak Yong-Ch'ŏl and produced on stage.[28] *Ghosts,* which deals with the problems of a loveless marriage, was translated in an abridged form in *New Woman (Sin yŏsŏng)* in 1932. *The Lady from the Sea* was translated by Yi Sang-Su in 1923, an abridged translation appeared in the magazine *Student (Haksaeng)* in 1930, and it was produced on stage in 1932. The articles on Ibsen tended toward wholehearted praise of his work, to the point of lacking critical judgment, and much of this writing was repetitive and lacking in originality. In spite of these limitations, the amount of writing about Ibsen testifies to the importance that his works had during this crucial phase of Korean cultural history, when modern literary forms were rapidly developing.

The Nora image gave great inspiration to Korean women. Nora offered a model for those who wanted to throw off the shackles of feudal society and explore new possibilities for women's lives.[29] However, while male intellectuals recognized Ibsen's role in criticizing the unreasonableness of traditional marriage customs, they criticized the followers of the New Woman ideal in their attempts to emulate Nora's quest for a more fully human existence. Certain critics even went so far as to claim that the so-called New Women were behaving in a way that was exactly opposite to the ideals represented by Nora. In an article that appeared in *New Woman (Sin yŏsŏng)* in 1926, Yu U-Sang commented that *Ghosts* and *A Doll's House* described with startling honesty the problems of modern family life. Women had lost their social rights and were little more than slaves to tyrannical husbands, and Nora accurately pointed out that she was a prisoner of man-made laws. However, Yu abruptly changed his tone when he wrote of the New Women in his own country, who, according to him, were indulging in wanton sexual excess and becoming victims of venereal disease. In this way male critics evoked the name of Nora to chastise the behavior of women who, they felt, were not following the proper path. In contrast to this contradictory view, Na Hye-Sŏk's poem, "A Doll's House," indicated how some women writers were identifying Nora's situation as similar to their own.

Among the many articles praising Nora as a representative of emancipated women was Hyŏn Ch'ŏl's 1921 *Creation (Kaebyŏk)* article, which pointed out that *A Doll's House* represented self-awakening.[30] In his May 1921 *Civilization (Kyemyŏng)* article, Kim Sŏk-Song pointed out that *A Doll's House* portrayed the anguish of a woman who sought to be liberated from the traditional family system so that she could live a more fully human life. Ibsen could be considered a proponent of individualism to the extent that his female characters developed their human qualities rather than fulfilling traditional roles.[31] Yŏm Sang-Sŏp in his 1922 *New Life (Sin saenghwal)* article pointed out that through her revolt Nora overcame generations of female oppression. Sim Hun, in a 1928 *Chosŏn Daily* article, contended that even if Ibsen did not present the answers to the problems posed in his plays, he was a pioneering author.[32] In the 1930s Koreans continued to comment on Ibsen's plays, and among his translators were Yi Hŏn-Gu, Kim Kwang-Sŏp, and Sŏ Hang-Sŏk. Yi Hŏn-Gu was one of the critics who recognized that Ibsen was a dramatist of genius, a proponent of freedom, and a supporter of women's rights.

Maupassant

Maupassant's works were first translated into Korean in the 1910s, and they continued to be among the most widely translated foreign works during the 1920s and 1930s. The works were popular in Korea for various reasons, such as Maupassant's international reputation as a writer and the clarity and brevity of his works. However, probably the most important reason was the fact that Maupassant's works had been widely translated into Japanese, and this provided a relatively accessible source for Korean translators.[33] The fact that *Une vie (Yŏja ŭi ilsaeng)* was translated into Korean twice during this period indicates the wide readership for the works.

Korean critics compared Ibsen's Nora, Maupassant's Jeanne *(Une vie),* and Kollontai's Vassilissa *(Red Love).* Most of the male intellectuals took Jeanne to resemble the traditional Korean woman, who endured suffering and hardship. Pak Yŏng-Hŭi wrote an article in 1928 in the *Chosŏn Daily* in which he compared Vassilissa and Jeanne. He contended that Vassilissa represented modernity, while Jeanne, sheltered by her family and educated in a convent, married a man of loose virtue who caused her a life of suffering. In contrast to Nora, who escaped the tyranny of her husband's house, Jeanne fatalistically accepted a life of servitude.[34] Kye Yong-Muk's 1939 article in *Woman* related Jeanne's suffering as an abused woman to the lives of many Korean women.

Tolstoy

Tolstoy's works have played a significant role in Korea since the early twentieth century, and a number of his works were translated in the 1920s and 1930s. Tolstoy was the most widely read Russian author in Korea from the 1910s through the 1930s.[35] Two of his female characters were particularly impressive for Korean readers: Anna Karenina and Katyusha from *Resurrection*. In the 1920s and 1930s many articles examined Tolstoy's ideas on religion, literature, and love (among other things). Many articles considered Tolstoy's works in light of the New Woman ideal, such as Kim Sŏk-Song's June 1921 *Civilization* article, which explained Tolstoy's views on chastity.[36] In a 1922 *Youth (Ch'ŏngnyŏn)* article, Uwhajikin explained Tolstoy's view that by controlling sexual desire and observing abstinence people could come closer to God.[37] As part of a series on famous people's ideas about love, Ch'ilbosanin explained in an article in 1926 in *New Woman (Sin yŏsŏng)* that Tolstoy valued spiritual rather than physical love and felt that divorce was impossible.[38] Korean critics identified Katyusha and Anna Karenina as Tolstoy's ideal women. In the 1930s Korean periodicals began to focus more on Tolstoy's views on literature.

Female Protagonists in Other Works

In addition to the female protagonists mentioned above, a number of others attracted Korean readers at the time. A 1939 article in *Woman* examined the female characters in Gustave Flaubert's *Madame Bovary*, Prosper Merimée's *Carmen*, and Pearl Buck's *The Good Earth*. One of the authors of this article, Yi Sŏn-Hŭi, praised the depiction of passionate love in *Carmen*, which she felt was more appropriate reading for women than the naturalist or Marxist works favored by male intellectuals. After Pearl Buck won the Nobel Prize for literature in 1938, many articles about her work appeared in Korea, including one by the poet Mo Yun-Suk in the *East Asia Daily* that explained that Buck's female characters represented Asian women who did not openly rebel but retained their innate beauty and strength in the face of hardships.[39]

Although most of the women translators whose work we examine in the following chapter did not focus on women authors, their contributions must be considered in the context of the introduction of foreign women writers that was taking place at the time.

chapter four

Women Literary Translators
in the 1920s and 1930s

The 1920s saw the publication of 124 volumes of literary translations into Korean—a significant increase over the 1910s. In addition, 671 literary translations appeared separately in newspapers and magazines. The breakdown by the countries whose works were most frequently translated is as follows: England, 151; Russia, 127; India, 126; France, 100; North America, 65.[1] Among the authors whose fiction works were most frequently translated are the following: Maupassant (twelve works), Chekhov (eleven), and Tolstoy (ten). English poets were the most frequently translated, including William Blake, Alfred Lord Tennyson, Arthur Symons, and Lord Byron; Byron's works were particularly popular, with three volumes of his poems appearing in Korean translation at the time.

In 1921 Kim Ŏk, one of the most prolific literary translators of the early 1920s, published *Dance of Agony (Onoe ŭi mudo),* the first volume of translated poetry in modern Korea. In 1924 he published a volume of Arthur Symons' poetry in translation that helped to introduce the works of this poet to Korean readers. During the 1920s most literary translations into

Korean were not done directly from the original, but rather used Japanese intermediate translations. At a time when most Korean translators depended on Japanese intermediate texts, Kim Ŏk was one of the few to translate directly from foreign languages such as English and French.[2]

During the 1930s the number of volumes of literary translations fell to only twenty-one. However, 894 such translations were published in newspapers and magazines, including 367 from England, 127 from Germany, 108 from France, 104 from North America, 101 from the USSR, and 21 from India. In 1935 Japan dropped out of the League of Nations and became isolated internationally, which led to a decline in the translation of foreign works in the Korean colony. In Korea foreign literature was denounced, and its importation was restricted by government controls.

In spite of this unfavorable climate, translation norms and procedures evolved during the 1930s, and translators with specialized training in foreign languages and literatures began to appear. Unlike in the 1920s, when the original title and author were frequently not identified, in the 1930s information was increasingly provided about a work and its author. At this time stress was placed on translating entire works directly. The 1930s can be considered a turning point in Korean literary translation because of the attempts of translators with specialized training to implement specific policies.[3]

In the late 1920s the members of the Foreign Literature Group (Haeoemunhakp'a) began to emphasize translating directly from the original and raising the level of Korean language and literature through the translation of foreign literary works. Translators who had studied foreign languages, such as Yi Ha-Yun, Ch'oe Jae-Sŏ, Yang Ju-Dong, and Pak Yong-Ch'ŏl, translated many foreign literary works, such as those of Thomas Hardy, Robert Louis Stevenson, Tolstoy, and Chekhov. During the 1930s English poetry was particularly emphasized, with 239 translations appearing.[4] Newspapers such as the *East Asia Daily* and *Chosŏn Daily* devoted sections to translations of Wordsworth, Blake, Shelley, Symons, and others. The 1930s have been termed the renaissance of literary translation in Korea.[5]

This chapter considers the work of the first group of modern women translators in Korea. The first section gives an overview of their work and is followed by an examination of norms and techniques. The next sections consider the innovative/conservative tendencies of the women translators and the institutional constraints they faced. In the concluding section I summarize how women translators contributed to the development of new forms of writing and to Korean literary and cultural development in the 1920s and 1930s.[6]

Background on the Women Translators

Women translators in the 1920s and 1930s were among the intellectuals who had benefited from a modern education. Also, a few foreign women missionaries translated into Korean in the late nineteenth and early twentieth centuries. Although research on Korean women writers has been expanding in the past few decades, almost no attention has been given to the work of women translators. My research has identified forty women literary translators who were active during the 1920s and 1930s (see the appendix for a list of translations). While Kim Myŏng-Sun, the most prolific of the women translators, published ten translations, many of the others published only one or two. The translations consist mostly of relatively short poems, particularly by British and American authors, but also include fiction works and fairy tales. The scarcity of information about most of the translators and the lack of scholarly interest in their translations can be explained by the fact that the output was limited and that as young women, the translators occupied a marginal position in the literary world. Although some of the women slipped into obscurity after publishing only one or two translations, at least several of them were relatively well known as writers, including Kim Myŏng-Sun, Mo Yun-Suk, No Ch'ŏn-Myŏng, and Kim Ja-Hye. Although Korean women translators at this time were not united under the banner of feminism—or any other ideology—there are some common features in most of their careers. Many of them graduated from Ewha Women's College and published translations and original works in women's magazines and literary periodicals such as *New Family, New Woman (Sin yŏsŏng), Woman, Three Thousand Li,* and *New East Asia (Sin Tonga).*

Three foreign women, at least two of whom were missionaries, appear in Kim Byŏng-Ch'ŏl's list of literary translators: Mary Hillman, Mrs. Norton, and Mrs. Underwood. Some scholars have concluded that the foreign missionaries translated in order to transmit a religious message.[7] Robert Louis Stevenson's *The Strange Case of Dr. Jekyll and Mr. Hyde* was used by preachers to illustrate the dangers of the evil side of the human psyche. Therefore missionaries were interested in this work, and it was translated into Korean in 1921 by Mrs. Underwood and again in 1926 by James Scarth Gale.[8] On the other hand, according to Kim Byŏng-Ch'ŏl, Mrs. Norton's translations of fairy tales go beyond didactic aims and display a concern for style.[9] It is, of course, possible that some of the anonymous translations from this period were done by Korean or foreign women.

Norms and Techniques in the Work
of Individual Women Translators

The concept of translation norms has been used by scholars of the so-called descriptive-explanatory school of translation studies as a tool in examining the translation process and the functions of translation within a target culture. Theo Hermans sums up the objectives of this kind of research: "The aim remains that of gaining insight into the theoretical intricacies and the historical relevance and impact of translation."[10] In this section I examine the ways in which the women translators followed certain norms, as well as the stylistic techniques they employed, such as the use of colloquial language or Chinese-character expressions.[11]

Chang Ki-Sŏn

Chang Ki-Sŏn translated Henry Wadsworth Longfellow's "The Rainy Day" in 1934. Since the version of this work by Kim Han-Suk, an Ewha student like Chang, was printed on the same page of the college magazine, *Ewha,* it appears that the students were practicing their skills in translation. Chang's translation is somewhat wordier than Kim's.

Chang Yŏng-Suk

Chang Yŏng-Suk translated the following works: John McCrae's "In Flanders Fields" (1933), O. Henry's story "The Cop and the Anthem" (1935), and Percy Shelley's "Stanzas Written in Dejection" (1935) and "To the Moon" (1936). In the late 1930s she also published articles and stories in women's magazines such as *New Family* and *Woman.* In the 1930s the Poetry Group (Simunhakp'a) published a journal and gave a distinctive direction to Korean poetry. The members of this group, like Pak Yong-Ch'ŏl and Yi Ha-Yun, had studied foreign literatures and were concerned with creating new poetic language expressive of modern emotions. Chang Yŏng-Suk showed a similar concern with refining poetic language in her translations. For instance, in her translation of Shelley's "Stanzas Written in Dejection" she employs predicate endings like *"-nora,"* and *"-iyŏ"* that create a mood of contemplation, and her version is more polished than one by Kim Yŏng-Ae that appeared in 1931 and did not follow a poetic form but rather the format of the newspaper column in which it was printed. Chang identifies the author of "In Flanders Fields" as an American but offers no further explanation of the background of the work. In her translation Chang avoids prose style and instead employs predicate endings like *"-ne"* that evoke the strong emotional appeal of the dead soldiers to their still living comrades.

Cho Jŏng-Sun

Cho Jŏng-Sun published her version of Thomas Carlyle's "Today" in 1932. In translating this poem, which deals with the importance of using time well, she renders "eternity" from the second stanza with the Buddhist term *"yŏnggŏp"* (endless time), which is opposed to *"ch'alna"* (instant). The original poem, of course, did not refer to a Buddhist view but to the pragmatic idea that time should not be wasted. The translator seems to be adapting the poem to the cultural background of the readers. In addition to her translation, Cho Jŏng-Sun published a few of her own poems in a 1933 issue of *New Woman (Sin yŏsŏng)*.

Ch'oe Jŏng-Rim

Ch'oe Jŏng-Rim published three poetry translations in 1933: Oscar Wilde's "Requiescat," Gerard Manley Hopkins' "Rest," and Alice Meynell's "At Night." In 1938 several of Alice Meynell's poems were translated by a male translator, Ch'oe Jae-Sŏ, including "At Night." Although generally foreign poems were translated first by men, Ch'oe Jŏng-Rim's Meynell translation preceded that of her colleague. Predicate endings are an extremely important part of the mood of Korean poems, and Ch'oe Jŏng-Rim's use of exclamatory endings such as *"-iŏra"* effectively conveys the tone of the original. At the same time, Ch'oe Jae-Sŏ employs predicate endings such as *"-inyŏ"* and *"-irŏda"* that were found in traditional poetry and are somewhat outmoded.

The woman translator Kim Han-Suk's translation of Hopkins' "Rest" appeared two years after Ch'oe Jŏng-Rim's version. Kim renders the first line, "I have desired to go,"[12] using a verbal form in the present tense that lends a sense of immediacy. In contrast, Ch'oe's use of a past tense creates the impression of an explanation of more distant events. This is an indication that the translators were trying different approaches or at least experimenting with different stylistic techniques. Ch'oe Jŏng-Rim's translation of Wilde's "Requiescat" presents a motif that was prevalent in Korean translations of foreign poetry at the time—namely, the feeling of despair experienced by a male poetic narrator when faced with the death of a pure and lovely young woman. Her rendering of "lyre" as *"kŏmungo"* (a traditional Korean stringed instrument) reveals a tendency to orient her translation more toward the expectations of the receiving culture than to follow the source text closely.

Ch'oe Sŏn-Hwa

Ch'oe Sŏn-Hwa published two translations in 1931: John McCrae's "In Flanders Fields" and William Wordsworth's "I Wandered Lonely as a Cloud." The fact that only the translator's initials were identified indicates a lingering tendency to view translation as a marginal activity. The Wordsworth poem was translated several times into Korean in the 1920s and 1930s. Another woman translator, No Jae-Suk, translated the work in 1926, but Ch'oe's version includes more Chinese-character expressions, which were associated with the formal literary style. Indeed the two translations by Ch'oe Sŏn-Hwa lean toward this style more than do the works of most of the other women translators. Ch'oe seems to have put emphasis on the source text since she includes the original title of McCrae's poem along with the Korean translation. In spite of this, she does not include any background information, so many Korean readers would have had difficulty interpreting the poem. Ch'oe's use of the predicate ending "-da," which is used in prose writing, and the Chinese-character expressions gives her version a somewhat dry mood in comparison with Chang Yŏng-Suk's 1933 rendition, which is couched in a more colloquial style.

Chŏn Yu-Dŏk

Chŏn Yu-Dŏk translated a fiction work by Alice Webster, *Daddy Long Legs,* which was serialized in the *East Asia Daily* in 1937. The work deals with the experiences of a young American woman university student and would have appealed to reader curiosity about life in foreign countries. Chŏn Yu-Dŏk also published articles and essays in *Women's World.*

Chu Su-Wŏn

Chu Su-Wŏn published some of her original poems in *New Family* and *Woman.* In a 1933 article in *New Family,* Ch'oe Jŏng-Hŭi listed Chu Su-Wŏn, Ch'oe Jŏng-Rim, and No Ch'ŏn-Myŏng as promising young poets from Ewha Women's College. Chu Su-Wŏn's 1933 translation of Robert Burns' "A Red, Red Rose" was included in a *New Family* series entitled "Western Love Poems." The translation is couched in the language of Korean love poems and employs the relatively new term *"ch'ŏnyŏ"* to refer to a young woman. Her use of the term *"mellodi"* (melody) helps to create a foreign atmosphere.

Han Ch'ung-Hwa

Han Ch'ung-Hwa translated a Joseph Cambell poem, "The Old Woman," in 1936. Han translates the first verse, "As a white candle / In a holy place, / So is the beauty / Of an aged face,"[13] as *"Churŭm chin ŏlkul ŭi arŭmdaum iyŏ"* (Beauty of a wrinkled face). Such a description of an old woman was quite unusual in Korea at the time. Han uses simple colloquial language to convey the images in a vividly descriptive way, avoiding more formal language.

Mary Hillman

Mary Hillman's abridged translation of Anna Sewell's *Black Beauty* was published in 1927.[14]

Kim Han-Suk

Kim Han-Suk translated Stevenson's "Requiem" (1933), Hopkins' "Rest" (1935), and Longfellow's "The Rainy Day" (1935). Her translation of Hopkins' "Rest" is more concise than Ch'oe Jŏng-Rim's version and conveys the narrator's longing for the ideal. Kim begins her translation with the phrase *"Na nŭn karyahane"* (I must go), which gives an impression of urgency, while Ch'oe's translation starts with an explanatory phrase that is somewhat flat. Alongside her translation of the Hopkins poem, Kim published her own poem with the same title, which indicates an attempt to link translations and original writing. She displays the same conciseness in her translation of Stevenson's "Requiem"; it uses native Korean expressions like *"tolaonda"* (return) to describe death as a kind of homecoming. (In Korean one of the expressions for dying, *tolakanda* [go back, return], reveals the circular pattern of traditional Korean thought.) As noted, her translation of Longfellow's "The Rainy Day" was published on the same page as Chang Ki-Sŏn's version in an issue of *Ewha*.

Kim Ja-Hye

Kim Ja-Hye published two poetry translations in 1933: Elizabeth Lincoln Otis' "An 'If' for Girls" and Robert Burns' "Highland Mary." She also published summaries of three fiction works: Maupassant's *Une vie,* Alexandre

Dumas *fils' La dame aux camélias,* and Kollontai's *Red Love,* which appeared in a *New Family* series purporting to present "summary translations" *(kyŏnggae yŏk)* of works focusing on female protagonists. Along with her summary translations, Kim Ja-Hye comments that Jeanne of *Une vie* represents feminine endurance in the face of hardship, while Marguerite of *La dame aux camélias* epitomizes sacrifice and service to others. Kim Ja-Hye's translation of *Red Love* helped to popularize this Russian work, which many Koreans understood as presenting a modern and independent woman. In a brief 1933 article in *New Woman* Kim Ja-Hye comments on her vivid memories of studying Tennyson's *Enoch Arden,* which highlights the absolute devotion of the female protagonist Annie Lee. Her translation of Burns' "Highland Mary" was one of four poems included under the heading of "Western Love Poems" in a 1933 *New Family* series. This translation preserves a foreign atmosphere by employing such terms as *"ch'ŏnsa nalgae"* (angel's wings). In addition to translating, Kim Ja-Hye worked as a reporter for *New East Asia* and contributed many articles and essays to women's magazines.

Kim Kŭm-Ju

Kim Kŭm-Ju translated Wordsworth's "She Dwelt among the Untrodden Ways" in 1933 and "The Solitary Reaper" in 1935. Although she employs simple, everyday language, her somewhat unusual use of topic particles gives her translations a distinctive flavor. In both translations she uses the term *"ch'ŏnyŏ,"* which was favored by several of the women translators to refer to a young, unmarried woman without reference to traditional class distinctions.

Kim Kyŏn-Sin

Kim Kyŏn-Sin translated Thomas Moore's "Oft, in the Stilly Night" in 1931. The *Chosŏn Daily* printed the poem without regard for the format of the lines, which would seem to indicate a disregard for translations.

Kim Me-Ri

Kim Me-Ri translated a portion of Tennyson's *Enoch Arden* in 1929. She included a brief introduction in which she claimed that she rendered her translation in prose because of her inability to do justice to such a long verse work. Compared to the language of most of the other women translators, that used by Kim Me-Ri displays more archaic features, such as introducing the main characters in a manner reminiscent of traditional narratives. At the time, Ewha was the only women's college to offer a literature program, and both Korean and foreign teachers encouraged students to read and memorize the works of authors such as Tennyson as a way of training young literary talent.

Kim Myŏng-Sun

Kim Myŏng-Sun, the most prolific of the women translators, published ten translations in 1922: Edgar Allan Poe's "The Assignation" and nine poems —Baudelaire's "Femmes damnées" and "La mort des pauvres"; Rémy de Gourmont's "La neige"; a poem called "Chujang" (Drinking place) by a poet listed as Horessŭ Horei; Hermann Kasack's "Die tragische Sendung"; Maurice Maeterlinck's "J'ai cherché trois ans mes soeurs"; Poe's "To Helen" and "The Raven"; and Franz Werfel's "Lächeln Atmen Schreiten." Kim Myŏng-Sun displayed originality in choosing some works that had not been translated into Korean, as well as in her scheme for classifying the poems as "Expressionist" (Werfel and Kasack), "Symbolist" (Maeterlinck and Gourmont), "late Impressionist" (Horei), and "Satanic" (Baudelaire and Poe). (Although in a commentary accompanying her translation of "The Assignation" she berates the Korean literati for their ignorance of Poe's extraordinary works, she has not received recognition for introducing his works into Korea.) She lists the original authors' names in *han'gŭl* but does not list the original titles or give any information about the works. Although she identifies the works with certain literary movements, she offers no explanations for the readers, and some scholars have criticized her unclear use of terms.[15] In the 1920s relatively few Korean readers would have had any knowledge about foreign literary and artistic movements such as Expressionism. While we cannot be sure of the extent of Kim Myŏng-Sun's grasp of these terms, she indicated the depth of her interest in the commentary on "The Assignation" when she expressed a distaste for Naturalism and claimed that Korean artists should create a new beauty through "Satanic Art." Her choice of texts and classification scheme are part of her search for new esthetic values through translation. Her translation emphasizes the search for self-identity, which also characterizes her original work.

In her poetry translations Kim Myŏng-Sun tends to avoid predicate endings that were traditionally used and instead to repeatedly employ endings such as *"-hara," "-anida," "-kŏsinga,"* and *"-issda,"* which create a brisk, rhythmic effect. In spite of the brisk pace, her tendency to use Chinese-character expressions would have caused difficulty for some readers. The fact that

Kim Myŏng-Sun translated Poe's "The Assignation" in its entirety was notable at a time when many Korean translators produced condensed or abridged versions. This translation offers examples of the ways in which Kim Myŏng-Sun contributed to a modern translation style—for example, her use of exclamatory phrases that produce an impression of vividness and her avoidance of the long explanations that were characteristic of traditional Korean fiction. In her study on fiction works translated into Korean in the 1920s, Kim Hyŏn-Sil points out that Kim Myŏng-Sun's translation does not properly distinguish between present and past verb tenses and that foreign works and quotations in the original work are not properly translated. These features might indicate that Kim Myŏng-Sun was referring to a Japanese intermediate translation.[16]

Kim Yŏng-Ae

Kim Yŏng-Ae translated Shelley's "Stanzas Written in Dejection" in 1931. Since another Ewha student, Chang Yŏng-Suk, also translated this poem, it seems that Shelley was one of the authors whose works were being emphasized at Ewha. Kim Yŏng-Ae's translation was published in a newspaper that appears not to have paid much attention to poetic form, especially in the case of translation, and instead fit the work in the space available in the column.

Kyu Sŏn

Kyu Sŏn published a translation of Wordsworth's "On a Summer Evening" in 1931.[17]

Mo Yun-Suk

Mo Yun-Suk's writing career spanned a period of over fifty years. In 1931 she published a story in *Ewha*, and during the 1930s she published a number of poems in *New Woman (Sin yŏsŏng)*, *New Family*, and *Three Thousand Li*. *The Wren's Elegy* (Ren ŭi aega), one of her representative works of the 1930s, on one level deals with the concerns of a young woman but on another level expresses the anguish of the Korean people under Japanese colonial rule. According to Song Yŏng-Sun, Mo Yun-Suk, using the pseudonym of Moaksanin, published a translation of Naidu's "To India" in 1933.[18] Her translation of an Irish folksong (1939) reveals a hopeful mood similar to the tone of some of her original works, in which she expresses the nationalist sentiments of her people. In 1941 she published a translation of an Italian poem praising war, which seems to suggest that she was supporting the Japanese war effort.

No Ch'ŏn-Myŏng

No Ch'ŏn-Myŏng published the following translations: a poem called "Kŭriun pada ro" (Longing for the sea) by an author listed as Epsŭsaken (1934); a poem by Winifred M. Letts listed as "'Akssŭp'otu' ŭi chŏmt'ap" (The sharp tower of Oxford, 1941); and a poem by Thomas Hardy listed as "Nalkŭn mal ŭl terigo" (Leading an old horse, 1941). In 1934 she published an article about Charles Lamb that described the hardships he endured and introduced a few of his works, including "The Old Familiar Faces," which was translated by the Ewha student Yi Sŏn-Hŭi. She attended Ewha Women's College in the early 1930s, where she was a student of the poet Chŏng Ji-Yong and the poet/translator Kim Sang-Yong. After graduation she worked as a newspaper reporter, and in 1938 she published her first volume of poetry, *Coral Reef (Sanhorim)*. The critic Ch'oe Jae-Sŏ compared this work to that of Alice Meynell. Along with Mo Yun-Suk, No Ch'ŏn-Myŏng is considered one of the representative women poets of the 1930s.

No Jae-Suk

No Jae-Suk translated Wordsworth's "I Wandered Lonely as a Cloud" in 1926. Her translation employs plain predicate endings such as "*-poassda*" and "*-hada*," which contribute to a dry and flat tone. No's translation uses more Chinese-character expressions than the version of this poem by Yi Gwang-Su that appeared a year earlier.

Mrs. A. H. Norton

Mrs. Norton was a foreign missionary who translated a volume of fairy tales, *Imkŭm ŭi saeot kwa tarŭn iyagi* (The emperor's new clothes and other stories), into Korean in 1925. While some of the missionaries were concerned mostly with transmitting an edifying message in their translations, Mrs. Norton displayed a concern for form.[19] An example of her sensitivity to language can be seen in her diverse renderings of "fairy"—for instance, *"sonyŏ"* (nymph) and *"kwisin"* (ghost).

Paek An-Ja

Paek An-Ja translated a fiction work with the Korean title of *Kawang* (False king); it was serialized in thirty-seven episodes in the *Chosŏn Daily* in 1925. Kim Byŏng-Ch'ŏl comments that although nothing is known about the translator, the translation reads more smoothly than many others of the period.[20] We can infer that there must have been many other unknown women translators at the time.

Paek Kuk-Hŭi

Paek Kuk-Hŭi translated Arthur Symons' "The Fisher's Widow" in 1935. An interesting stylistic feature is Paek Kuk-Hŭi's use of *"kŭ"* as a personal pronoun to refer to the widow. The modern Korean third-person pronoun, *"kŭnyŏ"* (she), was not in wide use at the time. Since personal pronouns are much less frequently used in Korean than in English, their translation is one of the problems that translators must solve. The Foreign Literature Group, which emphasized the importance of creating new vocabulary, coined the term *"kŭnae"* for the third-person feminine pronoun. Paek Kuk-Hŭi chose a different solution.

Pak Do-Ŭn

Pak Do-Ŭn published a translation of Shelley's "Stanzas Written in Dejection" in 1933. She was one of the students who took part in the Ewha Women's College English theatrical productions in the mid-1930s.

Pak In-Dŏk

Pak In-Dŏk published two poetry translations in 1921: Tennyson's "Columbus" and an anonymous poem with the Korean title of "Koaeu ŭi chŏng" (Lament for a dead friend). After graduation from Ewha Women's College, Pak In-Dŏk taught music and then went to the United States as an exchange student. In 1928 she received a B.A. from Wesleyan University and in 1930 an M.A. from Teachers College at Columbia University. In 1951 she published an autobiographical work in the United States, and with the proceeds from this work and from a lecture tour she raised funds to establish Indŭk Vocational School.

Pak Kyŏm-Suk

Pak Kyŏm-Suk translated Tennyson's "Break, Break, Break" in 1926. Although this work was translated several times in Korea in the 1920s and 1930s, Pak Kyŏm-Suk's version was the first to appear. Unlike the other translators, she included a brief explanation about the poem—that it deals with the loss of a good friend—which would indicate an effort to communicate an understanding of the background of the original work. Foreign Literature Group members Yi Ha-Yun and Kim Sang-Yong did not include any comments with their translations of this work. As Kim Byŏng-Ch'ŏl points out, many scholars feel that in the original poem the breaking of the waves on the rocks conveys the inner turbulence of the narrator, who is grieving for the loss of a friend.[21] Therefore when Pak Kyŏm-Suk renders the first line, "Break, break, break,"[22] with the imperative form *"Pusŏra, pusŏra, pusŏra,"* she appears to be attempting to convey the emotion of the original. While most of the women translators used simple, everyday language, Pak Kyŏm-Suk had a tendency to use somewhat difficult Chinese-character expressions that might have made the translation less clear for certain readers.

Shin Paek-Hŭi

Shin Paek-Hŭi translated Elizabeth Lincoln Otis' "An 'If' for Girls" in 1927 and a poem by Turgenev with the Korean title of "Sanyang gun" (The hunter) in 1932. Shin Paek-Hŭi's translation of the Otis poem is longer than Kim Ja-Hye's version of this work, and she has adapted some of the lines to suit the cultural background of the Korean readers, such as substituting Japanese and Korean for the Western languages in the original.

Sŏ Akada

Sŏ Akada translated a religious poem with the Korean title of "Hwangch'ok e pul ŭl palkhimyŏ" (Light the candle) by an author listed as Tenisŭ A. Maekkat'i in 1934.

Sŏ Ŭn-Suk

Sŏ Ŭn-Suk published a translation of Francis William Bourdillon's poem, "The Night Has a Thousand Eyes," in a 1933 issue of *New Family* that also included translations of Robert Burns' poems by Chu Su-Wŏn and Kim Ja-Hye. This issue printed comments on love and marriage by leading Korean literary figures, such as Kim Dong-In and Pak Hwa-Sŏng. Translations of foreign love poems responded to the continuing interest in new sexual mores that had begun with the New Woman ideal in the 1920s.

Sŏk Ran

Sŏk Ran published a translation of Virginia Woolf's story, "The Mark on the Wall," in 1934 and Jules Romain's poem, "Ode I," in 1935. The fact that both of her translations were published in the magazine *New Chosŏn (Sin Chosŏn)*, which was not specifically aimed at women, was somewhat unusual. It is noteworthy that Sŏk Ran translated Virginia Woolf's story in its entirety rather than limiting herself to the kind of plot summary of a foreign work that was prevalent in the women's magazines at the time.

Mrs. Underwood

Mrs. Underwood, a foreign missionary working in Korea, published translations of John Bunyan's *Pilgrim's Progress* (1920) and Robert Louis Stevenson's *The Bottle Imp* (1921) and *The Strange Case of Dr. Jekyll and Mr. Hyde* (1921). James Scarth Gale had translated the first part of *Pilgrim's Progress* in the 1890s, and Mrs. Underwood translated the second part, which deals with the journey of the Christian family toward heaven. Her translation uses long sentences that resemble traditional prose style. However, in her translation of *The Strange Case of Dr. Jekyll and Mr. Hyde* she uses short, simple sentences with few modifying phrases. She translated *The Bottle Imp* with Pak T'ae-Wŏn; Kim Byŏng-Ch'ŏl points out that they did not follow their stated aim of using a sparse style.[23]

Yi Kyŏng-Suk

Yi Kyŏng-Suk published a translation of Turgenev's prose poem "The Beggar" in 1932. This work, which was first translated into Korean in 1918 by Kim Ŏk, was translated several times in the 1920s and 1930s and was imitated by Korean writers of prose poems. Yi Kyŏng-Suk employs a simple style and uses the plain pronouns *"na"* (I, the narrator) and *"kŭ"* (he, the beggar) that do not indicate traditional class distinctions.

Yi Sŏn-Hŭi

Yi Sŏn-Hŭi published a translation of Charles Lamb's poem, "The Old Familiar Faces," in 1932. Her use of the traditional *sijo* poetic form situates the translation in a cultural context familiar to the readers. Each stanza ends with the verbal form "*-nora*," which gives the translation a distinctive rhythm.

Yi Sun-Hŭi

Yi Sun-Hŭi, an Ewha student, published five poetry translations: Wilfred Wilson Gibson's "To the Memory of Rupert Brooke" (1932); Shelley's "A Lament" (1933); Thomas Hood's "The Bridge of Sighs" (1933) and "The Song of the Shirt" (1932); and Walt Whitman's "O Captain! My Captain!" (1932). She employs a simple, colloquial style that is easy to read, and she avoids abstract terms and Chinese-character expressions. Both of the Hood poems deal with Christian themes; this would have appealed to some of the students of Ewha, where missionaries played a prominent role. Members of the Foreign Literature Group took an interest in Whitman's works, and the poet/translator Chu Yo-Han included explanatory notes with his 1925 translation of "O Captain! My Captain!" However, Yi Sun-Hŭi, the only woman translator to work on Whitman, does not provide the reader with any background information about this poem.

Yi Sun-Yŏng

Yi Sun-Yŏng was an Ewha student who translated part of Tennyson's "Lady Clare" in 1930. The translator employs predicate endings like "*-sŭpnida*" that create a natural conversational style, and she uses the relatively new term "*ch'ŏnyŏ*" to refer to a young, unmarried woman. As noted, the foreign missionaries at Ewha focused on the works of Tennyson, and several of the students translated his works.

Yi Wŏn-Hŭi

Yi Wŏn-Hŭi translated Wordsworth's "To the Cuckoo" in 1937.[24]

Yŏn Kap-Sun

Yŏn Kap-Sun translated Walter Savage Landor's poem, "Rose Aylmer," in 1933. Like many of the other women translators, she employs simple language and smooth rhythms that make the translation easy to read. Kim

Sang-Yong translated the same poem in 1931 using predicate endings, such as "*-muŏt hao*" and "*-tŭrigo issso,*" that create a rather flat impression. In contrast Yŏn Kap-Sun's use of exclamatory phrases conveys the emotions surrounding the death of the young woman of the title.

Yu Hyŏng-Suk

Yu Hyŏng-Suk translated a poem by Virginia Poe, "Ever with Thee I Wish to Roam," in 1929. The translator comments that Virginia Poe was the young and sagacious wife of Edgar Allan Poe.[25]

Yu Jŏng-Ok

Yu Jŏng-Ok translated two short tales in *Ewha* in 1930, one with the Korean title of "Kihoe" (Opportunity) by an author identified as "Jenkalssŭ" and the other with the Korean title of "Kŭ ch'amsae" (That sparrow) by an unidentified author. The first employs simple, short sentences and deals with the vicissitudes of destiny, while the second uses a conversational tone to portray a mother bird's concern for her young. Both works convey a moral lesson.

Anonymous

An unnamed woman reporter published an abridged translation of a work by Shakespeare in the magazine *New Novel (Sin sosŏl)* in 1929. The title of the translation is "Sarang kwa chukŭm" (Love and death).[26]

Translations for Theatrical Productions

In addition to the above translations that can be attributed to individual translators, a number of foreign theatrical works were produced at educational institutions for women during the 1920s and 1930s. Although precise information is not available, it can be assumed that women participated in translating these works (see appendix).

General Innovative / Conservative Tendencies

In this section I examine the work of the women translators in the larger context of the translation and literary activities of their time. I use the opposition innovative/conservative to contrast activities that set new precedents with those that followed dominant trends.

Choice of Texts

As noted, in the 1920s and 1930s translation activities increased, and translators with training in foreign languages and literatures began to appear. At this time literary translation in Korea was dominated by men who engaged in lively debates about translation policies and methods. A few privileged women took advantage of opportunities to study abroad, and some of these educated women became translators. While the translations of some works were first done by women, in most cases women chose works that had already been translated, indicating that they were following the trends of the literary establishment.

Kim Myŏng-Sun can be considered the most innovative in terms of choice of texts. She seems to have become acquainted with various trends in foreign literature as an exchange student in Tokyo. Many of the works that Kim Myŏng-Sun translated or cited in her original works had not been mentioned by others at this time, so it is clear that she exercised a certain originality in this respect. She was the first to translate Poe into Korean, and she translated Baudelaire's "Femmes damnées" and Maeterlinck's "J'ai cherché trois ans mes soeurs" for the first time. When Kim Myŏng-Sun translated two poems and one short story by Poe in 1922, there was little interest. The works of European Symbolist poets like Baudelaire began to be translated into Korean in the late 1910s. Kim Myŏng-Sun was aware of Baudelaire's interest in Poe, and therefore she classified their works as "Satanic poems." Some scholars have pointed out errors in Kim Myŏng-Sun's Poe translations.[27] Although she translated only three of the eighteen stanzas of "The Raven," her introduction of the work in Korea is significant. Kim Myŏng-Sun also demonstrated initiative in translating the works of authors such as Franz Werfel and Hermann Kasack, who seem to have been unknown in Korea at the time.

In addition to Kim Myŏng-Sun, some other women translators chose their texts in an innovative way, among them Pak Kyŏm-Suk, Kim Me-Ri, and Paek An-Ja. Pak Kyŏm-Suk was the first to translate Tennyson's "Break, Break, Break" in 1926. This work was later translated by Yi Ha-Yun in 1927 and Kim Sang-Yong in 1938. Although Kim Me-Ri's translation of Tennyson's *Enoch Arden* was only a summary, she was the only translator to approach the work at this time. While most other women translators focused on brief poems, Paek An-Ja's choice of a fiction work, *Ka wang*, was somewhat unusual. Also, Chŏn Yu-Dŏk's translation of Alice Webster's *Daddy Long Legs* presented the experiences of foreign women in a new light for Korean readers.

Translation Norms and Techniques

In the late 1910s and early 1920s Kim Ŏk was the preeminent translator, but in the 1920s and 1930s translation activities centered around those who had been exchange students in Japan. Among the new translators were Yi Ha-Yun, Yi Hŏn-Gu, Kim Sang-Yong, Kim Jin-Sŏp, Yang Ju-Dong, and Ch'oe Jae-Sŏ. Debates among them resulted in a reconsideration of translation norms and covered such issues as translating directly from the original source and avoiding reliance on intermediary sources, the limited capacities of the Korean language for the transmission of foreign literature and the need to develop a translation vocabulary and style, and effective translation methods. Before considering the work of the women translators, I will briefly review some of the main translation problems under discussion at the time: (1) the choice between literal and figurative translation; (2) the question of intermediate translations; and (3) the limits of translation language.[28]

Kim Ŏk and Yang Ju-Dong, two of the most important translators of the 1920s, engaged in debates on literal *(chikyŏk)* versus figurative *(ŭiyŏk)* translation. Kim Ŏk held to the principle of translation as creation, which he claimed could be accomplished through what he termed figurative translation. In contrast, Yang Ju-Dong favored direct translation and bitterly criticized the practice of relying on Japanese intermediary translations. When Yang translated French Symbolist poetry and the works of Tagore, he proclaimed that he was translating literally from the original. Yang and the other members of the literary journal *Venus (Kŭmsŏng)* group were strongly against indirect translation, and they held that it was the duty of the translator to translate directly and faithfully. They tended to accompany their translations with an indication of the original title and author and a brief explanation of the work. In the case of indirect translation, the translator was expected to indicate the intermediate source.

In the 1920s the Foreign Literature Group focused on translation language and the creation of new vocabulary. In 1926 the Foreign Literature Research Association (Oeguk Munhak Yŏnguhoe) proclaimed that its goals went beyond studying foreign literature and included developing Korean literature and expanding the boundaries of world literature.[29] The members of this group, including Chŏng In-Sŏp, Yi Ha-Yun, Kim Sang-Yong, and Yi Hŏn-Gu, aimed to contribute to the development of Korean literature by importing foreign literature.[30] Chŏng In-Sŏp claimed that when a country imports foreign literature through translation, the vernacular is strengthened and the boundaries of the national literature are broadened.[31] In the inaugural issue of *Foreign Literature* the following program was announced: (1) producing faithful translations; (2) avoiding indirect translations; and (3) developing the Korean language by researching traditional language and creating new terms.[32]

Kim Jin-Sŏp, a member of the Foreign Literature Group, held that it was permissible to use foreign words in a translation. Kim Ŏk criticized this view on the grounds that foreign words were undesirable in prose writing and completely unacceptable in poetry.[33] In contrast, Yang Ju-Dong felt that there were instances when the use of foreign words was acceptable. Taking the argument a step further, Kim Jin-Sŏp asserted that it was necessary to use newly created words to translate the particular sentiments of foreign poetry. He made the following suggestions about how to create a new vocabulary: (1) use foreign words in their original form; (2) translate foreign words literally; and (3) use existing Korean words with a new meaning.[34]

Although the women translators did not enter directly into these translation debates, for the most part they translated in simple, everyday language, avoiding a more formal style, and, for reasons we will explore more fully below, it is quite likely that many of them translated directly. As I mentioned above, Kim Myŏng-Sun was quite progressive in her views on translation. After her translation of Poe's "The Assignation," she expressed the hope that Koreans would develop the kind of literature represented by Poe, and she castigated the literary establishment for its inability to go beyond worn-out methods. She saw Satanic Art (under which she grouped Poe and Baudelaire) as a new method of pursuing esthetic goals that were appropriate for Korea's young writers. Kim Yong-Jik points out that although Ch'oe Jae-Sŏ's 1938 translation of Poe's "To Helen" is clearer than that of Kim Myŏng-Sun, Ch'oe employs outmoded language at a time when poets like Kim Yŏng-Rang, Yi Sang, and Kim Ki-Rim were using language in a more sophisticated way.[35]

Kim Myŏng-Sun's somewhat difficult style is in marked contrast with many of the other women translators, whose renditions create esthetically pleasing effects in simple, colloquial Korean. For example, Kim Han-Suk (Stevenson's "Requiem") and Ch'oe Jŏng-Rim (Meynell's "At Night") employed poetic language in a precise way and produced concise translations. Yŏn Kap-Sun produced a smooth, flowing, colloquial version of Landor's "Rose Aylmer," while the translations by her male colleagues, Kim Sang-Yong and Pak Yong-Ch'ŏl, are more difficult to understand.

Images and Motifs

Although the corpus of translations by women in Korea at this time is rather limited, certain images and motifs occur repeatedly: death, particularly that of a young woman; feminine ideals; religion; and nature. It is worthwhile considering how the women translators handle these images and motifs.

Death

Traditionally in Korea the sudden death of a young person was taken as an omen of misfortune for the family and sometimes imputed to the influence of evil spirits or the discontent of deceased ancestors. The women translators of the 1920s and 1930s were choosing a subject that was not common in traditional literature when they translated poems about death, particularly that of a young woman. Through their translations they were able to introduce new poetic images and moods. Several of the women translators effectively employ the paradoxical image of death as a release from a painful life. Kim Myŏng-Sun's translation of Baudelaire's "La mort des pauvres" transmits a more stark image than the one found in Yang Ju-Dong's version:

> Kim: Chukŏm iyamallo uri rŭl uirohanda / A a chukŏm iyamallo uri rŭl sallinda (Death, this indeed comforts us/Ah, death, this indeed allows us to live).[36]
>
> Yang: Wirohanŭn kŏs ŭn chukŭm, a sallinŭn kŏt do chukŭm (Comforting thing death, saving thing death).[37]
>
> Baudelaire: C'est la Mort qui console, hélas! et qui fait vivre.[38]

While we cannot be sure whether Kim was translating directly or referring to an intermediate translation, her intention to highlight the importance of death is clear. Yi Sun-Hŭi's translation of Thomas Hood's "The Bridge of Sighs" also shows the mysterious nature of death. (In this work a weary young woman jumps off a bridge and plunges into the mystery of death to escape from the misery of the world.) In her translation of Stevenson's "Requiem," Kim Han-Suk conveys the image of a peaceful death. The narrator's relaxed perception of death, without horror or fear, is in contrast with the common depiction of death in Korean literature at the time.

Several of the works of the women translators depict the death of a beautiful young woman as a way of reflecting on the meaning of life. Kim Myŏng-Sun translated Poe's works in order to explore the connection between the appreciation of beauty and death. Kim Ja-Hye's translation of Robert Burns' "Highland Mary" highlights the way death separates the male narrator from a beloved woman. Yi Sŏn-Hŭi's translation of Charles

Lamb's "The Old Familiar Faces" portrays the loss of beloved women in a nostalgic vein. In Ch'oe Jŏng-Rim's translation of Oscar Wilde's "Requiescat" the peaceful death of a beautiful young woman is contrasted with the anguish experienced by the male narrator. In a similar way, Kim Kŭm-Ju's translation of Wordsworth's "She Dwelt among the Untrodden Ways" depicts the profound changes in the life of the male narrator as a result of the death of a woman who had led an obscure life. Yŏn Kap-Sun translated Landor's "Rose Aylmer," which centers around the pathos of a young woman's death.

Feminine Ideals

As we have seen in the preceding chapters, during the Chosŏn period women, especially those of the upper classes, were expected to maintain their chastity above all else, and this was considered the highest feminine virtue. Regardless of their personal feelings they were bound by rules of strict obedience, and there were heavy penalties for any deviance from the rigid patterns of behavior imposed on them. These feminine ideals are promoted in many literary works and popular songs, such as *The Song of Ch'unhyang*, which depicts a woman's absolute loyalty to her spouse. In spite of the changes in attitudes toward women with the development of the New Woman ideal, traditional feminine ideals are still reflected in the works of many of the women translators. Oscar Wilde's "Requiescat" contains the line "Lily-like, white as snow" to describe a young woman who has died.[39] Ch'oe Jŏng-Rim's translation of the line reads *"Paekhap kach'i kokyŏlhago, nun kach'i sunkyŏlhadŏn"* (Lofty as a lily, pure as snow), using the terms *"kokyŏl"* (loftiness, purity) and *"sunkyŏl"* (purity, cleanliness).[40] The translator has placed the poem in the context of traditional Korean ideals of womanhood. The term *"sunkyŏl"* is also used by Kim Ja-Hye to refer to the female protagonist in her summary translation of Maupassant's *Une vie*. Also, in Kim Ja-Hye's summary translation of Dumas *fils' La dame aux camélias*, Marguerite is considered by her lover's father to be a woman who is not capable of becoming a *"sunkyŏlhan puin"* (chaste wife). Two of the women translators, Kim Ja-Hye and Shin Paek-Hŭi, chose to translate Otis' "An 'If' for Girls," which enumerates feminine virtues. Han Ch'ung-Hwa's translation of Campbell's "The Old Woman" highlights the inner beauty and serenity that shines through the countenance of the old woman. In Paek Kuk-Hŭi's translation of Symons' "The Fisher's Widow" the motif of the woman waiting for the return of her lost mate blends well with the values of traditional Korean society.

However, a contrasting image is found in Kim Ja-Hye's summary translation of Kollontai's *Red Love,* whose female protagonist, Vassilissa, does not follow the traditional model of feminine subservience but rather struggles to combine love and work. As we have already seen, Korean intellectuals were interested in Kollontai's views on the socialist woman, and in a 1928 article Pak Yŏng-Hŭi analyzed the modern values presented in *Red Love.*

Religious Images

While many of the works by the women translators present a view of women that is in line with traditional values, the religious images in their translations mostly deal with Christianity. This can be explained by the fact that a number of them had been introduced to foreign literature by Christian missionaries at Ewha Women's College. Generally these translations associate Christianity with compassion, rationality, and progress. In Yi Sun-Hŭi's translation of Hood's "The Bridge of Sighs," a young woman commits a sin of despair when she fails to discern Christ's compassion in the workings of the world. Yi's translation of Hood's "The Song of the Shirt" paradoxically also affirms Christian values by decrying their absence in contemporary secularized society. In Kim Me-Ri's translation of Tennyson's *Enoch Arden,* the Christian God gives hope and strength in the face of death and despair. Other than those relating to Christianity, very few religious images appear in these translations. However, in her translation of Carlyle's "Today," Cho Jŏng-Sun renders the phrases "out of eternity" and "into eternity" as *"yŏnggŏp esŏ"* and *"yŏnggŏp ŭro."* The Buddhist term *"yŏnggŏp"* (endless time) gives the translation a traditional flavor.

Nature

The depictions of nature in traditional Korean poetry are quite different from those found in the foreign poems that were translated at this time. One kind of image found in traditional Korean poetry is that of the peach blossom, which represents the perfection of nature.[41] In translating foreign poetry, the women translators had to devise new ways of depicting natural phenomena. An example is Chu Su-Wŏn's translation of Burns' "A Red, Red Rose":

O nae sarang ŭn yuwŏl e saero p'in/Pulko pulkŭn changmikkot.[42]
O, My luve's like a red, red rose, that's newly sprung in June.[43]

In a similar way Kim Ja-Hye's translation of Burns' "Highland Mary" situates love in an estival environment of trees and flowers, and the loveliness of the maiden in Kim Kŭm-Ju's version of Wordsworth's "The Solitary Reaper" is emphasized by her isolation in a natural setting. In the translations of Hopkins' "Rest" by Ch'oe Jŏng-Rim and Kim Han-Suk, an idyllic place is associated with good weather, blooming flowers, and clear water. In an article on English literature and Romanticism Ch'oe Jŏng-Rim contends that in the age of Romanticism authors like Wordsworth and Byron received new inspiration and searched for beauty in nature.[44] The translations of Wordsworth's "I Wandered Lonely as a Cloud" by Ch'oe Sŏn-Hwa and No Jae-Suk depict the healing power of nature, which the narrator experiences at the sight of daffodils. Similarly in Chang Ki-Sŏn's version of Longfellow's "The Rainy Day," gloomy weather coincides with the darker aspects of life. Chang Yŏng-Suk's translation of Shelley's "To the Moon" personifies nature, and her version of Shelley's "Stanzas Written in Despair" associates the narrator's feelings with the movements of wind, sun, and waves. In each case the women translators were creating new poetic expressions for the relationship between human emotions and the natural environment.

Institutional Constraints

Translation studies scholars have examined the constraints that govern the work of translators. For example, André Lefevere considers that patronage and ideology are important constraints on translators and that "translation can no longer be analysed in isolation, but . . . should be studied as part of a whole system of texts and the people who produce, support, propagate, oppose, censor them."[45] The following section considers the constraints on the women translators stemming from literary groups, media and publishers, educational institutions, and the government.

Literary Groups

In the 1920s and 1930s writers and translators with similar views formed literary groups. Most of these were composed of men who had studied in Tokyo, and they emphasized that translation should be a professional activity following high standards. Men like Kim Ŏk and Yang Ju-Dong, as well as the members of the Foreign Literature Group and the Poetry Group, combined the roles of translator, writer, and critic. Translation criticism aimed to enforce certain standards; in some cases—like the heated debates in which Yang Ju-Dong triumphed over Kim Ŏk—the course of a translator's career was altered.

Since women were for the most part excluded from the influential literary groups, they could not take part in the debates that set the standards for translation. Thus for them an avenue for influencing the direction of translation policy and practice was blocked. The exclusion of Kim Myŏng-Sun from such literary groups illustrates this difficulty. When Kim Myŏng-Sun published a poem, "Flower Dream of the Morning Dew" ("Choro ŭi hwa-mong") in *Creation (Ch'angjo)*, it was praised for a delicacy of sentiment, and she was welcomed as a member of *Creation's* literary group. However, in the next issue of the magazine it was announced that she had been banned from the group. Although we cannot know the reason for her exclusion, it is clear that the condition for a favorable assessment of her work was her acceptance as a *Creation* member. The literary critic Kim Ki-Jin also attacked Kim Myŏng-Sun for works that reflected the instability of the middle-class family. As an early feminist writer, Kim Myŏng-Sun was relegated to the periphery of the Korean literary world, and her contributions as a writer and translator were not recognized.

Pak Hwa-Sŏng was another woman writer of the time who resisted the attempts of men to create literary ghettos for women. She denied the rumor that when the well-known writer Yi Gwang-Su recommended her work for publication in *Chosŏn Literary World,* he corrected and revised her manuscript. There were few women writers like Kim Myŏng-Sun and Pak Hwa-Sŏng who resisted the dominance of men of letters. As noted, most of the women translators of this period tended to be rather cautious in their choice of texts and followed the norms dictated by the literary establishment. The male critics encouraged women writers to emulate the poetic techniques of foreign women writers like Christina Rossetti, Elizabeth Browning, and Sara Teasdale. The critic and writer Pak Yong-Ch'ŏl praised the lyricism of Sara Teasdale's works and contended that Korean women should contribute to the creation of lyric poetry.[46]

The Media and Publishers

During the 1920s and 1930s the Japanese colonial government encouraged the publication of newspapers and magazines. However, with the exception of the women's magazines, most publications devoted only limited space to women's issues and writing by women. In 1925 the *Chosŏn Daily* published a translation of a fiction work by Paek An-Ja without any introduction about the translator, original author, or work. This is an indication that even the well-known publications did not recognize the contributions of women translators.

Even the magazines of Korean exchange students in Japan were unfavorable toward women. For instance, Na Hye-Sŏk was the only woman writer whose works were published in the student magazine *Light of Learn-*

ing (Hakjikwang). In contrast, *Women's World,* which was published in Japan between 1917 and 1920, featured women writers and well-known male writers like Yi Gwang-Su and Ch'oe Namsŏn. Outlets for the works of women translators were provided by such women's magazines as *Ewha, New Family,* and *Three Thousand Li.*

Educational Institutions

In 1936 *Three Thousand Li* published an article, "A Discussion among Women Writers" ("Yŏryu chakka chwadamhoe"), in which seven women took part: Pak Hwa-Sŏng, Chang Dŏk-Jo, Mo Yun-Suk, Ch'oe Jŏng-Hŭi, No Ch'ŏn-Myŏng, Paek Sin-Ae, and Yi Sŏn-Hŭi. These women emphasized that writing by women should be promoted in newspapers and magazines, in the Literature Department of Ewha Women's College, and in society as a whole. Pak Hwa-Sŏng stated that she hoped that future students of Ewha, Korea's only liberal arts college for women, would become more serious and focus on the harsh realities facing their country. Mo Yun-Suk commented that it was unfortunate that Ewha was not properly fulfilling its crucial role in responding to the needs of young women writers. She pointed out that students fresh from high school did not have the ability to follow lectures in English given by foreign professors. No Ch'ŏn-Myŏng suggested that Ewha should invite well-known Korean writers to give creative writing courses. Others regretted the lack of practical guidance for women students launching professional careers. As noted, a number of the Korean women writers of the 1920s and 1930s were graduates of Ewha, including Mo Yun-Suk and No Ch'ŏn-Myŏng. They were highly critical of Ewha's literature program.

Ewha Women's College was originally founded by Christian missionaries, whose influence was strong in the 1920s and 1930s. At this time there was a department at Ewha referred to in English as the Literary Department or the English Literary Department. A number of foreign missionaries taught in this department, which aimed to introduce students to Western culture, and particularly to Christianity, in order to develop a new Korean culture. In addition, there was a policy of teaching creative writing and translation with the aim of opening up new paths for Korean literature. Since it was not possible to specialize in Korean literature during the colonial period, English was offered as an alternative. During the 1930s the Literary Department at Ewha produced plays in English under the direction of the foreign teachers. These plays attracted wide audiences and helped to raise the level of theatrical productions in Korea. Students worked on translating some of the plays that were produced, and generally the translation courses offered by the Literary Department for third- and fourth-year students contributed to the training of young translators.[47]

After the Manchurian invasion in 1931 the Japanese increased their preparations for war, and the Koreans were expected to participate in this effort. Compared to the national schools, the Christian schools had been relatively free from government surveillance, but as the demands for emperor worship increased, many schools closed down. Ewha and other Methodist schools agreed to observe the official worship, so they avoided suppression for a while. Because of the problem of emperor worship, the Christian missionaries were in conflict with the Japanese colonial authorities. To make matters worse, after the outbreak of hostilities between Japan and China, the United States supported Chiang Kai-Shek, and it became increasingly difficult for foreign missionaries to operate in Korea. In 1939 English was already considered the language of the enemy, and the teaching of English declined. Ewha was among the schools that were most affected by the ban on English. By the early 1940s there were few foreign missionaries left in Korea, and instruction at Ewha was conducted by Koreans who had been educated in the Japanese way. With the departure of the foreign missionaries and the worsening of relations between Japan and the United States, the translation and introduction of foreign literature came to be considered subversive activities.[48]

Government Controls under the Japanese Colonial Regime

After the March 1919 Independence Movement the Japanese colonial rulers began to pursue a policy of more openness for cultural activity while in reality tightening their control of Korean society.[49] During the 1920s many publications began to appear, including the *Chosŏn Daily* and *East Asia Daily* as well as over a hundred magazines of various kinds. *New Woman (Sin yŏsŏng)*, a magazine with socialist leanings, appeared in 1924. This publication boom encouraged literary and translation activities.

However, in the 1930s even these limited freedoms began to disappear, and more repressive policies were enforced. The Japanese needed to be able to exploit Korean resources as a step in their plan to gain control of Manchuria and the Chinese mainland. Therefore they tightened their grip on Korean politics, economics, and cultural activities. Everything that interfered with their aims was forbidden. *New Family* began to be published in the early 1930s under these repressive conditions. This magazine focused on what were considered to be women's issues, and it avoided discussions of political problems. Unlike *New Woman (Sin yŏsŏng)*, which was critical of social conditions, *New Family* emphasized literary activities and published translations, original works, and articles introducing foreign women writers. It helped to raise the profile of women writers in Korea and provided opportunities for women to publish their works.

Gradually the Japanese colonial government moved toward destroying the cultural identity of the Korean people. Agricultural regions became impoverished, and textile factories exploited the female labor force. In the 1930s women workers demonstrated for wage increases and the protection of maternal rights. Women's organizations worked to eradicate illiteracy, to educate the rural population, and to provide training for women in urban areas. Two women writers of the 1930s, Kang Kyŏng-Ae and Paek Sin-Ae, were active members of the Kŭnu Association, and their concern for the plight of women under colonialism is reflected in their literary works.[50] They and other women writers contributed to the development of feminist literature. Some of the writing by women in the 1930s gives vivid descriptions of the lives of women workers, as we will see in chapter 5, when we consider the work of Pak Hwa-Sŏng.

In the 1920s women writers like Kim Myŏng-Sun, Na Hye-Sŏk, and Kim Il-Yŏp wrote about the need to promote women's emancipation and develop new moral standards. In contrast, the women writers of the 1930s focused on the problems of women under colonialism, including poverty and economic exploitation. When criticism of the Japanese colonial government was indirect and subdued, their works were not censored. However, in Mo Yun-Suk's first volume of poetry, *The Bright Zone (Pich'nanŭn chiyŏk)*, almost half of the original two hundred poems were suppressed because they were perceived as containing anti-Japanese sentiments. At the same time that women were writing about the problems of workers and Mo Yun-Suk was challenging the censors, Ewha students were translating foreign poems focusing on love, religion, and the pathos of early death. This trend can partly be explained by the restrictions on young women students within the educational system. However, the choice of seemingly innocuous topics provided women translators with the opportunity to explore the resources of Korean literary forms and to develop the expressive possibilities of colloquial language.

Conclusions

In the 1920s and 1930s most of the women translators fit themselves cautiously into a male-dominated environment and either gained limited recognition as Ewha students or published a few translations as individuals. This marginal status is attested to by the fact that their works were not published in the leading literary magazines that focused on translations, such as *Venus* and *Foreign Literature*. With the exception of Kim Myŏng-Sun, who published her translations in *Creation (Kaebyŏk)*, and Sŏk Ran, who published in *New Chosŏn*, their works appeared in women's magazines only. In spite of these restrictions, we have seen that the women translators made contributions in several important areas: the use of colloquial style in writing, the introduction of new terms relating to foreign cultures, the treatment of topics relating to Christianity, the introduction of English and American literature, and the promotion of direct translation.

As the twentieth century progressed, more works were translated from Western languages, and this contributed to the development of writing style in Korean. As the importance of Chinese culture declined, Koreans developed a writing style that was more in line with everyday usage. After World War II Western culture was widely accepted, and finally the traditional, Chinese-based writing was replaced by writing in harmony with the spoken language. The works of the women translators, which tended to employ simple, colloquial language, helped to bridge the gap between writing styles during the transitional period. The women translators also participated in the effort to create new vocabulary by the use of foreign words in their translations. Some examples include: "kiss" (Kim Myŏng-Sun, Gourmont's "La Neige"); "manteau" (Kim Myŏng-Sun, Poe's "The Assignation"); "violet" (Kim Kŭm-Ju, Wordsworth's "She Dwelt among the Untrodden Ways"); "romance" (Kim Ja-Hye, Otis' "An 'If' for Girls"); "dance" (Shin Paek-Hŭi, Otis' "An 'If' for Girls"); "butter," "cake," and "pavement" (Chang Yŏng-Suk, O. Henry's "The Cop and the Anthem"); "veil" (Kim Ja-Hye, Dumas *fils' La dame aux camélias*); and "melody" (Chu Su-Wŏn, Burns' "A Red, Red Rose").

As students of Ewha College, many of the women translators had been introduced to Christian thinking, including humanitarianism and the philanthropic spirit. During the colonial period Christianity was associated with rationality and social justice. By translating works with Christian themes, many of the women translators contributed to the development of an important trend of twentieth-century thought in Korea.

The choices of texts were partially conditioned by the fact that under Japanese colonial domination political topics or social criticism would have been risky, so the translators opted for works that dealt with individual emotions such as love, despair, and solitude. During the 1930s Korean authors were increasingly compelled to avoid nationalist literature and to turn to so-called "pure literature" *(sunsu munhak)*. In this respect the women translators can be considered forerunners of the literature of individualism, which developed in the post–Korean War period.

At the time in Korea many translations were still being done indirectly through Japanese intermediate translations. Even translators who had studied foreign languages tended to refer to existing translations in Japanese since this language was more familiar to them. However, a number of the women translators had been taught by the foreign teachers at Ewha to translate English and American works directly from the original. Therefore their work was crucial in changing translation methods in Korea.

In chapter 5 I focus on three Korean women writers of the period whose works relate to translation trends and formulate nationalist sentiments from a feminist perspective.

1. Members of the YWCA commemorating the appearance of the inaugural issue of *Ewha* in 1929 (Ewha Archives)

EWHA AND WOMEN'S EDUCATION.

Few places in the world have undergone such rapid changes in a generation as has Korea. Perhaps no change is more startling than that which concerns education. While there was always reverence for the scholar, who held the highest offices in the land because of his attainments in learning, the masses of the people had not the leisure for study, which required a life—time of memorization and concentration on the Chinese classics. The people were largely illiterate, many of them not even knowing the "eunmun". All this applies only to men, for women were scarcely ever taught at all, and were generally considered incapable of learning.

Now in a few short years we see hundreds of schools crowded to the doors with boys and girls, and in primary schools they are together. There is a loud cry for more and more schools of all kinds, a cry which will not be satisfied until every child in Korea has a chance to go to school. Hundreds are turned away because there is not room for them. Many who can afford it send their children abroad for higher education and wider opportunities than are given here. There are great numbers of Korean students in Japan, competing with Japanese students in a foreign tongue and often standing high in their classes, overcoming great obstacles in their consuming desire for learning. Parents share in the effort by the sacrifices they make to send their children to school, often selling lands and valuable possessions in order to meet the heavy expenses, for free eduation is unknown here.

How intelligent is this mad rush for education ? What are the boys and girls seeking in this frenzied race for learning ? Probably the first motive is economic. They must have an education in order to find a place in the changed order of

——(1)——

2. First page of the introductory comments by Ewha president Alice Appenzeller in the inaugural issue of *Ewha* (Ewha Women's University Museum)

梨花

第一輯

一九二九年二月

梨花專門學校
學生基督教青年會 發行

3. Cover page of the inaugural
issue of *Ewha,* February 1929
(Ewha Women's University
Museum)

4. Poet/translator Mo Yun-
Suk, 1930 (Ewha Archives)

5. Poet/translator No
Ch'ŏn-Myŏng, 1934
(Ewha Archives)

6. Ewha Literary Department's production of *Ivanhoe* in English, 1930; Mo
Yun-Suk (first on left), Professor Conrow (middle), translator Ch'oe Sŏn-Hwa
to the right of Conrow (Ewha Archives)

7. On left, Paek Kuk-
Hŭi, Ewha student
and translator,
early 1930s (Ewha
Archives)

8. On left, Pak In-Dŏk, Ewha student and translator, early to mid-1910s (Ewha
Archives)

9. Professors' office, Ewha Literary Department, 1932 (Ewha Archives)

10. Ewha student and translator Ch'oe Sŏn-Hwa, foreground (Ewha Archives)

11. Ewha students on an outing, early 1930s; translator Ch'oe Jŏng-Rim in back on right (Ewha Archives)

12. Translator Ch'oe Jŏng-Rim, second from right, early 1930s (Ewha Archives)

13. Translator
Ch'oe Jŏng-
Rim on right,
1935 (Ewha
Archives)

14. The English House family, Christmas 1937 (Ewha Archives)

15. Ewha students with Professor Conrow and Professor Kim Sang-Yong, translator (Ewha Archives)

chapter five

Translation, Gender, and New Forms of Writing in the 1920s and 1930s

The preceding chapters have considered the links between the translation of foreign materials and the development of new feminine ideals from the turn of the twentieth century through the 1930s. We have seen that while the translation of heroic narratives at the beginning of the twentieth century fostered a feminine model of patriotic participation (chapter 2), the translation and introduction of foreign works in the 1920s and 1930s emphasized the ideal of the educated and emancipated New Woman (chapter 3). Chapter 4 demonstrated that while most of the women translators of this period were following the dominant trends of the literary establishment, they contributed to the development of a modern, colloquial writing style and introduced new images and motifs. This chapter deals with three women writers, Kim Myŏng-Sun, Pak Hwa-Sŏng, and Mo Yun-Suk, whose work reflects new trends imported through translation. After an overview of women writers of the 1920s and 1930s, I consider the work of these three writers in an attempt to answer the following questions: What are the connections between the work of women translators and original writing by women of the period? How do these writers combine feminist and nationalist concerns in their works? What role did the women translators and writers play in redefining the identity of their nation under colonialism?

Overview of Women Writers

In the 1920s women writers like Kim Myŏng-Sun, Kim Il-Yŏp, and Na Hye-Sŏk went beyond the restrictions of traditional, male-dominated society and expressed themselves forcefully in their works. These women, who were exchange students in Japan in the 1910s and 1920s, were exposed to the ideas of foreign writers like Ellen Key and Henrik Ibsen. Their experiences as exchange students awakened them to the need for the emancipation of women, and they advocated free choice in marriage and a new view of sexual morals. During the 1930s more women writers began to appear in Korea, and, in contrast with those of the 1920s who promoted the rights of women as individuals, they focused on women's issues in the broader context of nationalism, the class struggle, and colonialism.[1]

Fiction Writers

In the 1920s Kim Myŏng-Sun, Kim Il-Yŏp, and Na Hye-Sŏk wrote works in which characters fundamentally challenged the traditional system of marriage and morals. These works criticized loveless marriage and centered around the searching and self-awakening of those who adhered to the New Woman ideal.

Kim Myŏng-Sun (1896–1951) was born of an upper-class father and a concubine mother. In 1911 she graduated from Chinmyŏng Girls' School in Seoul, and in 1913 she went to Tokyo, where she studied for two years. In 1917 she graduated from Sukmyŏng Girls' High School, and in the same year she published "A Suspicious Young Girl" in *Youth (Ch'ŏngch'un)*. In 1920 she again went to Tokyo, where she studied French and German. After her return in 1925 she published a volume of her works, *The Fruits of Life (Saeng-myŏng ŭi kwasil)*. In the late 1920s she began to work as a film actress, and her literary activities declined until she went to Japan in 1939, where she died in 1951.[2]

Kim Il-Yŏp (1896–1971) was born into a fervent Christian family, and her father was a Protestant minister. She lost her parents at an early age but managed to graduate from Ewha Girls' School with difficulty. After editing the magazine *New Woman (Sin yŏja)*, she went to Tokyo to study in 1919. In

1920 she became the only woman in the literary group that published the journal *Ruins (P'yehŏ)*. After a decade of intense activity, in 1928 she became a Buddhist nun, and her period as a proponent of the New Woman ideal ended. Kim Il-Yŏp wrote several articles in 1920 that emphasized the need for women's emancipation: "The Need for Women's Education" ("Yŏja kyoyuk ŭi p'ilyo"), "Women's Self-Awakening" ("Yŏja ŭi chagak"), and "Our Demands and Claims as New Women" ("Uri sin yŏja ŭi yogu wa chujang"). In one of her most controversial articles, "My Views on Chastity," she claimed that fidelity was not a fixed concept but applied only when people were in love. Her story "Love" ("Sarang") stressed that people should not be bound by their past relationships but rather should seek happiness in their current situations.[3] In "The Death of a Young Girl" ("Ŏnŭ sonyŏ ŭi sa"), a woman finds herself overwhelmed by the difficulties of a traditional marriage and commits suicide.

Na Hye-Sŏk (1896–1946) graduated from Chinmyŏng Girls' School in 1913 and went to Tokyo to study art at the Tokyo Women's Art School. She began to write articles promoting women's rights for periodicals such as *Light of Learning* and *Women's World*. In 1920, after spending five months in prison as a result of her participation in the March 1919 Independence Movement, she married a lawyer, Kim U-Yŏng. Between 1920 and 1927 she traveled around the world with her husband, who was in the foreign service, and in 1930, after having given birth to four children, she was divorced. Two of her works, "Divorce Confession" ("Ihon kobaek sŏ" [1935]) and "Entering a New Life" (1939), were written during the difficult period after her divorce. Her later years were lived in obscurity.

Na Hye-Sŏk is noted for her precise examination of the injustices faced by women. In 1914 she wrote a strong defense of women's rights, "Ideal Woman," which was published in *Light of Learning*. Her works of fiction, poetry, and criticism focus on gender equality and appeared in newspapers like the *Chosŏn Daily* and the *Daily News* and periodicals like *Chosŏn Literary World* and *New Woman (Sin yŏsŏng)*. In "Entering a New Life," she outlined a radical approach to morality, arguing that sexual behavior should follow natural instincts instead of being artificially restricted.[4] Although her literary works are not as highly regarded as her art works, she left behind five poems, four fiction works, about forty essays, three travel sketches, and one play. In 1921 she published two poems in the *Daily News,* "A Doll's House" and "Nora," which proposed the emancipation of women and the restoration of their human rights.[5] Her fiction work "Kyŏng-Hŭi," named after the female protagonist, illustrates the urgent need for women's awakening. In contrast to the superficial portrayal of the New Woman by male authors such as Yi Gwang-Su and Kim Tong-In, "Kyŏng-Hŭi" represents the views of many of the educated women of the time.[6]

In the 1930s the dominant trend among women writers changed from a focus on emancipation and individual rights to a concern with the injustices of colonialism. Kang Kyŏng-Ae (1906–1944) lost her father at an early age and spent her childhood with her mother in poverty. She made her literary debut in 1931, when she published a story, "The Broken Harp" ("P'akŭm"), in the *Chosŏn Daily*. During the Japanese colonial period she immigrated to Manchuria with her family, and by the mid-1930s her health had begun to deteriorate, leading to her early death. In the 1980s Kang Kyŏng-Ae's works began to be reevaluated, and she gained recognition as a realistic feminist writer. Instead of criticizing the patriarchal family directly, Kang Kyŏng-Ae's works describe the harsh realities of life under colonialism. In describing the situation of women during the colonial period in the 1930s, she indirectly encouraged a spirit of resistance. Her works deal with the tragic lives of women at the bottom of society and display sensitivity for their suffering. "The Two Hundred Wŏn Manuscript Fee" ("Wŏngoryo ibaek wŏn") is about a poor woman who becomes embroiled in a dispute with her husband over a fee she has earned for a manuscript. This story criticizes the New Women for their attention to outward appearances and luxury.[7] Among her representative works are "Salt" ("Sokŭm" [1934]) and "The Underground Village" ("Chiha ch'on" [1936]).

Paek Shin-Ae (1908–1939) was a novelist and anti-Japanese activist who died while still only in her thirties. In 1927, while crossing the border into Manchuria, she was captured by the Japanese police, who submitted her to torture; as a result, she was left sterile. She made her literary debut in 1929, when her story "My Mother" ("Na ŭi ŏmŏni") was given the *Chosŏn Daily* award for new writers. Her works display sympathy for the lives of women who suffer from poverty and oppression. Many of her works deal with the inner conflicts of women who are trying to live according to their own will, such as "A Beautiful Sunset" ("Arŭmdaun nol") and "In the Darkness" ("Honmyŏng esŏ").[8]

Yi Sŏn-Hŭi (1911–?) attended Ewha Women's College and began to work as a reporter for *New Woman (Sin yŏsŏng)* in 1933 and also contributed to *Creation*. In the 1930s she continued to write for various magazines, began writing fiction, and in 1938 went to work for the *Chosŏn Daily*. After World War II she went to North Korea, and not much is known about her later years. Most of her works deal with the dark side of women's lives and the suppressed dreams of married women. In the late 1930s she focused on depicting tragic circumstances in an emotive and poetic style.[9] Yi Sǒn-Hŭi's works do not deal directly with politics or social problems but rather with the conflicts between women who follow tradition and those who attempt to realize the New Woman ideal, such as two stories that appeared in 1937, "The Seal" ("Tojang") and "The Bill" ("Kyesansǒ").

Kim Mal-Bong (1901–1961) attended a girls' school and went to Japan, where she studied English literature. After returning to Korea in 1927, she began to work as a newspaper reporter and gained recognition as a writer when her story "Wild Rose" ("Tchillekot") was serialized in the *Chosǒn Daily*. In 1932 she won the *Central Daily (Chungang ilbo)* new writer's award for her story "Woman in Exile" ("Mangmyǒng nyǒ"). By the mid-1930s she had become known as a leading writer of popular fiction. Her works have been criticized for an excessive use of coincidental occurrences, but her depiction of emotions and various social problems attracted many readers.[10]

Like Kim Mal-Bong, Pak Hwa-Sǒng (1904–1988) also went to Japan in the 1920s as an exchange student to study English. While there, she married the socialist activist Kim Kuk-Jin. She received favorable reviews for her 1925 short story, "The Eve of the Harvest Moon Festival" ("Ch'usǒk chǒnya"), which depicts the struggles of a woman worker against colonial oppression. While women writers like Kim Myǒng-Sun, Kim Il-Yǒp, and Na Hye-Sǒk focused on the emotional needs of women, Pak Hwa-Sǒng explored the problems of women workers.[11]

Ch'oe Jǒng-Hŭi (1912–1990) began to publish stories in 1931 in *Three Thousand Li*. While many of the Korean women writers in the 1920s and 1930s had short lives because of illness or political oppression, Ch'oe Jǒng-Hŭi's writing career spanned more than fifty years. Unlike Kang Kyǒng-Ae and Pak Hwa-Sǒng, who dealt with social problems, Ch'oe Jǒng-Hŭi, like Yi Sǒn-Hŭi and Paek Shin-Ae, focused on roles within the family and the inner lives of women. For example, *Ways of Heaven (Ch'ǒnmaek)* deals with the attempts of women to overcome prejudice, oppressive social conditions, and inner conflicts. The use of first-person narration in many of her works vividly portrayed the points of view of the women characters. Many of her works depict the conflict between sexuality and motherhood.[12]

Poets

Representative women poets in Korea in the 1920s include Kim Myǒng-Sun, Na Hye-Sǒk, and Kim Il-Yǒp. In the 1930s Mo Yun-Suk and No Ch'ǒn-Myǒng are considered to represent the beginning of modern poetry by women in Korea. A number of other women poets at the time, such as

Paek Kuk-Hŭi and Chu Su-Wŏn, left behind interesting works. In addition, some women poets contributed to the revitalization of the traditional *sijo* form—for example, Chang Jŏng-Sim, Kim O-Nam, and O Shin-Hye.

Kim Myŏng-Sun was the first modern woman writer to publish a collection of her works, *The Fruits of Life*. This work, which appeared only two years after Kim Ŏk published the first volume of original modern Korean poetry, *The Song of the Medusa (Haep'ari ŭi norae)*, contains twenty-four poems, four essays, and two short stories. It signals Kim Myŏng-Sun's intention to play a leading role in the literary world.[13]

Na Hye-Sŏk published six stories and four poems. Her poem "Nora" starkly presents the struggle to achieve the New Woman ideal. Kim Il-Yŏp, one of the most outspoken proponents of the emancipation of women, wrote modern poems, *sijo,* and short stories. While most of her poems deal with the struggle for women's rights, some evoke the longing for a spiritual ideal.

Mo Yun-Suk (1909–1990) began her writing career in the 1930s during the formative phase of modern Korean poetry. Over a period of more than fifty years she published several collections of essays and seven volumes of poetry, including *The Bright Zone* (1933), *The Wren's Elegy* (1937), *A Jade Hairpin (Okpinyŏ* [1947]), *The Waves (P'ungrang* [1951]), *A Touching Scene (Chŏngkyŏng* [1962]), and *Nongae* (1975). No Ch'ŏn-Myŏng (1912–1957) made her literary debut in 1933 and published a total of 172 poems. The 1930s critic Ch'oe Jae-Sŏ praised her for the conciseness and delicacy of her poetic style.[14] Her poems are noted for their restrained language and the image of women as lonely and socially alienated beings. Her volumes of poetry include *Coral Reef* (1938), *At the Window (Ch'angbyŏn* [1945]), and *Gazing at Stars (Pyŏl ŭl ch'yŏdabomyŏ* [1953]). Paek Kuk-Hŭi (1915–1940) graduated from the literature department of Ewha Women's College and published poems such as "Cosmos" ("K'osŭmosŭ"), "The Shade of Trees" ("Nokŭm"), and "Solitude" ("Kojŏk") in *New Family*. As noted above, she also published a translation of Arthur Symons' poem, "The Fisher's Widow." Chu Su-Wŏn (1909–?) was also a graduate of the literature department of Ewha Women's College and translated Robert Burns' "A Red, Red Rose." Her poems, which were published in the 1930s, include "Knitting" ("P'yŏnmul"), "Pondering " ("Chŏuljil hanŭn mamiyŏ"), and "The Fallen Tower" ("Munŏjin t'ap").

Chang Jŏng-Sim (1898–1938) published a volume of religious poetry, *Victory of the Lord (Chu ŭi Sŭngri),* in 1933 and was one of the first women to write modern *sijo*. Kim O-Nam (1906–?) studied English at a women's college in Japan and made her literary debut in 1931. She was one of the most prolific writers of modern *sijo* and left behind around four hundred works.

O Shin-Hye (1913–1978) made her literary debut in 1938 with the *sijo* "Weeping Willow" ("Suyang bŏdŭl"). Her works contain images of an ideal, contented life, in contrast with the images in the works of the other women writers of *sijo* at the time.[15]

Journalists and Social Commentators

In the 1920s women began to work as journalists and to contribute articles to magazines; this provided opportunities to express opinions about the New Woman ideal, as well as about the obstacles to improving the status of women. *New Family, New Woman* (both *Sin yŏsŏng* and *Sin yŏja*), *Woman,* and *Three Thousand Li* (among others) published women's essays, translations, and original fiction. *Ewha,* the magazine of Ewha Women's College, appeared in 1929, and it provided a forum for young women writers and translators. In the 1930s women writers formed associations and engaged in discussions on the promotion of writing by women in a male-dominated literary establishment. In the 1936 "Discussion among Women Writers," Pak Hwa-Sŏng claimed that it was unreasonable to expect women writers to limit themselves to topics deemed appropriate for women, and she protested against the inequality implied by the designation "woman writer" *(yŏryu chakka)*. In the same article Mo Yun-Suk pointed out that since women had to overcome so many handicaps in a male-centered society, they should strive to avoid the marginalization of women's writing. Women writers also argued that they should receive higher fees for their writing, and they pledged to attempt to correct erroneous views about women through their works.

Some well-known male writers, such as Yi Gwang-Su and Kim Tong-In, took a great interest in some of the newly emerging women writers, although they tended not to consider works by women on the same level as those by men. Yi Gwang-Su evaluated the works of Kim Myŏng-Sun, Pak Hwa-Sŏng, and Mo Yun-Suk very highly. As noted, Ch'oe Jae-Sŏ praised No Ch'ŏn-Myŏng's poems, claiming that they showed a skillful use of language and a "feminine" concern for detail. However, even these relatively successful women writers did not always receive favorable evaluations from the literary establishment. Kim Tong-In's "The Story of Kim Yŏn-Sil" ("Kim Yŏn-Sil chŏn") is supposed to have used Kim Myŏng-Sun as a model to criticize the New Woman ideal. Certain critics, like Kim Mun-Jip, urged women writers to avoid topics that were inappropriate for their sex.[16]

Na Hye-Sŏk, who was one of the first women in Korea to gain recognition as a painter, became a reporter for the *Daily News* in 1925, after several years of publishing translated and original works. In 1920 Kim Il-Yŏp founded *New Woman (Sin yŏja)*, which printed many articles about women's emancipation. In "Our Demands and Claims as New Women," printed in the magazine, she pointed out that since men and women were equal, there was only one set of morals for both, so men should not enslave women nor abuse them. She argued that women needed to go beyond traditional customs, and she attributed the low status of women to their lack of education and independent careers. All of her work emphasized the need for new moral values and sexual emancipation.

Other women journalists at this time included Kim Ja-Hye, who contributed essays to *New East Asia* and *New Family* and was particularly noted for the perspicacity of her style; Song Kye-Wŏl and Chang Dŏk-Jo, socialist writers who contributed to *Creation (Kaebyŏk)*; Yi Sŏn-Hŭi, who wrote for both *Creation (Kaebyŏk)* and *New Woman (Sin yŏsŏng)*; Ch'oe Jŏng-Hŭi, who wrote for *Three Thousand Li*; No Ch'ŏn-Myŏng, who contributed to various newspapers and *Woman*; Kim Mal-Bong, who worked for the *Domestic and International Daily (Chungoe ilbo)*; Hwang Sin-Dŏk, who worked for the socialist women's movement and wrote for the *Domestic and International Daily, The Times (Sidae ilbo)*, and *East Asia Daily*.

As discussed above, the works of Korean women writers of the 1920s and 1930s reflected an interest in foreign women writers and thinkers such as Ellen Key, Alexandra Kollontai, and Sarojini Naidu. While writers like Pak Hwa-Sŏng, who treated socialist themes, were interested in Kollontai's works, Mo Yun-Suk's nationalist concerns can be related to the writings of Naidu. Chŏng Ch'il-Sŏng, a courtesan who took part in the March 1919 Independence Movement, became known for her contributions to the nationalist cause. When the sexual morality of Kollontai's *Red Love* was being discussed, she wrote an article about this topic that appeared in *Three Thousand Li* in 1929. Hŏ Jŏng-Suk, a reporter for *Creation (Kaebyŏk)* and the *East Asia Daily*, wrote about the activities of the various women's organizations. She advocated a new sexual morality based on Kollontai's concept of men and women as ideological partners. Pak Wŏn-Hŭi, an active member of several important women's organizations, strongly advocated socialist reforms. These women, who were active participants in social organizations, aimed to awaken the women of Korea to their potential and to free them from the limits of traditional society.

Writers on Education

In the 1920s educated Korean women were beginning to find employment as teachers. Such writers as Pak Hwa-Sŏng, Mo Yun-Suk, and Paek Shin-Ae worked for a while as teachers, and some women founded their own schools and set new trends in education. Upon her return to Korea from the United States, Pak In-Dŏk became involved with the education of women in rural areas. She wrote articles on the women's movement and on the American educational system—for example, "American Lecture Tour: Black Schools and Outstanding Women Educators" (1938), in which she introduced American black women educators. Kim Hwal-Ran graduated from Ewha Women's College in 1918, went to the United States to study, and obtained a teaching position at Ewha in 1925. As noted above, in 1922 she founded the Korean YWCA along with Kim P'il-Rye and Yu Kak-Kyŏng. She returned to the United States and received a doctorate from Columbia University in 1931. In 1939 she became the first Korean president of Ewha Women's College. Kim Hwal-Ran and Yu Kak-Kyŏng wrote many articles about women's education that appeared in such magazines as *New Woman (Sin yŏsŏng)* and *Youth (Ch'ŏngnyŏn)*. In "Higher Education for Women" (1932), Kim Hwal-Ran emphasizes that women's education is important for the development of Korean society.

Translating Feminist Nationalism: The Approaches of Three Women Writers

The works of Kim Myŏng-Sun, Pak Hwa-Sŏng, and Mo Yun-Suk are related to new trends imported through translation, and they represent different ways of combining feminist and nationalist concerns. In her work as a translator Kim Myŏng-Sun strove to overcome the limitations of the Korean literary world, and in her original works she linked the problems of gender inequality and discrimination against the Korean people. Pak Hwa-Sŏng, though not a translator herself, took an interest in Alexandra Kollontai's works, which presented socialism from a feminist point of view. In her own works, Pak Hwa-Sŏng placed the problems of women workers at the center of the struggle for social equality and national liberation. Mo Yun-Suk was one of the Ewha College students who was taught to read and translate English and American poetry by their foreign professors. Her poetry displays some of the stylistic features of many of the women translators of the time. Mo Yun-Suk's originality consists in transforming the traditional ideal of the self-sacrificing woman into a modern woman who devotes herself to the betterment of her nation.

Kim Myŏng-Sun: Foreignness and the New Feminine Identity

Kim Myŏng-Sun's life and works reflect the search for a new feminine identity. Although she was brought up in an upper-class household, since her mother was a concubine she faced severe discrimination, and her pursuit of education was motivated at least partially by the desire to overcome the disadvantages of her background. In her several trips to Japan she came into contact with the Japanese version of European culture. These forays abroad are reflected in the depictions of foreign culture and the exchange student's experience that appear in works written between 1917 and the late 1930s. The following section focuses on the appropriation of elements of foreign culture in Kim Myŏng-Sun's work as part of her attempt to compensate for a sense of gender and national inferiority, as well as to go beyond the limits of patriarchal traditions. Her work as a translator was crucial in this process of importing and assimilating foreign culture.

Kim Myŏng-Sun's Literary World

In recent years scholars have been conducting research on Kim Myŏng-Sun's oeuvre, which includes approximately sixty poems, fourteen stories, seven essays, and ten translations. The overarching themes of her works include a protest against the restrictions of the traditional family, the promotion of free choice in love and marriage, and a fascination with foreign culture as a way of overcoming the disadvantages of her background. Kim Myŏng-Sun's debut work, "A Suspicious Young Girl," received a favorable review from Yi Gwang-Su, who claimed that it contributed to the agreement of written and spoken language and displayed a realistic contemporary approach.[17] However, later he reversed his opinion and attacked Kim Myŏng-Sun for imitating a Japanese work. Pŏm-Rye, the protagonist of the story, has lost her mother, who committed suicide rather than endure mistreatment from her traditional husband. The motherless girl leads a wandering life in the care of her maternal grandfather and rejects her cruel father, who caused her mother's death.[18] While some scholars compare this concisely written story to Kim Myŏng-Sun's later works and conclude that it may well have been modeled on a Japanese work, others point out that there is no conclusive evidence that the work was an imitation.[19] "Turkey" ("Ch'ilmyŏnjo"), which appeared in *Creation (Kaebyŏk)* from December 1921 to January 1922 and received a good deal of attention from literary people, employs an epistolary style giving detailed descriptions of the psychological state of the female protagonist. In "The Maiden's Path" ("Ch'ŏnyŏ ŭi

kanŭn kil"), published in *New Woman (Sin yŏja)* in March 1920, Ch'un-Ae refuses to marry the man picked out by her parents and leaves home to follow
the man she loves. Ryu So-Yŏn, the protagonist of "Looking Back" ("To-
ladabol ttae"), published in *Chosŏn Daily* in 1924, is an English teacher in a
girls' high school. When she goes on a school picnic, she meets and falls in
love with a young married scientist. "T'an-Sil and Ju-Yŏng" ("T'an-Sili wa
Ju-Yŏngi"; *Chosŏn Daily*, 1924) deals with the struggle against the restrictions of traditional family life.

The works in *The Fruits of Life* are characterized by the search for a new
feminine identity and the expression of anticolonial feelings.[20] "A Night to
Question Dreams" ("Kkum mutnŭn nal pam"; *Chosŏn Literary World*, 1925)
deals with the psychological conflicts of a woman who is emotionally involved with her friend's husband, a father of three children. Another story
that deals with a love triangle, "I Am in Love" ("Na nŭn saranghanda"; *East
Asia Daily*, 1926), presents a young woman, Yŏng-Ok, who receives advice
from a friend to end her loveless marriage since women in this sort of situation are little more than prostitutes.

Kim Myŏng-Sun's poetic production can be divided into three periods.
She published her first poem, "Flower Dream of the Morning Dew"
("Choro ŭi hwamong"), in 1920 in *Creation (Ch'angjo)*. *The Fruits of Life* anthology was published during her peak period. The poems that appeared
from 1928 to 1939 can be considered among Kim Myŏng-Sun's later works.[21]
Since Kim Myŏng-Sun translated some poetry in the 1920s, her works of
this period can be related to foreign literary trends. While some of her
poems focus on remembrances of her mother and deal with individual
emotions, she also wrote works that convey the hope of regaining national
independence and escaping from colonial domination.[22] Kim Myŏng-Sun
also wrote essays, such as "Beyond Myself" ("Nae chasin ŭi wie" [1925]), in
which she complained of being caught between banishment *(ch'ubang)* and
confinement *(yup'ye)*.

Images of Foreign Culture

The images of foreign culture in Kim Myŏng-Sun's works take various
forms: the inclusion of foreign names and words, as well as foreign authors
and works, and praise for foreign culture. A number of characters with foreign names appear in Kim Myŏng-Sun's stories. In "The Maiden's Path" a
woman named Maria encourages Ch'un-Ae to avoid an unwanted marriage.
Maria advises her to think of her future rather than making the fatal mistake
of marrying simply to please her parents. Although Maria is Korean, the
fact that a character with a Christian name argues strongly for a woman's

right to control her own destiny indicates a favorable view toward Western culture. In "Turkey" the protagonist, Sun-Il, writes letters to a German teacher, Nina Schultz, whom she met as an exchange student in Tokyo. Through this correspondence Sun-Il describes the difficulties she endured and complains of the insecurities of the situation in her homeland. Sun-Il comes to rely on the sagacious advice of her foreign teacher. In "The Guest" ("Sonnim") the names of several famous Westerners appear, including Bach, Woodrow Wilson, and Kant. "The Orphanage" ("Koawŏn"), "The Orphan's Decision" ("Koa ŭi kyŏlsim"), and "A Friend in the Orphanage" ("Koawŏn ŭi tongmu") center around a young foreign boy named Simon who loses his parents and comes to stay in an orphanage in Tokyo.

In "Looking Back" Ryu So-Yŏn is in love with the married Song Hyo-Sun. They take inspiration for their unrealizable love in the works of the German author Gerhart Hauptmann, according to whom it is not necessary for people in love to be joined physically. In their attempt to emulate the ideal lovers of Hauptmann's "Lonely Lives," they escape from traditional morality and pledge undying loyalty.[23] In "I Am in Love" Yŏng-Ok is inspired by a motto attributed to the French scientist Henri Poincaré about remaining hopeful in the face of difficulties. These words encourage Yŏng-Ok to leave her loveless marriage. Kim Myŏng-Sun also mentions Poincaré's motto in her essay "Writing Experiment" ("Sip'il"). Although the literary references in Kim Myŏng-Sun's works tend to be somewhat vague, she presents Western culture as providing a more reasonable environment than does her native land, where women faced many disadvantages.

Experiences of Foreign Students

Kim Myŏng-Sun's works focus on two aspects of being a foreign exchange student: the desire for self-improvement and the financial difficulties. Kim Myŏng-Sun gives an indication of the complexity of her own motives for undertaking studies in Japan in "Beyond Myself," in which she wonders if she will ever feel comfortable again in her native land. Although foreign studies offered new possibilities for learning, going abroad was a kind of exile from her own country.[24] In spite of the difficulties, her women characters are strongly motivated to pursue studies in Japan not just to acquire new learning, but also to overcome traditional limits (such as those concerning illegitimate children) and to compensate for the disadvantages they face in their native land. In "T'an-Sil and Ju-Yŏng," which contains autobiographical elements, T'an-Sil's desire to study in Japan is linked to her efforts to overcome her individual handicaps as well as those of her country.

T'an-Sil firmly resolves to overcome the disgrace of being a concubine's daughter. T'an-Sil values education not so much for its own sake as for the possibility it offers of gaining social acceptance, and she strives to become a cultivated woman who will rise above the scorn heaped upon those of lowly birth. She envies students who go abroad and dreams of her stay in Tokyo as a step up the social ladder.[25]

Women students who did not take their work seriously are presented in an unfavorable light in Kim Myŏng-Sun's stories. In "The Guest" Ŭl-Sun is a somewhat spoiled girl from a prosperous family. She fails to graduate from the music school she attends in Tokyo but returns to Korea pretending to be a properly trained musician. Her only ambition is to marry a wealthy man and settle down to a life of comfort. In contrast, her younger sister, Sam-Sun, approaches her work enthusiastically and is praised for her piano studies at a women's college in Tokyo. She studies late into the night and considers becoming a worker in order to help the common people. This work presents both a favorable and an unfavorable view of the New Woman. Many people thought that Kim Myŏng-Sun herself had followed the latter pattern, although the story proposes an ideal New Woman who is deeply involved in both studying and contributing to her nation.

Kim Myŏng-Sun presents a poignant picture of the discrimination and poverty faced by women exchange students in Tokyo. At this time foreign studies—especially the musical studies pursued by Kim Myŏng-Sun—were assumed to be for wealthy intellectuals; some scholars have identified the women writers of the 1920s as members of the upper middle class. However, an examination of Kim Myŏng-Sun's works indicates that such assumptions need to be reexamined. Some of her works depict female characters who are not adequately supported by their families and who struggle to find financial sponsors for their studies. These pioneering young women leave their native land and strive to develop their capacities, but as women, their possibilities are limited, and they urgently need to find patrons to provide financial support. In "Turkey" the narrator, identified as "I" *(na)*, is an exchange student in Tokyo who struggles to find a financial backer and expresses her anxieties about survival: "I became more and more worried about finding a financial sponsor, and I started to cry."[26] She finally obtains aid from a man by the name of Pak Hŭng-Guk, but when his visits become more frequent, she realizes that he was not motivated by generosity but by a desire for sexual conquest. In "T'an-Sil and Ju-Yŏng" the financial difficulties of foreign study are vividly described; T'an-Sil barely manages to eke out a living. The image of the struggling exchange student can also be seen in some of Kim Myŏng-Sun's poems, such as "Half a Life, in a Poem" ("Siro ssŭn pansaenggi"), in which the narrator complains of the penury and debts of exchange students in Tokyo.

Love Triangles and International Affairs

Kim Myŏng-Sun's works criticize patriarchal traditions, particularly the system of concubinage and the restrictions on free choice in love and marriage. In traditional Chosŏn society the practice of concubinage was accompanied by discrimination between children of primary and secondary wives.[27] Under such conditions women faced enormous pressures, and Kim Myŏng-Sun herself suffered from these inequalities since her mother was a secondary wife. The fact that she became an actress, which was considered a morally ambivalent career in the 1920s, is an indication of the difficulties she faced in transcending her background and establishing herself as a professional writer.[28] The link between Kim Myŏng-Sun's concerns about gender and national discrimination can be seen in her use of terms such as "disdain" *(ŏpsin yŏkim)*, "the weak and the strong" *(yakhanja, kanghanja)*, and "revenge" *(p'umkap'ŭm)*. She depicts Chosŏn as a weak country that historically lacked the power to prevail over others and therefore was treated with disdain. In "T'an-Sil and Ju-Yŏng" the female protagonist vows to overcome her disadvantaged situation through study, and she contends that Chosŏn will ultimately achieve independence through the efforts of people like her whose struggle for self-improvement contributes to the betterment of the nation.[29]

In Kim Myŏng-Sun's works there is a connection between the discrimination against women in general, the children of concubines in particular, and the colonial domination of Korea. On one level her works depict the unfair treatment of concubines and their children as playthings of men; on another level they represent the disadvantaged situation of Korea, which was exploited and deprived of national sovereignty under Japanese colonial domination. Kim Myŏng-Sun links the betrayal experienced by the daughter of a concubine with the exploitation and colonial domination of the nation. Learning is the path for women to overcome their social disadvantages, and nationalism is the way for Koreans to regain their dignity.

Strong condemnations of patriarchal practices can be found in Kim Myŏng-Sun's works. In traditional society suicide was the only avenue of protest against the lascivious misconduct of men, and in "A Suspicious Young Girl" Ka-Hŭi, denied freedom and dignity, ends her life to escape abuse and degradation. The heroine of "T'an-Sil and Ju-Yŏng," suffering from the stigma attached to being a concubine's daughter, rejects her mother and prays that she will repent and become a Christian. For herself she chooses studies as the way to overcome the disadvantages of her background and strives to become a cultivated woman who will not have to suffer the indignities of concubinage. In contrast to the self-destructive approach of Ka-Hŭi in "A Suspicious Young Woman," T'an-Sil takes her destiny in her own hands and resolves to forge a new path in life.

In several of Kim Myŏng-Sun's stories the depiction of young women attempting to gain a certain amount of sexual freedom is reminiscent of the work of Ellen Key. As discussed in chapter 3, some scholars have pointed out that there is a relationship between the thinking of Ellen Key on women's rights and the work of Korean women writers of the 1920s and 1930s with regard to free choice in love and marriage.[30] This first generation of modern Korean women writers recommended changing the system that bound women to loveless and even abusive marriages. While they emphasized Ellen Key's ideas on the unity of spiritual and physical love, they were not interested in her ideas on the importance of motherhood.[31] "The Maiden's Path" criticizes the traditional custom of arranged marriages, which allowed no room for individual choice. "Looking Back" illustrates the principle of free choice in love, even if the lovers cannot marry. In "A Night to Question Dreams" Nam-Suk connects emotional ties between individuals with patriotism and national development. Yŏng-Ok in "I Am in Love" ends her unsatisfactory marriage to build a life based on self-respect.

Many of Kim Myŏng-Sun's female protagonists are in some way marginalized, while their lovers maintain socially acceptable traditional marriages. Although the men choose to remain in loveless marriages in order to fulfill their social obligations, the women strive to overcome the restrictions against them and want the freedom to make decisions about their lives. Moreover, as noted, in Kim Myŏng-Sun's stories triangular relationships go beyond the difficulties of individual women and are linked with the struggle of Koreans who were caught between the injustice of Japanese colonialism and the indifference of Western powers. Her works represent the strivings of the oppressed, on both an individual and an international level. Just as Kim Myŏng-Sun's women are constrained by rigid rules, so were the Koreans prevented from properly governing themselves. The women characters cannot obtain help from the men they love any more than the Koreans could gain recognition from the Western countries they admired. In "Looking Back" So-Yŏn is criticized for behaving like her mother; in this respect she is like many of Kim Myŏng-Sun's other women, who meet with disapproval as they attempt to live their lives on their own terms. The triangular relationships in "T'an-Sil and Ju-Yŏng" and "A Night to Question Dreams" unveil attempts to live freely and overcome discrimination. The characters' efforts to go beyond prejudice mirror the struggle of Koreans to regain national sovereignty and international respect.

If we look more closely at Kim Myŏng-Sun's triangular relationships, we can identify two general patterns: female protagonist–male protagonist–Western person (or Western books) and Korea–Japan–Western countries. The first pattern is illustrated by female protagonists who are deeply concerned about their own lives as well as the future of their country. The situation of Korea under colonial domination was analogous to the plight of women attempting to overcome social disadvantages. In spite of the difficulties they face, the women characters remain optimistic about their ability to triumph over prejudice and outmoded customs. Although the male characters tend to be intellectuals who have studied in Japan, they prove incapable of helping the women in a practical way or even providing emotional support. In "The Maiden's Path" Ki-Su, the male protagonist, adopts a fatalistic attitude as he advises his lover, Ch'un-Ae, that she cannot escape her destiny and must accept the marriage planned for her by her family. In contrast, Ch'un-Ae's friend Maria takes a far more progressive stance in advising her to leave her parents' house and take charge of her own life. In "Looking Back" another male protagonist, Hyo-Sun, has no plans to solve the dilemma of his emotional attachment to So-Yŏn, although he is married to someone else. In these stories rather than obtaining help from their lovers, the women draw strength from reading foreign books or having contact with foreign culture.

The second pattern is helpful in understanding Kim Myŏng-Sun's portrayal of her country's international standing. Although Koreans were deeply resentful of Japanese colonial domination, Japan was a haven for promising young students. In "T'an-Sil and Ju-Yŏng," we read: "I was born into a lowly situation, the daughter of a concubine, and I was treated with scorn. And the country where I grew up is weak and ignorant and historically was rarely victorious over others. It has always been scorned by others. I must escape from this situation. I must escape."[32] Kim Myŏng-Sun also depicts the physical and emotional oppression of the Koreans by the Japanese colonizers. In "Turkey" Sun-Il enters a woman's school in Japan where she is complimented on the fact that she does not act like a Korean. In "T'an-Sil and Ju-Yŏng" Ju-Yŏng is described as being mistreated by selfish Japanese people.[33]

While Koreans resented Japan, they tended to look upon Western countries in a positive light, and in Kim Myŏng-Sun's stories the unfavorable portrayal of the Japanese is contrasted to a favorable one of Westerners. In

"Turkey" T'an-Sil writes Nina Schultz that if she had studied in Germany rather than Japan, she would have become much more self-sufficient and capable of managing her own life. Kim Myŏng-Sun presents Western countries like Germany as much more advanced than Japan.

Links between Kim Myŏng-Sun's Translated and Original Works

Although Kim Myŏng-Sun left behind only ten translations, she is the most prolific of the women translators of the 1920s and 1930s. The fact that she classified her translations under the headings of Expressionism, Impressionism, Satanic Art, and Symbolism—we leave aside the question of the accuracy of her classifications—indicates that she had a strong interest in foreign literary movements that is also reflected in her original works. This section focuses on how her understanding of foreign literary movements relates to her original writing.

As we have seen, Kim Myŏng-Sun labeled her translations of the works of Franz Werfel and Hermann Kasack as Expressionist. When *Creation (Kaebyŏk)* published these translations in 1922, it also featured an article by Im No-Wŏl that claimed that Expressionist art transformed nature and focused on the sensibilities of modern city dwellers. Other critics of the time, such as Kim U-Jin, recommended Expressionism as an appropriate method for Korean writers and artists.[34] Kim Jin-Sŏp also published an article about Expressionism in *Foreign Literature* in 1927, and Sŏ Hang-Sŏk translated some Expressionist works in 1933. These critics and translators understood Expressionist art as conveying a loneliness and despair that was well suited to the precarious situation of Korea under colonialism. A good example is the lamentations and painful outcries in Kim Myŏng-Sun's translation of Baudelaire's "La mort des pauvres."

Kim Myŏng-Sun classified her translations of a poem by Maeterlinck and one by Gourmont as Symbolist. She followed Kim Ŏk, who was one of the first to translate Symbolist works into Korean and who emphasized the suggestiveness and musicality of the works of such poets as Verlaine and Baudelaire. Some scholars feel that the vocabulary and style of Kim Myŏng-Sun's poem, "Flower Dream of the Morning Dew," which expresses the frustrations of disappointed love, reflect her interest in foreign poetry. This is a long poem of 133 lines—at a time when short works were more prevalent—and the poet experiments with a new poetic drama form.[35]

Kim Myŏng-Sun classified her Baudelaire and Poe translations as Satanic Art. She understood Baudelaire's esthetics to imply that art consists in the search for beauty amid the degradation and despair of everyday life. In her translations Kim Myŏng-Sun uses original vocabulary to depict the particularly arduous lives of women—for example, *pauvres soeurs (pich'amhan chamae dŭl)* and *douleurs (kot'ong)* in "Femmes damnées" and "sad, uncertain" *(sŏlŭm, pulanhan)* in "The Raven." Similar images of women's anguished lives can be found in some of Kim Myŏng-Sun's original poems that appeared in *The Fruits of Life.* The female narrator of "In the Glass Palace" ("Yurigwan soke") is trapped in an isolated space and is overcome with feelings of rejection and frustration. "Alter Ego" ("Punsin") depicts a young woman beggar who struggles against depression and helplessness. In "Testament" ("Yuŏn") the narrator laments her mistreatment in her native land. While death is ironically associated with hope in her translation of Baudelaire's "La mort des pauvres" *("et c'est le seul espoir" [yuilhan hŭimang]),* some of her original poems present a much more stark image of the threat of death for those who are socially marginalized.

As noted, Kim Myŏng-Sun was the first to introduce Poe into Korea, and her comments on his works reveal her conviction that Korean writers could benefit from emulating his esthetic principles. According to Kim Myŏng-Sun, Poe's focus on the supernatural was an important factor in the development of European art. By translating Poe's works, she was attempting to contribute to the creation of a new kind of art in Korea. Kim Myŏng-Sun held the view that one of the main aims of literature was the exploration of the self, and she claimed to have discovered this in Poe's writing. In the 1920s in Korea writers of both nationalist and socialist leanings upheld the principle that literature should give priority to broad social issues. In contrast, Kim Myŏng-Sun's method of exploring human emotions as the key to an understanding of social and national problems can be related to her interest in Poe.

Pak Hwa-Sŏng: Women, Work, and Colonial Oppression

Pak Hwa-Sŏng gained recognition in the 1930s for the treatment of socialist themes in her works. In the following I relate her writing about women workers and colonial oppression to new ideas about feminism and socialism found in the works of foreign writers like Alexandra Kollontai.

Pak Hwa-Sŏng's Literary World

Pak Hwa-Sŏng was born in 1904 and went to Japan as a young woman to study English. She made her literary debut in 1925 when she published "The Eve of the Harvest Moon Festival" in *Chosŏn Literary World.* She continued to gain recognition with the appearance of *White Flower (Paekhwa)* in 1932, which was serialized in the *East Asia Daily,* and other publications during the 1930s. In the 1930s she wrote fiction about the exploited classes and was considered a fellow traveler by socialists.[36] After World War II she published mostly longer works and established herself as an author of major importance.

Pak Hwa-Sŏng's writing reached a turning point in the mid-1930s: the earlier works mainly focused on ideological questions, while the later ones shifted to the effects of poverty on the everyday lives of ordinary people. The protagonists of Pak Hwa-Sŏng's early works tended to be intellectuals whose thinking was influenced by leftist movements and who considered ideology to be more important than individual happiness. The following works are included in this group: "The Eve of the Harvest Moon Festival" (1925), *The White Flower* (1932), and *Daybreak of the Northern Country (Pukkuk ŭi yŏmyŏng* [1935]). Works in the later group include: "A Snowy Night" ("Nun onŭn pam" [1935]), "Before and After the Flood" ("Hongsu chŏnhu" [1934]), "The Barber" ("Ibalsa" [1935]), "Drought Spirit" ("Hankwi" [1935]), "An Auspicious Day" ("Chungkusnal" [1935]), and "Homeless People" ("Kohyang ŏpnnŭn saram dŭl" [1936]).

"The Eve of the Harvest Moon Festival" deals with a woman worker, Yŏng-Sin, who injures her arm as she is protesting the harassment of a fellow worker. She does not get proper treatment for the injury and must bear the pain as she spends the night sewing to earn extra money for the Harvest Moon Festival. The climactic scene, when the landlord takes her hard-earned money, contributes to the sharp criticism of the gap between rich and poor. At the time, some male critics such as Kim Mun-Jip and An Hŭi-Nam criticized Pak Hwa-Sŏng's writing for a lack of "femininity" and urged her to write works of fiction that extolled the traditional womanly virtues of tranquility, delicacy, and beauty.[37] Pak Hwa-Sŏng emphasized that the traditional weakness of women must be overcome through class and gender emancipation. Along with Kang Kyŏng-Ae and Paek Shin-Ae, she belongs to the group of women writers of the 1930s who vividly described the difficult living conditions under colonialism, and she explains poverty as the result of both human and natural factors.[38] Feminist scholars have pointed out that Pak Hwa-Sŏng explores in a realistic fashion the impact of poverty and colonialism on the lives of women.

The Colonizer's Long Shadow

Since her days as an exchange student in Japan, Pak Hwa-Sŏng was determined to play a leading role in defending her country against the injustices of colonialism.[39] She had witnessed the plunder of her country by colonial invaders, and she felt that the way for her people to overcome this situation was to develop class consciousness. In the 1920s and 1930s the Japanese exploitation of their Korean colony was so devastating that many people in rural communities, who were already struggling to survive, were forced to become migrant workers or to emigrate to Manchuria. Many of Pak Hwa-Sŏng's works deal with the problems of exploited workers, especially women, under the colonial regime.[40]

In order to remedy the problems of widespread unemployment in the 1930s the colonial government undertook large construction projects. Pak Hwa-Sŏng's story "Sewer Construction" ("Hasudo kongsa") is built around the confrontations of the exploitative Japanese officials and the persecuted construction workers on a large construction project in Mokp'o, which was Pak Hwa-Sŏng's home town. The Japanese construction supervisor takes 40 percent of the construction fee for himself and even uses some of the money intended for workers' wages for his own purposes. (This kind of exploitation was common during the colonial period.) The male protagonist, Tong-Kwŏn, drops out of business school and goes to Tokyo, where he becomes acquainted with socialist thinking. When he returns to Korea, he becomes active in a labor group, explains socialist theories in simple terms to his fellow workers, and guides them in developing class consciousness. He does not have a favorable opinion about the proponents of free choice in love and marriage, and he views relations between men and women from a socialist viewpoint. He instructs his lover, Yong-Hŭi, about socialism, and she completely accepts his view that ideological commitments take precedence over individual feelings.

The problems of migrant workers are treated in "Homeless People," which details the plight of a group of impoverished farmers who have been encouraged to head north by some pro-Japanese officials. When they reach their new home, they realize that the land is arid and inhospitable, but their petition to be allowed to return is not answered.

"The Avengers" ("Pulgasari" [1935]) shows how family relationships were distorted during the colonial period. Although the protagonist comes from a family that has curried favor with the Japanese authorities, he develops a critical stance toward his family after being expelled from high school and investigated by the police. At his father's sixtieth birthday party his brothers invite police agents to spy on him; as a result, he leaves the house, warning the family that it will pay a price for its collaboration with the Japanese oppressors. This work criticizes the collaborators, who gained wealth and powerful positions in government and industry, and decries the destruction of family life under colonial oppression. Many of Pak Hwa-Sŏng's characters display strongly nationalistic sentiments.

It is the women characters, however, who exemplify the injustices of colonialism in the most striking way. In "The Eve of the Harvest Moon Festival" when Yŏng-Sin speaks out against the Japanese bosses who exploit workers and sexually assault women, she is also protesting the colonial domination of her country. In "Spring Night" ("Ch'un so" [1936]) we see the suppression and economic exploitation of lower-class women. This work focuses on the burdens of poverty and discrimination that weigh on working-class mothers. Although Yang-Rim's mother vigorously struggles against harsh conditions, she is surrounded by women who are too poor to care for their children properly and face harassment by Japanese police officers. The story ends with the piercing cry of a mother who loses her child because of poverty.

Women's Work and Socialism

Pak Hwa-Sŏng became interested in socialism during her studies in Japan, where leftist thinking was widespread, and when she returned to Korea, leftist intellectuals were concerned with the problem of social inequality. Many dealt with problems of poverty under colonialism, and they linked class and national liberation. To these concerns Pak Hwa-Sŏng added gender equality, emphasizing that women needed to go beyond traditional limits and participate in broader social processes. In a 1933 *New Woman (Sin yŏsŏng)* article Pak Hwa-Sŏng wrote that without class emancipation there could be no emancipation of women.[41] In spite of these feminist tendencies most of the social activists in her works are men, and women function in secondary roles as comrades.

During the colonial period women had to cope with such adverse conditions as the lack of legal protection for workers, long working hours at low pay, abusive and often violent treatment at home and in the workplace, and various other conditions that threatened their very existence. Under conditions of extreme poverty the only work available for women was in factories. Since Chosŏn had a long tradition of training women to be patient and submissive to the will of men, factory managers used male workers to control young female workers.[42] "The Eve of the Harvest Moon Festival" was the first literary representation of a woman worker under conditions of colonial oppression. With Yŏng-Sin as the victim of national, class, and gender discrimination, it represents a new trend in Korean literature.

Red Love

Although Pak Hwa-Sŏng was not a translator herself, her work can be linked to trends of socialist thinking that were being imported into Korea through translation. In particular, many of the problems raised in Pak Hwa-Sŏng's works of the 1920s and 1930s relate to those found in the works of Alexandra Kollontai, introduced into Korea by intellectuals who were interested in promoting socialist views on women.[43] In a 1933 *Rising Chosŏn (Sinhŭng Chosŏn)* article Chu In-Suk claimed that it was a mistake to interpret Kollontai's *Red Love* as a work that dealt with a woman's lascivious adventures. Rather it should be recognized as a work treating the problems of contemporary women and pointing the way toward their emancipation in a socialist society. Pak Hwa-Sŏng considered Kollontai's thought helpful in formulating an approach linking women's emancipation with class emancipation.[44] She was especially interested in the way *Red Love* presented male-female relations based on intellectual companionship. It would seem that in her own life Pak Hwa-Sŏng may have been trying to emulate some of the ideas gleaned from Kollontai's work. As noted, she married Kim Kuk-Jin, who was a poor but brilliant socialist. (Her family was opposed to the match, and the marriage was kept secret until their first child was born.)

The female protagonists in Pak Hwa-Sŏng's earlier works represent variations on the theme of ideological comradeship. "Sewer Construction" puts sexual love in a socialist perspective. Yong-Hŭi refuses to marry the university student picked out by her parents because she does not love him. In this respect the work is similar to others at the time that were promoting free choice in love and marriage. However, Pak Hwa-Sŏng's characters emphasize intellectual companionship. Tong-Kwŏn criticizes individualistic love and leaves Yong-Hŭi so that he can pursue his socialist goals, demonstrating that ideological commitment is more important than individual feelings. He tells her that he would rather think of her as a comrade than a lover, and he hopes that she will develop her own capabilities. To the extent that Yong-Hŭi accepts her lover's point of view and is content to remain behind while he pursues his career, the work presents only a somewhat modernized version of the traditional woman's endurance. "The Cliff" ("Pit'al") also presents two lovers who focus on their work rather than on private meetings. The heroine, Ju-Hŭi, forgoes emotional pleasures and takes pride in her lover Jong Ch'an's work in organizing a strike. In "The Avengers" one of the daughters of the family goes beyond conventional morality and lives with a socialist.

In contrast with some of Pak Hwa-Sŏng's works, *Daybreak of the Northern*

Country presents a woman who eschews individual relationships for her own work as a socialist. Hyo-Sun, an exchange student in Tokyo, breaks off an engagement with a man she does not love and starts to live with a socialist intellectual, Jun-Ho, concealing the relationship from her parents until after the birth of their daughter. When they return to Korea, Jun-Ho is sent to prison for his socialist activities but renounces his ideological commitments and is released. Hyo-Sun, shocked by Jun-Ho's renunciation, rejects him and leaves home to pursue her work for the socialist cause. This work presents a striking image of a woman who overcomes emotional conflicts in her personal life and gives priority to her work.[45]

Mo Yun-Suk: A Chosŏn Daughter Sings of Her Nation

Although Mo Yun-Suk is widely acknowledged as one of the most important women poets in Korea in the 1930s, so far little attention has been paid to the ways in which her works relate to trends in translation. Here I place Mo Yun-Suk's writing in the context of the translation of foreign works dealing with nationalism.

Mo Yun-Suk's Literary World

Mo Yun-Suk continued writing until her death in 1990, and she earned a reputation as a poet who expressed nationalist concerns in passionate tones. She was born in 1910 in Wŏnsan (in the northern part of the Korean peninsula) and entered Ewha Women's College in 1928, where she became active as a student leader in the Independence Movement.[46] At Ewha she studied writing with the poet Kim Sang-Yong and along with No Ch'ŏn-Myŏng (and others) participated in the publication of a poetry magazine, *The Poetry Garden (Siwŏn)*.

Before 1945 Mo Yun-Suk's works displayed a tendency toward ardent nationalism that continued to appear in her later works to a lesser degree. When her first volume of poetry, *The Bright Zone,* appeared in 1933, it attracted wide attention in the Korean literary world. In his introduction Yi Gwang-Su praised the work, but opinions about it varied. Pak Yong-Ch'ŏl defended the emotional expressiveness of Mo Yun-Suk's poems, claiming that the best artistic effects were reached by boldly revealing emotions. He contended that women had a great potential to write lyric poetry.[47] Yi Hŏn-Gu, another well-known critic, praised Mo-Yun-Suk's works, saying that the tears of the poet were the tears of the nation and of the age.[48] However, some criticized her poetry for being overly sentimental. The translator and scholar Yang Ju-Dong warned that Mo Yun-Suk's creativity might be stifled by too much dependence on her literary mentor, Yi Gwang-Su.[49]

Mo Yun-Suk's second book, *The Wren's Elegy,* which appeared in 1937, was sold out within a few days, and a second edition was quickly printed; by 1985 the work had been reprinted fifty-eight times. This work is considered representative of Mo Yun-Suk's early period and is noted for a refined use of language and moving images. When the work came out, it created a sensation. It was first seen as a love poem that elevated the spiritual over the physical.[50] Although it seems to be a simple love poem, it expresses a deep concern for the future of the Korean people that earned Mo Yun-Suk a reputation as a poet of nationalism.[51] Her later works include *A Jade Hairpin* and *The Waves.* After World War II she became active in political and cultural organizations, participating as a Korean delegate in meetings of the United Nations in 1949 and UNESCO in 1955, and she assumed a leadership role in the international PEN and the Modern Korean Poets' Association.

"First Woman Poet of the Chosŏn Spirit"

From the early phase of her career Mo Yun-Suk displayed strong nationalist tendencies that reflected the mood of the country under colonial domination. However, with the exception of a few works she wrote in Manchuria, rather than criticizing the colonial situation directly, she presented nationalistic ideals. She did not focus on the class struggle and never became involved in the proletarian movement of the 1920s and 1930s.[52] Mo Yun-Suk's view that literature should contribute to social improvement is related to the teachings of her father and of her mentor, Yi Gwang-Su. From her father, who was an independence fighter, she learned the traditional view that literary works should have didactic aims, and this approach to artistic creation was further strengthened as a result of her contact with Yi Gwang-Su's brand of nationalism. When Yi Gwang-Su first evaluated her poems, he emphasized that the guiding spirit of a work was primary, and this encouraged her to focus on conveying a patriotic message.[53] Yi Gwang-Su, whose early fiction works appeared in the 1910s, was a self-proclaimed nationalist who linked literary production with patriotism. In the 1920s he rejected the proletarian literature movement and promoted social, political, and cultural improvement. Some scholars have pointed out that Yi Gwang-Su's nationalism was not primarily geared toward achieving independence in the short run but rather toward seeking the freedom to pursue cultural activities under the foreign occupation.[54]

Some aspects of Yi Gwang-Su's thought are reflected in *The Bright Zone,* particularly the combination of nationalism and humanism. As noted, almost half of the original two hundred poems were eliminated by government censors. In his introduction Yi Gwang-Su wrote: "In the Chosŏn period there was a woman poet named Hŏ Nansŏlhŏn. However, Mo Yun-Suk is the first woman poet to use the Korean language to express the spirit of the Korean people."[55] The poems in this volume are not concerned with free choice in love and marriage, as are the works of some of the women writers of the 1920s, nor do they display a socialist bent. Mo Yun-Suk's originality consists in linking the image of self-sacrificing women with nationalism.

While some of the women writers of the time rebelled against the tradition of viewing women as sacrificial victims, Mo Yun-Suk's poetry depicts Chosŏn as a lover to be embraced. "Letting Down My Black Hair" ("Kŏmŭn mŏri p'ulŏ"), one of Mo Yun-Suk's earliest works that was not included in her first volume, goes beyond the image of the traditional woman who waits passively for her lover to return. We see a woman who is willing to sacrifice herself but at the same time plays a very active role. Loosening her hair, the woman forgoes safety and goes forth to pour her energies into saving her nation. "This Life" ("I saengmyŏng ŭl") also presents the image of a woman willing to sacrifice her life for her country. The narrator expresses her absolute love for her native land in terms that are reminiscent of a love song and vows to dedicate herself to regaining the lost sovereignty of her people. Of course images of feminine sacrifice can be seen in traditional Korean literary works, such as the Koryŏ poem "The Song of Pyŏngyang" ("Sŏkyŏng pyŏlgok"), in which the female narrator is willing to abandon everything to follow her lover. However, in her poem Mo Yun-Suk employs the startling image of the woman who is willing to drain the blood from her heart and offer it to her beloved. This type of passionate expression of nationalist sentiment was not common in poetry by Korean women. Narrators who are willing to sacrifice their blood for the sake of the nation also appear in "This Heart" ("I mam ŭl") and particularly in "A Wife's Wish" ("Anae ŭi sowŏn"), which depicts a woman of the Silla period thinking of her husband, who has gone off to war for the fatherland. "Woman Drawing Water" ("Mulkitnŭn saeksi") links the image of a woman drawing water from a well to serve her family with the willingness to sacrifice for the nation. In "A Daughter of Korea" ("Chosŏn ŭi ttal"), one of the representative works in Mo Yun-Suk's first volume of poetry, the beloved (Nim) is equated with the nation. The daughter of Chosŏn rises above everyday concerns and heeds the call of nationalism.

The Anxiety of Foreign Culture

While Mo Yun-Suk gained a reputation as a poet of nationalism very early in her career, her work was also closely connected with newly imported trends of foreign literature. As a student, she was greatly interested in the works of foreign authors such as Tolstoy, Yeats, Rossetti, Shelley, and Burns. She was particularly impressed with the works of the Indian poets Tagore and Naidu. In spite of her fascination with foreign literature, she was highly critical of the pedagogical approach of the Literary Department at Ewha Women's College. She complained about the faculty's methods and particularly about the difficulty of the English books that the students were required to read. She would have preferred to devote her time to the study of Korean language and literature.[56] Nevertheless, her own writing was clearly marked by her reading of poetry in English, especially Naidu's works.

After graduation from Ewha in 1931, Mo Yun-Suk went to Manchuria to work as an English teacher in a girls' high school, and she joined a group that read the works of foreign poets such as Yeats, Poe, Tagore, and Naidu. During her stay in Manchuria she immersed herself in the study of literature and broadened her outlook through contact with a foreign society. At this time she concentrated on writing poetry, producing the works that would be included in *The Bright Zone*. When she returned to Seoul in 1932, she took part in the activities of the Foreign Literature Group and other literary associations and became known for her commentaries on foreign authors such as Anatole France.[57]

The important influence of foreign literature on Mo Yun-Suk's work can be understood by considering the differences between her first volume of poetry and her second, *The Wren's Elegy*. A brief comparison of these two works reveals that when she wrote her second book, Mo Yun-Suk had absorbed many of the techniques being imported through translation, and she employs a more modern and colloquial style. Her first volume is characterized more by traditional stylistic features than by new elements brought in through the translation and introduction of foreign poetry. This volume uses relatively few foreign loan words in comparison with some of the other works being written in Korea at the time, and the vocabulary includes archaic, folkloric, and dialectal terms. In her study of Mo Yun-Suk's work, Kim Yu-Sŏn comments that this poet's emphasis on native Korean vocabulary, rather than terms of Chinese origin, contributed to the development of writing style in Korean. On the other hand, the archaic vocabulary gives the volume an aura of quaintness at a time when new poetic techniques were being developed.[58]

Mo Yun-Suk continued to add to *The Wren's Elegy* over a period of almost forty years. The 1937 edition, which some consider a prose poem, consists of eight letters and five diary entries in which the narrator, referred to as Wren, expresses the conflicting emotions resulting from her love for a married man, Simon.[59] Concerning the names of the two main characters, the author explains that the wren is a bird of Africa that cries alone deep in the forest. Simon, named after Peter from the New Testament because he easily has a change of heart, is the narrator's beloved teacher. Scholars have commented that although on the surface this work deals with the longing of the narrator for an absent lover, on a deeper level it indicates the ideal path for the Korean people.[60]

The Wren's Elegy can be linked to trends being developed through translated literature on at least two levels: the development of colloquial style and the use of a feminine narrative voice. As noted, Kim Ŏk had emphasized that translations should be undertaken in a creative way that conveyed mood and poetic emotion. In addition to his translations, he also wrote poems himself, and he is recognized for his contributions to modern Korean poetic style. Kim Ŏk began to translate European Symbolist poets in the late 1910s, and in the 1920s he also translated the works of Tagore and Naidu. In terms of both colloquial style and feminine narrative voice Mo Yun-Suk's original poetry relates closely to the translation techniques of Kim Ŏk. Her work can also be connected to that of Han Yong-Un, who is noted for his contributions as a poet, Buddhist reformer, and member of the Independence Movement.[61]

We have already seen that in the 1920s and 1930s writers and translators like Kim Ŏk and the women translators helped to develop a writing style more in harmony with everyday usage. Kim Ŏk pointed out that Tagore's own English translations of his Bengali originals were quite natural, and therefore in translating works like Tagore's *The Gardner,* he employed a colloquial style to come close to the original.[62] In translating the poems of Tagore and Naidu, Kim Ŏk repeatedly used the colloquial predicate endings *juseyo* and *sŭpnida,* and the repetition of these verbal forms gives unity and rhythm to the poetic translations. The following show Kim's translations of Tagore and Naidu:

The night is dark. The stars are lost in clouds.[63]
Pam ŭn ŏdŭpsŭpnida. Pyŏl dŭl ŭn kurŭm soke ilŏjyŏssŭpnida.[64]

Mine eyes that are weary of bliss. . . .
My lips that are weary of song.[65]

Nae nun ŭn ch'ukbok e p'ikonhaessŭpnida. . . .
Nae ipsul ŭn norae e p'ikonhaessŭpnida.[66]

Mo Yun-Suk's *Wren's Elegy* contains many examples of a similar use of col-loquial style—for example, "I cannot yet look at the rose in the front yard" *(Ajik na nŭn ttŭl ap'e changmi rŭl polsuŏpsŭpnida).*[67]

Kim Ŏk translated several of Naidu's poems in the early 1920s and ac-companied these with a brief commentary on her life and work. He claimed that while both Tagore and Naidu express nationalistic feelings, Naidu's works displayed a delicate feminine sensibility.[68] Kim Ŏk's translation of Naidu's "If You Were Dead" presents the paradox of an absolute love that is strengthened through death:

> For life is like a burning veil
> That keeps our yearning souls apart.[69]
> Kŭ kŏs ŭn chŏ saengmyŏng ŭn uri ŭi kŭriwŏhanŭn yŏng dŭl ŭl mŏlli
>   ddŏlŏjige hanŭn,
> pul put'ŭn myŏnsa wa kat'go.[70]

Much like Kim Ŏk in his Naidu translations, Han Yong-Un and Mo Yun-Suk employ a feminine narrative voice to express a longing for a beloved that is related to the yearning for national independence. In Han Yong-Un's poetry anthology, *The Silence of Love,* the narrator expresses her yearning for her beloved in terms that have generally been interpreted to refer on an-other level to the longing for the return of national sovereignty:

> Yet I know that to make parting the source of vain tears is to sunder
>   myself my love, so I transformed the unruly power of sorrow
>   and poured it over the vertex of new hope.
> As we fear parting when we meet, so we believe we will meet again
>   when we part.
> Ah, love is gone, but I have not sent my love away.
> My song of love beyond song shrouds the silence of love.[71]

The lover who has departed in *The Silence of Love* can be compared to the distant lover in *The Wren's Elegy*. While Han Yong-Un's beloved (Nim) is more abstract than Mo Yun-Suk's Simon, both works are characterized by paradox. By his very absence the lover takes on an almost sacred quality, and it is through striving to overcome this separation that the narrator grows spiritually: "Simon! Can you hear the increasingly anguished song of the women of Korea? Our sorrow as we grow in the gloomy shadow of this entangled society, in disarray! Are you the leader who will truly lead us by the hand?"[72]

The use of the feminine voice to talk about love in *The Silence of Love* has sometimes been interpreted as an aspect of a supposed maternal instinct or life force. However, a much more fruitful way of understanding the dynamics of the feminine narrator in the translations of Kim Ŏk and the poetry of Han Yong-Un and Mo Yun-Suk is to relate this technique to the desire for regaining national sovereignty. The female voice functions as an image of the traditions of the people and as an indication of the power discrepancies in gender relations as well as in international affairs.

Soaring on *The Broken Wing*

One of the foreign writers to have made a lasting impression on Mo Yun-Suk was Sarojini Naidu, who was born into a family of scholars in 1879. From 1895 to 1898 she studied at King's College, London, and at Girton College, Cambridge, and met a number of important figures in the English literary world, including Edmund Gosse and Arthur Symons, both of whom encouraged her aspirations to be a writer. She published three volumes of poetry: *The Golden Threshold* (1906), *The Bird of Time* (1912), and *The Broken Wing* (1917). In addition to being a writer, she was also noted for her political activities: she was elected president of the Indian National Congress in 1925, worked with Mahatma Gandhi, and was governor of Uttar Pradesh from 1947 to 1949.

Mo Yun-Suk first read Naidu's works as a student, and she reread *The Broken Wing* many times during the 1920s and 1930s. For Mo Yun-Suk, Naidu's works suggested possibilities for ameliorating the Korean situation, and she admired Naidu herself for combining writing and political activities. Throughout her life Mo Yun-Suk continued to be fascinated with her Indian counterpart.

When Mo Yun-Suk's poetry began to appear in the 1930s, some critics commented on the similarities between her works and Naidu's. These two poets can be compared with respect to their views on literature and their expression of nationalist sentiments. Both Naidu and Mo Yun-Suk held the view that literature should take account of contemporary social conditions. In a 1936 article Mo Yun-Suk revealed her determination to write poetry that expressed her passionate concern about the situation of her country.[73] She strongly emphasized the didactic aspect of literature, claiming that the reading of poetry should bring about enlightenment and social improvement.[74] Naidu took a stance against art for art's sake and felt that one of the ways to dedicate herself to the emancipation of her motherland was through her poetry.[75]

Although it would be difficult to establish a direct link between Naidu and Mo Yun-Suk in terms of style or technique, both of them express nationalist concerns in simple and moving images. When Mo Yun-Suk's first volume of poetry appeared, the critic Kim Ki-Rim remarked that some of her poems displayed the vigorous rhythm of Naidu's works.[76] Mo Yun-Suk wrote many of the works in this volume while she was teaching English in Manchuria in 1931, and at this time she was greatly impressed with the way Naidu's *Broken Wing* treated the suffering of a colonized people.[77] *The Broken Wing* contains mostly love poems that convey a mood of religious devotion and a few pieces memorializing well-known personages. The second stanza of the title piece, "The Broken Wing," indicates the way some of the works in the volume convey the patriotic aspirations of an oppressed people:

> Shall spring that wakes mine ancient land again
> Call to my wild and suffering heart in vain?
> Or Fate's blind arrows still the pulsing note
> Of my far-reaching, frail, unconquered throat?
> Or a weak bleeding pinion daunt or tire
> My flight to the high realms of my desire?
> Behold! I rise to meet the destined spring
> And scale the stars upon my broken wing![78]

In the introduction to *The Bright Zone* Mo Yun-Suk explains that she is dedicated to writing about the destiny of her people and that in her poems the image of the homeland is intimately connected with the fate of each person. The last stanza of "The Bright Zone" conveys this concern with the destiny of the homeland:

> Like ten thousand arrows shot into the air
> Distant days ahead dance in our heart.
> In this blessed zone where silver breeze ripples
> Be the life of twenty million souls everlasting.[79]

In the poetry of Naidu and Mo Yun-Suk there is a recognition that although their countries are downtrodden at the moment, a bright future is on the way. Their works are also similar in that they propose women as the bearers of the torch of nationalist hopes. In the preface to *The Broken Wing* Naidu writes: "The Indian woman of today is once more awake and profoundly alive to her splendid destiny as the guardian and interpreter of the Triune Vision of national life—the Vision of Love, the Vision of Faith, the

Vision of Patriotism."[80] "A Daughter of Korea" gives us an example of how Mo Yun-Suk also depicts women as the key to national aspirations:

When I feel miserable in a shabby skirt
His face floats gleaming from nowhere
And he whispers at a window crack:
"Aren't you a daughter of Korea?"[81]

Conclusions

Kim Myŏng-Sun, Pak Hwa-Sŏng, and Mo Yun-Suk, who took different approaches to combining feminist and nationalist concerns in their works, have provided models for women writers of the latter half of the twentieth century. While Kim Myŏng-Sun's work has inspired those writing on issues of gender discrimination and Pak Hwa-Sŏng's stories and novels are considered antecedents of works dealing with social problems, Mo Yun-Suk's work helped to open the way for women to excel in poetry in a country where, for many centuries, writing in verse was generally not considered appropriate for upper-class women.

In Kim Myŏng-Sun's writing the themes of free choice in love and marriage and the protest against patriarchal traditions are related to raising the status of women. Her works make a strong statement about the need to free women from a rigid pattern of social expectations. During her lifetime her message was misunderstood, but as feminist scholarship has developed, there has been a renewed interest in her work. She has gained recognition as one of the pioneering writers who boldly denounced gender discrimination in an age when women still had few options.

At present many women writers are depicting the sacrifices of women in a male-dominated society—for example, fiction writers O Jŏng-Hŭi and Chŏn Kyŏng-Rin and the poet Ch'oe Sŭng-Ja. O Jŏng-Hui began her writing career in 1968, and a number of her works, including "Evening Game" ("Chŏnyŏk ŭi keim" [1979]), deal with a rebellion against male authority.[82] Chŏn Kyŏng-Rin's works, such as "Desert Moon" ("Samak ŭi tal" [1995]), also depict gender discrimination and the problems associated with patriarchal values.[83] The poetry of Ch'oe Sŭng-Ja, such as For the Sake of Y (Y rŭl wihayŏ [1984]), presents the sacrifices of women and a desire for revenge against men for their mistreatment of women.[84] Ch'oe takes this desire for revenge a step further and rejects compromise in a society that represses the behavior of women.

Pak Hwa-Sŏng's contribution was to depict women who were committed to ameliorating social conditions rather than being limited to the household. The women in her works are educated, and they do not hesitate to criticize social injustice. Contemporary writers have continued to depict women characters who are committed to bringing about social change concerning the North-South division and the problems of rapid industrialization (among other issues). While in several of Pak Hwa-Sŏng's works the women learn about socialism from their male friends or lovers and are inspired by it, this is not the case with most contemporary works. Instead, more recent works present women who are deeply involved in eliminating such problems as urban ghettoization and rural impoverishment. In the works of Pak Wan-Sŏ, Yang Kwi-Ja, and Kang Sŏk-Kyŏng (among others), we see women struggling to cope with the absurdities of their society and attempting to define themselves in a society where traditional values have crumbled.[85] Pak Wan-Sŏ's works, such as *The Beginning of Days Being Lived* (*Salaissnŭn nal ŭi sijak* [1980]) and *The Standing Woman* (*Sŏissnŭn yŏja* [1985]), depict authoritarianism within the family as a microcosm of broader social inequalities. Yang Kwi-Ja's 1987 work, *The People of Wŏnmi Dong* (*Wŏnmi Dong saram dŭl),* portrays the effects of urbanization on marginalized people. In Kang Sŏk-Kyŏng's 1986 novella, *A Room in the Woods (Sup sok ŭi pang),* So-Yang is a university student who struggles with deep feelings of alienation from her peers as well as from the established generation. She fails to find meaning in studies or in the student protest movement, and she is unable to communicate with the members of her prosperous family. Her demise results from her feelings of helplessness in the face of lingering gender prejudice and the persistence of social inequality.

Mo Yun-Suk wrote many poems that revealed patriotic sentiments. In *The Wren's Elegy* in particular, Mo Yun-Suk goes beyond the traditional themes of poetry by women, such as the lassitude and longing for the return of the lover or the pent-up emotions of the upper-class wife. In this respect she opened up the way for more widespread participation for women writing poetry. She can be considered a precursor for many contemporary women poets, among them Ko Jŏng-Hŭi and Mun Jŏng-Hŭi. In many of her works, such as "The Pumpkin" ("Hobak"), Ko Jŏng-Hŭi depicts the oppression of the common people, echoing Mo Yun-Suk's socially engaged poetic voice.[86] Mo Yun-Suk's poetic legacy regarding the candid revelation of emotions can be traced to Mun Jŏng-Hŭi, who began publishing poetry in the 1970s and is noted for the bold and direct use of language in works such as "The Storm" ("P'okp'ungu") and "Song of Life" ("Moksum ŭi norae").[87]

conclusion

In Korea, at least since the Chosŏn period, translation activities have been linked to various literary works that aimed to promote feminine ideals related to state or nationalist goals. While at the turn of the twentieth century legends about European heroines were translated in order to encourage women to participate in patriotic activities, the translators in succeeding decades introduced new feminine ideals that promoted both the emancipation of women from traditional restrictions and the formulation of a new national identity.

In this book I have explored three phases of cultural change through translation. During the Chosŏn period the invention of *han'gŭl* made it possible to translate Chinese works in order to educate women. These texts aimed to instill the feminine virtues that were considered necessary for women to fulfill their roles as wives and mothers. In this rigidly hierarchical Neo-Confucian society women were expected to produce sons to perpetuate the patriarchal family and to act as guardians of the social values that were the underpinning of the state. Thus the translation of Chinese educational texts for women was considered to be crucial in maintaining social and political stability. However, we have seen that during this period there were other types of translations that were of interest to women. Women were actively involved in promoting the translation of Buddhist scriptures.

Also, starting in the seventeenth century women became avid readers of translated Chinese fictional works. These religious and fictional works presented feminine images that were radically different from those found in educational works. The precise role played by women translators in the complex cultural development of the Chosŏn period is an area that remains to be explored.

During the late nineteenth and early twentieth centuries Korea underwent a period of rapid change, and translation was one of the main ways of absorbing foreign culture. At the turn of the twentieth century Koreans faced the threat of Japanese colonial domination, and translations of legends about the lives of European heroines aimed to encourage women to participate in patriotic activities. The traditional ideal of the wise mother and dutiful wife *(hyŏnmo yangch'ŏ),* which was taken as the cornerstone of Chosŏn society, was being supplemented with a new ideal of feminine sacrifice for nationalist goals.

By the 1920s the translation of foreign literary works into Korean was beginning to expand, and translators engaged in lively debates about policies and techniques. The development of the New Woman ideal was closely related to translations of the works of foreign male authors like Ibsen and Tolstoy and to the introduction of women writers like Alexandra Kollontai and Ellen Key. Women writers like Kim Myŏng-Sun, Kim Il-Yŏp, and Na Hye-Sŏk adopted some of these new ideas and promoted the emancipation of women. Although the output of many of the women translators of the 1920s and 1930s was limited and the women tended to follow the dominant trends of the literary establishment, they contributed to the development of colloquial writing style, as well as to the introduction of new forms of poetic expression, through translations of British and American works. The tendency of these women translators to write in a colloquial style links their work to that of the women writers of the Chosŏn period, who contributed to the development of vernacular writing while their male counterparts preferred to employ Chinese writing.

The three women writers whose works are considered in chapter 5—Kim Myŏng-Sun, Pak Hwa-Sŏng, and Mo Yun-Suk—each in her own way dealt with nationalist concerns from a feminist perspective. Kim Myŏng-Sun links the discrimination against women with the disadvantaged position of Korea under Japanese colonial domination. Pak Hwa-Sŏng relates the problems of women workers to the exploitation of the lower classes and the subjection of the Korean people as a whole under colonialism. In Mo Yun-Suk's poetry the traditional self-sacrificing woman is transformed into the modern patriot who devotes herself to the salvation of her country.

In our increasingly interconnected world, where globalizing trends compete with rising local tensions, it is crucial to recognize that translation has been and will continue to be one of the underlying factors in the confrontations among cultures. We can no longer afford to overlook the rich storehouse of knowledge in the works of women writers and translators as we seek to understand the constantly shifting differences that define us.

Appendix: Women Literary Translators and Translations in the 1920s and 1930s

*A copy of the translation has not been found.

**Name of the original author cannot be verified.

***Original title cannot be verified. Titles in parentheses without quotation marks or italics are renderings of the title of the translation.

1. Chang Ki-Sŏn (Ewha graduate)
   Henry Wadsworth Longfellow, "The Rainy Day" ("Kujin Pi"). *Ewha* 5 (1935): 56.

2. Chang Yŏng-Suk (Ewha graduate)
   (a) O. Henry, "The Cop and the Anthem" ("Sunsa wa ch'anmiga"). *New East Asia,* January 1935, 259–262.
   (b) John McCrae, "In Flanders Fields" ("P'ŭraendŏsŭ esŏ"). *New Family,* December 1933, 147.
   (c) Percy Bysshe Shelley, "Stanzas Written in Dejection" ("Silmang ŭi norae"). *New Family,* August 1935, 129.
   (d) Percy Bysshe Shelley, "To the Moon" ("Tal ege"). *New Family,* January 1936, 85.

3. Cho Jŏng-Sun (Ewha graduate)
   Thomas Carlyle, "Today" ("Onŭl"). *International Women,* October 1932, 651.

4. Ch'oe Jŏng-Rim (Ewha graduate)
   (a) Gerard Manley Hopkins, "Rest" ("Na nŭn karyŏ hayŏssne"). *New Family,* August 1933, 129.
   (b) Alice Meynell, "At Night" ("Pam e"). *New Family,* August 1933, 129.
   (c) Oscar Wilde, "Requiescat" ("Chinhonga"). *New Family,* February 1933, 76.

5. Ch'oe Sŏn-Hwa (Ewha graduate)
   (a) John McCrae, "In Flanders Fields" ("P'ŭraendŏssŭ chŏnji esŏ"). *Ewha* 3 (1931): 149.
   (b) William Wordsworth, "I Wandered Lonely as a Cloud" ("Susŏnhwa"). *Ewha* 3 (1931): 148.
6. Chŏn Yu-Dŏk
   Alice Webster, *Daddy Long Legs (Yŏhaksaeng ilgi)*. *East Asia Daily,* 21 October–December 1937.
7. Chu Su-Wŏn (Ewha graduate)
   Robert Burns, "A Red, Red Rose" ("Pulkŭn changmi"). *New Family,* June 1933, 18–19.
8. Han Ch'ung-Hwa (Ewha graduate)
   Joseph Campbell, "The Old Woman" ("Nobu"). *Ewha* 6 (1936): 49.
9. Hillman, Mary
   *Anna Sewell, *Black Beauty (Hŭkjun Ma)*. Chosŏn Christian Publishing Company (Chosŏn Yasokyo Sŏhoe), 5 November 1927 (Kim Byŏng-Ch'ŏl, *Han'guk kŭndae pŏnyŏk munhaksa yŏngu,* 670).
10. Kim Han-Suk (Ewha graduate)
    (a) Gerard Manley Hopkins, "Rest" ("Na nŭn karya hane"). *Ewha* 5 (1935): 56.
    (b) Henry Wadsworth Longfellow, "The Rainy Day" ("Pi onŭn nal"). *Ewha* 5 (1935): 56.
    (c) Robert Louis Stevenson, "Requiem" ("Chinhonga"). *New Family,* December 1933, 56.
11. Kim Ja-Hye (Ewha graduate)
    (a) Robert Burns, "Highland Mary" ("Hairaendŭ Meri"). *New Family,* June 1933, 19–20.
    (b) Alexandre Dumas *fils, La dame aux camélias* ("Ch'un-hŭi"). (Abridgement.) *New Family,* March 1933, 190–195.
    (c) Alexandra Kollontai, *Red Love* ("Chŏkyŏn"). (Abridgement.) *New Family,* April 1933.
    (d) Guy de Maupassant, *Une vie* ("Yŏja ŭi ilsaeng"). (Abridgement.) *New Family,* February 1933, 137–141.
    (e) Elizabeth Lincoln Otis, "An 'If' For Girls" ("Manil yŏja ka"). *Three Thousand Li,* March 1933.
12. Kim Kŭm-Ju (Ewha graduate)
    (a) William Wordsworth, "She Dwelt among the Untrodden Ways" ("Injŏk tŭmun kose san ch'ŏnyŏ"). *New Family,* December 1933, 144.
    (b) William Wordsworth, "The Solitary Reaper" ("Kodokhan suhwakja"). *Ewha* 5 (1935): 57.
13. Kim Kyŏn-Sin (Ewha graduate)
    Thomas Moore, "Oft, in the Stilly Night" ("Chinan nal ŭi ch'uŏk"). *Chosŏn Daily,* 30 June 1931.
14. Kim Me-Ri (Ewha graduate)
    Alfred Lord Tennyson, "Enoch Arden" ("Inak Adŭn"). *Ewha* 1 (1929): 157–175.

15. Kim Myŏng-Sun
    (a) Charles Baudelaire, "Femmes damnées" ("Chŏju ŭi yŏin dŭl"). *Creation (Kaebyŏk)* 28 (October 1922): 54.
    (b) Charles Baudelaire, "La mort des pauvres" ("Pinmin ŭi sa"). *Creation (Kaebyŏk)* 28 (October 1922): 54.
    (c) Rémy de Gourmont, "La neige" ("Nun"). *Creation (Kaebyŏk)* 28 (October 1922): 51.
    (d) **(Horessŭ Horei), ***"Chujang" (Drinking place). *Creation (Kaebyŏk)* 28 (October 1922): 52.
    (e) Hermann Kasack, "Die tragische Sendung" ("Pikŭkjŏk unmyŏng"). *Creation (Kaebyŏk)* 28 (October 1922): 51.
    (f) Maurice Maeterlinck, "J'ai cherché trois ans mes sœurs" ("Na nŭn chajassda"). *Creation (Kaebyŏk)* 28 (October 1922): 51.
    (g) Edgar Allan Poe, "The Assignation" (Sangbong"). *Creation (Kaebyŏk)* 28 (November 1922): 25–36.
    (h) Edgar Allan Poe, "The Raven" ("Taeo"). *Creation (Kaebyŏk)* 28 (October 1922): 52–53.
    (i) Edgar Allan Poe, "To Helen" ("Hellen ege"). *Creation (Kaebyŏk)* 28 (October 1922): 53.
    (j) Franz Werfel, "Lächeln Atmen Schreiten" ("Usŭm"). *Creation (Kaebyŏk)* 28 (October 1922): 50.
16. Kim Yŏng-Ae (Ewha graduate)
    Percy Bysshe Shelley, "Stanzas Written in Dejection" ("Nap'oli haebyŏn esŏ"). *Chosŏn Daily,* 30 June 1931.
17. Kyu Sŏn
    *William Wordsworth, "On a Summer Evening" ("Ŏnŭ yŏrŭmnal chŏnyŏk e"). *New Life* 4, 6 (1931) (Kim Byŏng-Ch'ŏl, *Han'guk kŭndae pŏnyŏk munhaksa yŏngu,* 980).
18. Mo Yun-Suk (Ewha graduate)
    (a) Anonymous, ***"Aeran minyo" (Irish folksong). *Three Thousand Li,* January 1939, 89–90.
    (b) Sarojini Naidu, "To India" ("Indo ege"). *Eastern Light Collection (Tonggwang ch'ŏnsŏ),* June 1933 (Song Yŏng-Sun, *Mo Yun-Suk yŏngu,* 27).
    (c) **(P'aot'o Pp'ŭttchŭi), ***"Samsaek ki" (Three-colored flag), *Three Thousand Li,* December 1941, 144.
19. No Ch'ŏn-Myŏng (Ewha graduate)
    (a) Thomas Hardy, ***"Nŭlkŭn mal ŭl terigo" (Leading an old horse). *Three Thousand Li,* December 1941, 146.
    (b) **(Epsŭsaken), ***("Kŭriun pada ro") (Longing for the sea). *Center* 2, 8 (1 August 1934) (Kim Byŏng-Ch'ŏl, *Han'guk kŭndae pŏnyŏk munhaksa yŏngu,* 994).
    (c) Winifred M. Letts, ***"Aksŭp'odo ŭi ch'ŏmt'ap" (The sharp tower of Oxford). *Three Thousand Li,* December 1941, 144–145.

20. No Jae-Suk

   William Wordsworth, "I Wandered Lonely as a Cloud" ("Susŏnhwa"). *Youth (Ch'ŏngnyŏn)* 6, 5 (May 1926): 16.

21. Mrs. A. H. Norton

   ***"Imgŭm kwa sae ot kwa tarŭn iyagi" (The emperor's new clothes and other stories). Chosŏn Christian Publishing Company (Chosŏn Yasokyo Sŏhoe), 29 July 1925 (Kim Byŏng Ch'ŏl, *Han'guk kŭndae pŏnyŏk munhaksa yŏngu*, 963).

22. Paek An-Ja

   Anonymous, ***"Kawang" (False king). *Chosŏn Daily*, 8 November–2 December 1925 (Kim Byŏng-Ch'ŏl, *Han'guk kŭndae pŏnyŏk munhaksa yŏngu*, 964).

23. Paek Kuk-Hŭi (Ewha graduate)

   Arthur Symons, "The Fisher's Widow" ("Ŏbŭ ŭi hŏlŏmi"). *New Family*, June 1935, 24–25.

24. Pak Do-Ŭn (Ewha graduate)

   *Percy Bysshe Shelley, "Stanzas Written in Dejection" ("Silmang"). *New Life* 6, 7 (July 1933) (Kim Byŏng Ch'ŏl, *Han'guk kŭndae pŏnyŏk munhaksa yŏngu*, 989).

25. Pak In-Dŏk (Ewha graduate)

   (a) Anonymous, ***"Ko aeu ŭi chŏng" (Lament for a dead friend). *New World* 2, 1 (18 November 1921) (Kim Byŏg Ch'ŏl, *Han'guk kŭndae pŏnyŏk munhaksa yŏngu*, 949).

   (b) Alfred Lord Tennyson, "Columbus" ("K'ollombŏsŭ"). *Rose Village* 1, 1 (May 1921) (Kim Byŏng-Ch'ŏl, *Han'guk kŭndae pŏnyŏk munhaksa yŏngu*, 948).

26. Pak Kyŏm-Suk

   Alfred Lord Tennyson, "Break, Break, Break" ("Pusŏra pusŏra pusŏra"). *Youth (Ch'ŏngnyŏn)* 6, 9 (1926): 42.

27. Shin Paek-Hŭi (Ewha graduate)

   (a) Elizabeth Lincoln Otis, "An 'If' for Girls" ("Manil yŏja ka"). *Youth (Ch'ŏngnyŏn)* 7, 1 (1927): 88.

   (b) Ivan Turgenev, ***"Sanyanggun" (The hunter). *Yŏron* 1, 8 (1 November 1932) (Kim Byŏng-Ch'ŏl, *Han'guk kŭndae pŏnyŏk munhaksa yŏngu*, 985).

28. Sŏ Akada

   (Tenisŭ A. Maekkat'i), *"Hwangch'ok e pul ŭl palkhimyŏ" (Light the candle). *Catholic Youth* 2, 2 (January 1934) (Kim Byŏng-Ch'ŏl, *Han'guk kŭndae pŏnyŏk munhaksa yŏngu*, 992).

29. Sŏ Ŭn-Suk (Ewha graduate)

   Francis William Bourdillon, "The Night Has a Thousand Eyes" ("Norae"). *New Family*, June 1933, 18.

30. Sŏk Ran

   (a) Jules Romains, "Ode I" ("Tanjang"). *New Chosŏn* 12 (1935): 105–106.

   (b) Virginia Woolf, "The Mark on the Wall" ("Pyŏk ŭi ojŏm"). *New Chosŏn*, 1 June 1934, 106–113.

31. Mrs. Underwood
   (a) John Bunyan, *Pilgrim's Progress (Ch'ŏnro yŏkjŏng),* vol. 2. Chosŏn Christian Publishing Company (Chosŏn Yasokyo Sŏhoe), 10 September 1920 (Kim Byŏng-Ch'ŏl, *Han'guk kŭndae pŏnyŏk munhaksa yŏngu,* 529).
   (b) Robert Louis Stevenson, *The Bottle Imp (Pyŏng chung soma).* Chosŏn Christian Publishing Company (Chosŏn Yasokyo Sŏhoe), 20 May 1921 (Kim Byŏng-Ch'ŏl, *Han'guk kŭndae pŏnyŏk munhaksa yŏngu,* 947).
   (c) Robert Louis Stevenson, *The Strange Case of Dr. Jekyll and Mr. Hyde* ("Tchikŭl kwa Haidŭ"). Chosŏn Christian Publishing Company (Chosŏn Yasokyo Sŏhoe), 28 October 1921 (Kim Byŏng-Ch'ŏl, *Han'guk kŭndae pŏnyŏk munhaksa yŏngu,* 948).
32. Yi Kyŏng-Suk (Ewha graduate)
   Ivan Turgenev, "The Beggar" ("Kŏlin"). *International Women,* October 1932, 649–650.
33. Yi Sŏn-Hŭi (Ewha graduate)
   Charles Lamb, "The Old Familiar Faces" ("Kŭriun yet ŏlgul"). *International Women,* October 1932, 650.
34. Yi Sun-Hŭi (Ewha graduate)
   (a) Wilfrid Wilson Gibson, "To the Memory of Rupert Brooke" ("Ttŏnam"). *International Women,* October 1932, 650.
   (b) Thomas Hood, "The Bridge of Sighs" (T'ansik ŭi tari"). *Three Thousand Li* 5, 7 (1 July 1933): 122–123.
   (c) Thomas Hood, "The Song of the Shirt" ("Syassŭ ŭi norae"). *Ewha* 4 (1932): 95.
   (d) Percy Bysshe Shelley, "A Lament" (Pit'an"). *New Family,* March 1933, 196.
   (e) Walt Whitman, "O Captain! My Captain!" ("O sŏnjang, na ŭi sŏnjang"). *Ewha* 4 (1932): 94.
35. Yi Sun-Yŏng (Ewha graduate)
   Alfred Lord Tennyson, "Lady Clare" ("Nedi K'ŭlleŏ"). *Ewha* 2 (1930): 139–141.
36. Yi Wŏn-Hŭi
   William Wordsworth, "To the Cuckoo" ("Kwakgongjo yŏ"). *Evangelical Movement,* 1 June 1937 (Kim Byŏng-Ch'ŏl, *Han'guk kŭndae pŏnyŏk munhaksa yŏngu,* 710).
37. Yŏn Kap-Sun (Ewha graduate)
   Walter Savage Landor, "Rose Aylmer" ("Nojŭ Eilmŏ"). *New Family,* December 1933, 145.
38. Yu Hyŏng-Suk
   Virginia Poe, "Ever with Thee I Wish to Roam" ("Na ŭi kajang saranghanŭn iyŏ"). *New Life,* 2, 10 (1 October 1929) (Pak On-Ja, "Miguk munhak chakp'um ŭi han'gukŏ pŏnyŏkbon e kwanhan sŏji yŏngu," 44).
39. Yu Jŏng-Ok (Ewha graduate)
   (a) Anonymous, ***"Kŭ Ch'amsae." *Ewha* 2 (1930): 145–146.
   (b) **(Jenkalssŭ), ***"Kihoe" (Opportunity). *Ewha* 2 (1930): 138.

*40. Anonymous woman writer

    *William Shakespeare, ***"Sarang kwa chukŭm"(Love and death). *New Novel* 1, 2 (December 1929) (Kim Byŏng-Ch'ŏl, *Han'guk kŭndae pŏnyŏk munhaksa yŏngu*, 973).

41. Translations for Theatrical Productions

    During the 1920s and 1930s a number of theatrical works based on translations of foreign plays were produced at women's educational institutions and by women's associations. Women students were actively involved in these productions, and it can be assumed that they also contributed to the translation process. Such works included George Bernard Shaw's *Saint Joan* and William Shakespeare's *Taming of the Shrew* at Ewha College; Maurice Maeterlinck's *L' oiseau bleu*, Anatole France's *La comédie de celui qui épousa une femme muette,* and Anton Chekhov's *The Cherry Orchard* at Ewha High School; Karel Capel's *The Insect Play* at Chŏngsin Women's School; and Henrik Ibsen's *Ghosts* at the Kyŏng Sŏng Women's Christian Association (Kim Byŏng-Ch'ŏl, *Han'guk kŭndae pŏnyŏk munhaksa yŏngu,* 968–994).

Notes

Preface

1. Theresa Hyun and José Lambert, eds., *Translation*.
2. Homi Bhabha, ed., *Nation*.

Introduction

1. Except in cases where a previously accepted form of romanization exists, I have followed the McCune-Reishauer system of romanizing Korean.

2. Kim Byŏng-Ch'ŏl, *Han'guk kŭndae pŏnyŏk munhaksa yŏngu.*

3. Kim Mi-Hyŏn, *Han'guk yŏsŏng sosŏl kwa p'eminijŭm;* Sŏ Jŏng-Ja, *Han'guk kŭndae yŏsŏng sosŏl yŏngu;* Ch'oe Hye-Sil, *Sin yŏsŏng dŭlŭn muŏs ŭl kkumkkuŏssnŭnga.*

4. Lois A. West, *Feminist Nationalism,* xv.

5. Alice Yun Chai, "Integrative Feminist Politics," 177.

6. In Korea from the late nineteenth century until the end of World War II various nationalist movements arose in response to pressures from foreign powers. Japanese aggression toward Korea in the late nineteenth century prompted the formation of various nationalist groups such as the Independence Club (Tongnip Hyŏphoe), founded by Sŏ Jae-P'il and Yi Sang-Jae. This group published *The Independent (Tongnip sinmun)* and joined forces with political and religious groups to promote national independence and go beyond the limits of traditional society. Many newspapers and periodicals promoting the nationalist cause also began to appear. After the signing of the 1905 Protectorate Treaty, granting the Japanese Foreign Office full authority over all aspects of Korea's international relations, protest movements developed and demonstrations took place. After the official Japanese takeover in 1910, tens of thousands of Koreans were arrested by the Japanese police. The Independence Movement, which culminated in demonstrations on March

1, 1919, included the participation of over two hundred thousand people and was one of the largest manifestations of nationalism. It ultimately grew even larger as demonstrations spread over the entire country and continued for several months.

In April 1919 the Korean Provisional Government was established in Shanghai with Yi Sŭng-Man as the first president. The Communist Party was founded in 1925, and in 1927 it joined with the nationalist groups to form the New Korea Society (Singanhoe), which aimed to promote political and economic progress and to strengthen national solidarity. The Kwangju student movement began with a struggle between Korean and Japanese students in 1929 and escalated into widespread fighting in the streets of Kwangju. The demonstrations spread throughout the country and included many thousands of students, making this the largest nationalist movement since 1919. The New Korea Society was involved in the Kwangju student movement, and as a result its key members were arrested and the organization was dissolved in 1931 (Kuksa Taesajŏn P'yŏnch'an Wiwŏnhoe, *Han'guksa taesajŏn*, 495–497). In spite of the failure of the Independence Movement, resistance movements continued to operate overseas. For details, see, for example, Lee Ki-Baik, *Han'guksa sin ron*, 364–367.

7. Hermans, ed., *Manipulation*, 10–11.

8. Simon, *Gender*; Flotow, *Translation*.

Chapter One: Cultural Background

1. Pak Byŏng-Ch'ae, "Han'gŭl munhwa hyŏngsŏng kwa minjok chŏngsin," 55.

2. Cho Dong-Il, *Han'guk munhak t'ongsa*, 1: 96.

3. Yi Yong-Ju, "Hanjaŏ ŭi saengsŏng kwa paldal," 304.

4. Ibid., 303.

5. Pak Byŏng-Ch'ae, "Han'gŭl munhwa hyŏngsŏng kwa minjok chŏngsin," 56.

6. Ibid., 55.

7. Yi Ik-Sŏp, Yi Sang-Ŏk, and Ch'ae Wan, *Han'guk ŭi ŏnŏ*, 64–71.

8. Yi Hye-Sun and her co-researchers have attempted to correct some of the misunderstandings about women writers in Korea before the twentieth century, including the misconception about the scarcity and poor quality of works by women, as well as the overgeneralization that women were completely excluded from writing in Chinese. For a detailed examination of the genres and writing styles employed by women writers in Korea before the twentieth century, see Yi Hye-Sun et al., *Han'guk kojŏn yŏsŏng chakka yŏngu*.

9. Hŏ Mi-Ja, *Han'guk yŏsŏng munhak yŏngu*, 16.

10. Ibid., 20.

11. Ibid., 21–26.

12. Ibid., 31.

13. Cited in Lee Ki-Baik, *A New History of Korea*, 192.

14. During the Chosŏn period the core curriculum required to pass the examination for entry into government service focused on the Sasŏ Samkyŏng (The Four Books and the Three Classics). The Four Books were *The Analects of Confucius, The*

Works of Mencius, The Doctrine of the Mean, and *The Great Learning;* the Three Classics were *The Book of Odes, The Canon of History,* and *The Book of Changes.*

15. At this time in Korea, the Chinese language was referred to as *hwaŏ* and the Korean language as *ŏnŏ* (vernacular language); Chinese writing was referred to as *jinsŏ* (true writing) and Korean writing as *ŏnmun* (vernacular writing). The term *"ŏnhae"* (vernacular annotation) was used only when the source text was in Chinese, whereas a number of terms referred to the translation of texts from other languages, such as *pŏnyŏk, sinbŏn,* and *sinyŏk* (Yi Sung-Nyŏng et al., eds., *Kukŏ kukmunhak sajŏn,* 423).

16. In the Chosŏn period foreign relations were governed by *sadae chuŭi,* or reverence for political power. Chosŏn paid tribute to the Chinese courts and in return was granted protection from foreign invasions.

17. Cho Dong-Il, *Han'guk munhak t'ongsa,* 2: 259.

18. Ibid., 275.

19. Chŏn Kyu-Tae, *Han'guk kojŏn munhaksa,* 222.

20. Cho Dong-Il, *Han'guk munhak t'ongsa,* 2: 276.

21. Ibid., 277.

22. Ibid.

23. Yi Sung-Nyŏng et al., eds., *Kukŏ kukmunhak sajŏn,* 268.

24. Cho Dong-Il, *Han'guk munhak t'ongsa,* 2: 278.

25. In 1592 the Japanese under Hideyoshi Toyotomi launched a series of attacks against Chosŏn that lasted until 1598. Although the countryside was devastated and the social system was disrupted, new possibilities for cultural exchange were opened among the countries of East Asia.

26. Cho Dong-Il, *Han'guk munhak t'ongsa,* 2: 278.

27. Toury writes: "Thus, whereas adherence to source norms determines a translation's adequacy as compared to the source text, subscription to norms originating in the target culture determines its acceptability" (*Descriptive Translation Studies,* 56–57).

28. Cho Dong-Il, *Han'guk munhak t'ongsa,* 3: 102.

29. Yi Hye-Sun, "Hanjung sosŏl ŭi pigyo munhak," 304–305.

30. Yi Sung-Nyŏng et al., eds., *Kukŏ kukmunhak sajŏn,* 236.

31. Martina Deuchler, "Tradition," 1.

32. Song Ji-Hyŏn, *Tasissŭnŭn yŏsŏng kwa munhak,* 43–44.

33. Song Myŏng-Hŭi, *Munhak kwa sŏng ŭi ideollogi,* 41–42.

34. Deuchler, "Tradition," 5.

35. Ch'oe Suk-Kyŏng and Ha Hyŏn-Kang, *Han'guk yŏsŏngsa,* 572.

36. The Practical Learning Movement (seventeenth to nineteenth centuries) comprised a group of scholars who attempted to go beyond the metaphysical approaches of Neo-Confucianism in order to find practical solutions to the agricultural, economic, and social problems facing Chosŏn.

37. Ch'oe Suk-Kyŏng and Ha Hyŏn-Kang, *Han'guk yŏsŏngsa,* 582.

38. Yi Kyŏng-Sŏn, *Han'guk munhak kwa chŏnt'ong munhwa,* 209.

39. Ibid., 191.

40. Cho Dong-Il, *Han'guk munhak t'ongsa,* 3, 422.

41. Kim Hŭng-Kyu, *Han'guk munhak ŭi ihae,* 141.

42. Kim Hŭng-Su, "Munch'e ŭi pyŏnhwa," 993.

43. Kim Hae-Sŏng, *Yŏsŏng kwa munhak*, 42.

44. Yi Hye-Sun and Chŏng Ha-Yŏng, *Han'guk kojŏn yŏsŏng munhak ŭi segye*, 43–62.

45. Hŏ Mi-Ja, *Han'guk yŏsŏng munhak yŏngu*, 190.

46. Yi Hye-Sun and Chŏng Ha-Yŏng, *Han'guk kojŏn yŏsŏng munhak ŭi segye*, 17–31.

47. Cho Dong-Il, *Han'guk munhak t'ongsa*, 3, 111.

48. "Firm believers in the principle of equality, the Progressives (as they are sometimes called) sought to abolish class distinctions, reform the political process by following the model of Japan's Meiji Restoration, and achieve genuine national independence for Korea by ending China's interference in Korean affairs. They believed that their goals could be achieved only by extraordinary measures, and they hoped to obtain foreign support for their plans. Although few in number, the Progressives were a conspicuous element in the politics of the time and were referred to as the Enlightenment Party, or the Independence Party" (Eckert et al., *Korea Old and New*, 208–209).

49. Kim Yŏng-Jŏng, "Han'guk kŭndae ŭi yŏsŏng undong," 208.

50. Kim Ju-Su, "Han'guk kŭndae yŏsŏng ŭi pŏpjesang ŭi chiwi," 7.

51. Yun Hye-Wŏn, "Kaehwagi yŏsŏng kyoyuk," 178.

52. Yung-Hee Kim points out that the Ch'angyanghoe played a pioneering role in encouraging women's political and social participation ("Under the Mandate," 129–130).

53. Yun Hye-Wŏn, "Kaehwagi yŏsŏng kyoyuk," 157.

54. Ibid., 170–172.

55. Han'guk Yŏsŏng Yŏnguhoe, *Han'guk yŏsŏngsa*, 20.

56. Ibid., 21.

57. Kim Yŏng-Jŏng, "Han'guk kŭndae ŭi yŏsŏng undong," 205–229; Pak Yong-Ok, "1920 nyŏndae han'guk yŏsŏng tanch'e undong," 240.

58. Kim Hyŏn and Kim Yun-Sik, *Han'guk munhaksa*, 83.

59. Kwŏn O-Man, *Kaehwagi siga yŏngu*, 84–96.

60. Pak Yŏng-Shin, "Kidokkyo wa Han'gŭl undong," 55.

61. Although Catholicism had begun to take root in Chosŏn at least a century before Protestantism, the Protestants placed a much greater emphasis on translation of the Bible into *han'gŭl* and the Catholics focused more on works dealing with church doctrines.

62. Kim Byŏng-Ch'ŏl, *Han'guk kŭndae pŏnyŏk munhaksa yŏngu*, 71.

63. Cho Dong-Il, *Han'guk munhak t'ongsa*, 4, 426.

64. Theresa Hyun, "Byron Lands," 289–296.

65. Kim Byŏng-Ch'ŏl, *Han'guk kŭndae pŏnyŏk munhaksa yŏngu*, 282–283.

66. Ibid., 309.

Chapter Two: European Heroines in Translation: The Search for New Models

1. Paik Nak-Chung, "Nations," 226.

2. Lee Ki-Baik, *New History*, 315–317.

3. The terms *"kojŏn sosŏl"* (classical fiction narrative) and *"kodae sosŏl"* (ancient fiction narrative) refer to works before the end of the nineteenth century, as opposed to those that began to be written around the turn of the twentieth century. Terms such as *"ko sosŏl"* and *"ku sosŏl"* (old fiction work), *"Yi sosŏl"* (Yi dynasty fiction work), and *"chŏngi sosŏl"* (life story) are also used. Fiction works of the traditional period tended to be richer in fantastic details than modern works. One of the earliest of these traditional works was Kim Si-Sŭp's fifteenth-century work, *New Stories from Golden Turtle Mountain (Kŭmo sinhwa)*, which was written in Chinese. Traditional fiction narratives tended to be divided into those written in Chinese and those written in Korean, but many works appeared in both languages. So far approximately 530 traditional fiction narratives (including translations) have been identified. The authors of traditional fiction works were not limited to a single social class. While some of the authors were known to be of the upper classes, many works were anonymous, owing to the fact that fiction writing was not considered respectable. The readers were not limited to one social group either, and fiction works were popular among the upper classes as well as the common people. The great majority of these fiction works followed a chronological order in the life of the protagonist. Works dealing with the lives of aristocrats tended to be set in China, while those dealing with the lives of common people were mostly set in Korea (Yi Sung-Nyŏng et al., eds., *Kukŏ kukmunhak sajŏn*, 89–90).

4. There was a close link between the development of traditional Korean fiction works and Chinese fiction. Fiction works from Ming and Ching China were widely read in Korea, and many Chinese works were translated throughout the Chosŏn period, using methods that were quite different from the annotation of Chinese classics. Kim Si-Sŭp was well acquainted with *New Tales Written while Cutting the Wick (Chien-teng hsin-hua)*, by the Chinese author Ch'u Yu. This close connection between the fiction works of China and Korea continued until the end of the Chosŏn period, when Japan became the intermediary in bringing European culture to Korea and new fiction forms developed (Yi Kyŏng-Sŏn, *Han'guk munhak kwa chŏnt'ong munhwa*, 246–250).

5. So Jae-Yŏng, *Chosŏnjo munhak ŭi t'amgu*, 23.

6. Cho Dong-Il, *Han'guk munhak t'ongsa*, 3: 462.

7. Ibid., 472.

8. Ibid., 473.

9. Ibid., 475.

10. Song Min-Ho, *Han'guk Kaehwagi sosŏl ŭi sajŏk yŏngu*, 45.

11. Kang Yŏng-Ju, "Aeguk kyemonggi ŭi chŏngi munhak," 179.

12. Kim Tong-Uk and Hwang P'ae-Kang, *Han'guk kososŏl ipmun*, 104.

13. Kim Byŏng-Kuk, *Han'guk kojŏn munhak ŭi pip'yŏngjŏk ihae*, 203.

14. Fiction works in the early twentieth century can broadly be divided into the following categories: historical and biographical works, New Novels, short stories of the 1910s, and longer fiction works of the 1920s. The historical and biographical works had their roots in traditional biographies and military tales. The New Novels mixed traditional elements with new approaches partially developed through contact with Western literature. Yi Gwang-Su's novel *The Heartless (Mujŏng)*, which

appeared in 1917, is considered representative of the new trends in fiction writing (Kim Yŏng-Min, *Han'guk kŭndae sosŏlsa*, 481–496).

15. Jayawardena *(Feminism and Nationalism)* examines various strategies of adopting foreign models to fight foreign aggression.

16. Yi Jae-Sŏn, Kim Hak-Tong, and Pak Jong-Ch'ŏl, *Kaehwagi munhak ron*, 137.

17. Kang Yŏng-Ju, "Aeguk kyemonggi ŭi chŏngi munhak," 173.

18. Pak Ŭn-Sik contributed to the development of nationalist thought in his work as editor for various Korean publications. After the March 1919 demonstrations he sought refuge in Siberia, where he participated in the anti-Japanese movement. Subsequently he traveled to Shanghai and worked for nationalist publications such as *The Independent* and the *Korea Bulletin (Hanjok hoebo)*. In 1925 he was chosen for a leadership position in the Korean Provisional Government but stepped down shortly afterward because of constitutional changes. Chang Ji-Yŏn became involved in the activities of the Independence Club, and with Yi Sŭng-Man and Nam Kung-Ŏk he established the Assembly of All People (Manmin Kongdonghoe), which denounced government policy. In 1905 he was imprisoned for an editorial in the *Capital Gazette* in which he warned the Korean people of the nefarious designs of the Japanese. In 1906 he formed the Korea Self-Strengthening Society (Taehan Chakanghoe). In 1908 he sought exile in Vladivostok and later Shanghai. He returned to Korea in 1909. Shin Ch'ae-Ho's editorials aimed to foster patriotism among the Korean people. He became a member of the New Citizens' Society (Sinminhoe) in 1907, and he took part in the movement to repay the national debt. He participated in activities of the Independence Movement in Shanghai and Beijing, and in the 1920s he participated in the establishment of the Korean Provisional Government. He was arrested by the Japanese police in 1929 and died while serving a ten-year prison sentence. Shin Ch'ae-Ho is noted for his efforts to promote the knowledge of Korean history (Kuksa Taesajŏn P'yŏnch'an Wiwŏnhoe, *Han'guksa taesajŏn*, 516, 785, 1161).

19. Cho Dong-Il, *Han'guk Munhak t'ongsa*, 4, 322.

20. Mun Sŏng-Suk, *Kaehwagi sosŏlron yŏngu*, 90.

21. Kim Hak-Ju, "Yang Kye-Ch'o ŭi munhak sasang," 311–312.

22. Ibid., 314–328.

23. Yi Jae-Sŏn, *Han'guk Kaehwagi sosŏl yŏngu*, 152.

24. At the age of eighteen, An Ch'ang-Ho delivered a rousing speech at a meeting of the Independence Club, which launched his long career as a political activist. He participated in the founding of the Assembly of All People and the New Citizens' Society. He also contributed to the field of education and founded several schools. In 1911 An Ch'ang-Ho sought refuge in the United States, where he formed the Society for the Fostering of Activists (Hŭngsadan). After the March 1919 demonstrations, he went to Shanghai, where he held administrative positions in the Korean Provisional Government. In 1932 he was arrested in connection with a bombing incident that killed or wounded a number of Japanese officials, and he was sent back to Korea, where he was put in prison. Yang Ki-T'ak participated in various anti-Japanese activities such as the founding of the *Taehan Daily News (Taehan maeil sinbo)* in 1905 and the New Citizens' Society. After the Japanese annexation of

Korea he established the Manchurian Military School (Manju Mugwan Hakkyo) to train resistance fighters. After returning to Korea from exile in Manchuria, he was arrested and spent two years in prison. He is noted for his efforts to unite the various factions of the Independence Movement. In 1930 he took on a leadership role in the Korean Provisional Government but resigned shortly afterward (Kuksa Taesajŏn P'yŏnch'an Wiwŏnhoe, *Han'guksa taesajŏn,* 823–824, 831).

25. Yi Hyo-Jae, *Han'guk ŭi yŏsŏng undong,* 39.

26. Yi Jae-Sŏn, *Han'guk Kaehwagi sosŏl yŏngu,* 152.

27. Yi Hyo-Jae, *Han'guk ŭi yŏsŏng undong,* 40–43.

28. David McCann situates poetry by professional women entertainers within the dualistic structure of Chosŏn society, "characterized on the one hand by a formal, 'Confucian' mode of hierarchical interaction, and on the other by an informal, egalitarian mode" ("Formal and Informal Korean Society," 129).

29. West, ed., *Feminist Nationalism,* xv–xviii.

30. Partha Chatterjee, *Nation,* 120.

31. There has been some debate among scholars about whether *Aeguk puin chŏn* should be considered an adaptation, an original work, or a translation. Kang Yŏng-Ju ("Aeguk kyemonggi ŭi chŏngi munhak," 176) holds that the work should be considered an adaptation. Yi Jae-Sŏn, Kim Hak-Tong, and Pak Jong-Ch'ŏl (*Kaehwagi munhak ron,* 147) consider that the work is an original composition that Chang Ji-Yŏn wrote with reference to Schiller's play, *The Maid of Orleans.* Kim Yŏng-Min (*Han'guk kŭndae sosŏlsa,* 112) classifies the work as an original historical novel. On the other hand, Kim Byŏng-Ch'ŏl (*Han'guk kŭndae pŏnyŏk munhaksa yŏngu,* 245) classifies the work as a translation whose source text cannot be identified. Cho Dong-Il (*Han'guk munhak t'ongsa,* 4, 325) also considers the work as a translation from a Chinese text.

32. Jonathan D. Spence, *Search,* 240.

33. For an explanation of how the cult of Joan of Arc related to the development of nationalism in nineteenth-century France, see Guillemin, *True History,* 195–197.

34. Kang Yŏng-Ju, "Aeguk kyemonggi ŭi chŏngi munhak," 178.

35. Kim Yŏng-Min, *Han'guk kŭndae sosŏlsa,* 118.

36. Kang Yŏng-Ju, "Aeguk kyemonggi ŭi chŏngi munhak," 180.

37. Kim Byŏng-Kuk (*Han'guk kojŏn munhak ŭi pip'yŏngjŏk ihae,* 184–191) analyzes authorial voice and point of view in certain early twentieth-century Korean works that have a strong ideological focus.

38. Chang Ji-Yŏn, *Aeguk puin chŏn,* 348, 352, 367, 379. Citations from the Korean texts examined in this volume have been translated into English by the author.

39. Chang Ji-Yŏn also compiled a two-volume textbook for girls, *Women's Reader (Yŏja tokbon),* which contained selections about the lives of women who performed patriotic deeds. The second volume, focusing on foreign women who sacrificed themselves for their countries, aimed to encourage young women to go beyond traditional feminine ideals and contribute to the betterment of their nation (Pak Yong-Ok, "1905–10, Sŏgu kŭndae yŏsŏngsang ŭi ihae wa insik, Chang Ji-Yŏn ŭi *Yŏja dokbon* ŭl chungsim ŭro," 231).

40. Chang Ji-Yŏn, *Aeguk puin chŏn,* 349.

41. Yu Kwan-Sun (1904–1920) was a student at Ewha Girls' School who took part in the March 1919 demonstrations in Seoul. When she returned to her native town in the countryside, she helped organize demonstrations and distributed Korean flags to the local people. She was arrested by the Japanese and given a seven-year prison sentence. In prison she was known for her efforts to encourage fellow prisoners by chanting patriotic slogans. She died in prison (Kuksa Taesajŏn P'yŏnch'an Wiwŏnhoe, *Han'guksa taesajŏn*, 927).

42. Kim Byŏng-Ch'ŏl, *Han'guk kŭndae pŏnyŏk munhaksa yŏngu*, 231–234.

43. Gilmartin et al., eds., *Engendering China*, 195.

44. *Raran puin chŏn*, 385.

45. Ibid., 424.

46. Ibid., 395.

47. Ibid., 389, 395.

48. Yi In-Jik's (1862–1916) *Tears of Blood* was serialized in the *Independence News (Mansebo)* in 1906, and it appeared as a separate volume the following year. There has been a considerable amount of scholarly research on this work. *Tears of Blood* deals with themes such as national independence; the reform of social, political, and educational structures; problems of gender inequality; and the abolition of child marriage. Like many of the New Novels, this work rests on the assumption that by adopting a pro-Japanese stance, Koreans would be able to overcome Sino-centric traditions and promote their interests as a modern nation (Kim Yŏng-Min, *Han'guk kŭndae sosŏlsa*, 207).

49. Elaine H. Kim and Chungmoo Choi, eds., *Dangerous Women*, 2.

50. For an analysis of progressive thought in *Freedom Bell*, see Yi Yong-Nam, *Han'guk kŭndae munhak kwa chakka ŭisik*, 53–58.

51. Sŏng Hyŏn-Ja, *Sin sosŏl e mich'in manch'ŏng sosŏl ŭi yŏnghyang*, 115.

52. Ibid., 121.

53. Ibid., 157–159.

Chapter Three: Translation and New Feminine Ideals in the 1920s and 1930s

1. Eckert et al., *Korea Old and New*, 260–264.

2. Kim Byŏng-Ch'ŏl, *Han'guk kŭndae pŏnyŏk munhaksa yŏngu*, 411–413.

3. One of the early Japanese feminist writers, Raicho Hiratsuka, was well known for her pronouncements, such as the following: "The new woman is not satisfied with the life of the kind of woman who is made ignorant, made a slave" (cited in Jayawardena, *Feminism and Nationalism*, 246). The career of Raicho, who organized feminist publications and was actively involved in the women's movement, is quite similar to that of the early Korean feminists Na Hye-Sŏk, Kim Il-Yŏp, and Kim Myŏng-Sun (Ch'oe Hye-Sil, *Sin yŏsŏng dŭlŭn muŏs ŭl kkumkkuŏssnŭnga*, 164–165).

4. The "New Woman" concept, which was employed in many countries during periods of modernization, was a complex one, as Jayawardena points out: "In their search for a national identity, the emergent bourgeoisies also harked back to a national culture: the new woman could not be a total negation of traditional culture.

Although certain obviously unjust practices should be abolished, and women involved in activities outside the home, they still had to act as guardians of national culture, indigenous religion and family traditions—in other words, to be both 'modern' and 'traditional'." Jayawardena examines the connection between feminism and the cultural renaissance in China in the late 1910s: "The new ideas were expressed most effectively in radical journals like *New Youth* and *The Renaissance* and in women's magazines such as *The New Woman, Women's Bell, Girls' Daily of Canton* and *The Women's Monthly*. These journals raised all the issues of women's subordination and attacked the old customs regarding marriage; in addition, they publicized the militant activities of British suffragists, translated their articles and, influenced by the visit to China of feminists and birth control pioneers like Margaret Sanger (of the USA) and Ellen Key (of Sweden), published articles on birth control and motherhood" (*Feminism and Nationalism,* 14, 184).

5. Yi Jong-Wŏn, "Ilje ha Han'guk sin yŏsŏng ŭi yŏkhal kaldŭng e kwanhan yŏngu, 1920 nyŏndae rŭl chungsim ŭro," 29.

6. Ibid., 32.

7. Ibid., 60.

8. Ibid., 61.

9. Ibid., 42.

10. Ibid., 62–65.

11. Ch'oe Ŭn-Hŭi, *Han'guk Kaehwa Yŏsŏng Yŏljŏn,* 51.

12. Kim Yŏng-Jŏng, "Han'guk Kŭndae ŭi Yŏsŏng Undong," 218.

13. Ibid., 224.

14. Ibid., 222.

15. Ch'oe Ŭn-Hŭi, *Han'guk Kaehwa Yŏsŏng Yŏljŏn,* 78.

16. Ibid., 66.

17. Kim Yŏng-Jŏng, "Han'guk Kŭndae ŭi Yŏsŏng Undong," 222.

18. Ch'oe Ŭn-Hŭi, *Han'guk Kaehwa Yŏsŏng Yŏljŏn,* 86.

19. Ibid., 97.

20. For a detailed account of translated literature in Korea in the 1920s, see Kim Byŏng-Ch'ŏl, *Han'guk kŭndae pŏnyŏk munhaksa yŏngu,* 414–691.

21. Amy Dooling and Kristina Torgeson describe the situation of women writers in China in the early twentieth century (Dooling and Torgeson, eds., *Writing Women in Modern China,* 1–38).

22. Another Japanese feminist, Takamure Itsue, in her 1926 study on the condition of women, *Renai sosei* (Genesis of love), identified Ellen Key's idea that love was the foundation of marriage as an important step in the development of feminism (Jayawardena, *Feminism and Nationalism,* 250).

23. Pak Yŏng-Hye and Sŏ Jŏng-Ja, "Kŭndae yŏsŏng ŭi munhak hwaldong," 195.

24. Kim Byŏng-Ch'ŏl, *Kŭndae sŏyang munhak iipsa yŏngu,* 678–680.

25. Pak Yŏng-Hye and Sŏ Jŏng-Ja, "Kŭndae yŏsŏng ŭi munhak hwaldong," 196–197.

26. Kim Byŏng-Ch'ŏl, *Han'guk kŭndae sŏyang munhak iipsa yŏngu,* 159.

27. Kim Byŏng-Ch'ŏl, *Han'guk kŭndae pŏnyŏk munhaksa yŏngu,* 727.

28. Ibid., 569–578.

29. Nora was adopted as a symbol of women's struggles in many countries. In a speech at a women's college in Allahabad in 1928, Jawaharlal Nehru said: "I wonder if any of you here have read Ibsen's 'Doll's House,' if so, you will perhaps appreciate the word 'doll' when I use it in this connection. The future of India cannot consist of dolls and playthings and if you make half the population of a country the mere plaything of the other half, an encumbrance on others, how will you ever make progress?" (cited in Jayawardena, *Feminism and Nationalism*, 98).

30. Kim Byŏng-Ch'ŏl, *Kŭndae sŏyang munhak iipsa yŏngu*, 719.

31. Ibid., 722.

32. Ibid., 770.

33. Kim Byŏng-Ch'ŏl, *Han'guk kŭndae pŏnyŏk munhaksa yŏngu*, 437.

34. Kim Byŏng-Ch'ŏl, *Kŭndae sŏyang munhak iipsa yŏngu*, 508.

35. Kim Byŏng-Ch'ŏl, *Han'guk kŭndae pŏnyŏk munhaksa yŏngu*, 738.

36. Kim Byŏng-Ch'ŏl, *Kŭndae sŏyang munhak iipsa yŏngu*, 603.

37. Ibid., 607.

38. Ibid., 635.

39. Kim Byŏng-Ch'ŏl, *Han'guk kŭndae sŏyang munhak iipsa yŏngu*, 314–315.

Chapter Four: Women Literary Translators in the 1920s and 1930s

1. Kim Byŏng-Ch'ŏl, *Han'guk kŭndae pŏnyŏk munhaksa yŏngu*, 681–682.

2. Ibid., 689–690.

3. Ibid., 697–698.

4. Ibid., 711.

5. Ibid., 799.

6. In organizing this chapter, I have to a certain extent followed the approach outlined by Lambert and Van Gorp *(Manipulation of Literature),* which suggests the following steps for translation studies research aiming to consider individual translations within the larger context of translation activities: (1) preliminary data; (2) the macro level; (3) the micro level; and (4) the context. I have reversed steps (2) and (3).

7. Kim Byŏng-Ch'ŏl, *Han'guk kŭndae pŏnyŏk munhaksa yŏngu*, 539.

8. Ibid., 417.

9. Ibid., 652.

10. Theo Hermans, *Translation*, 36. The concept of norms that I use in this chapter is based on the work of Gideon Toury *(Descriptive Translation Studies*, 53–69), who identifies three kinds of translation norms: "Preliminary norms" concern such decisions as the choice of text to translate, whether to translate directly from the original language or work with an intermediate translation in another language, and whether to translate into the native language or a second language. "Initial norms" relate to the choice of orienting the translation toward the source or target culture. "Operational norms" concern the decisions made during the actual translation process.

11. As indicated above, traditionally in Korea there was a discrepancy between written and spoken language, resulting in a division in writing styles that persisted

into the early twentieth century. Formal literary style *(munŏch'e)* tended to rely heavily on Chinese-character expressions, while colloquial style *(kuŏch'e)* was close to the patterns of everyday speech. Kim Ŏk was one of the translators of the early twentieth century who was particularly sensitive to this division. When he translated Rabindranath Tagore's *The Gardner,* he avoided formal literary style and employed a colloquial style that he felt was more appropriate for transmitting the rhythms of Tagore's work (Kim Byŏng-Ch'ŏl, *Han'guk kŭndae pŏnyŏk munhaksa yŏngu,* 635).

12. Gerard Manley Hopkins, *Poetical Works,* 29.

13. Joseph Campbell, *Poems,* 166.

14. Kim Byŏng-Ch'ŏl, *Han'guk kŭndae pŏnyŏk munhaksa yŏngu,* 670–671.

15. Kim Yong-Jik, *Han'guk hyŏndae si yŏngu,* 159.

16. Kim Hyŏn-Sil, "1920 nyŏndae pŏnyŏk Miguk sosŏl yŏngu, kŭ suyongyangsang mit yŏnghyang ŭi ch'ŭkmyŏn esŏ," 40–41.

17. Kim Byŏng-Ch'ŏl, *Han'guk kŭndae pŏnyŏk munhaksa yŏngu,* 980.

18. Song Yŏng-Sun, *Mo Yun-Suk yŏngu,* 27.

19. Kim Byŏng-Ch'ŏl, *Han'guk kŭndae pŏnyŏk munhaksa yŏngu,* 653.

20. Ibid., 655.

21. Ibid., 500.

22. Alfred Lord Tennyson, *Tennyson,* 303.

23. Kim Byŏng-Ch'ŏl, *Han'guk kŭndae pŏnyŏk munhaksa yŏngu,* 539.

24. Ibid., 710.

25. Kim Byŏng-Ch'ŏl, *Kŭndae sŏyang munhak iipsa yŏngu,* 418.

26. Kim Byŏng-Ch'ŏl, *Han'guk kŭndae pŏnyŏk munhaksa yŏngu,* 973.

27. Kim Yong-Jik, *Han'guk hyŏndae si yŏngu,* 161.

28. Korean translators in the 1920s and 1930s were seriously concerned with the question of intermediate sources. According to Kim Byŏng-Ch'ŏl (*Han'guk kŭndae pŏnyŏk munhaksa yŏngu,* 798), among the 124 separate volumes of translations published in the 1920s, 27 were translated directly from the original source. Sixteen of these were translated by foreign missionaries. Fifty-one of them relied on an intermediate Japanese source, indicating that Japanese translations provided important models for Korean translators. Kim Byŏng-Ch'ŏl maintains that among the 21 translations published in the 1930s, 12 were translated directly. Although the number of translated volumes decreased, the higher percentage of direct translations indicates a decrease in reliance on intermediate sources. During the 1930s the specialists in foreign languages and literatures who were becoming more active as translators tended to translate an entire work directly from the source.

29. Kim Byŏng-Ch'ŏl, *Han'guk kŭndae pŏnyŏk munhaksa yŏngu,* 481.

30. Even-Zohar considers the case of a literature that adopts elements from another literature in order to compensate for a lack within the native system: "A 'need' may arise when a new generation feels that the norms governing the system are no longer effective and therefore must be replaced. If the domestic repertoire does not offer any options in this direction, while an accessibly adjacent system seems to possess them, interference will very likely take place" ("Laws of Literary Interference," 69).

31. Chŏng In-Sŏp, "P'oo rŭl nonhayŏ oeguk munhak yŏngu ŭi p'ilyo e kŭphago, *Haeoe munhak* ŭi ch'anggan ham ŭl ch'ukham."

32. Kim Byŏng-Ch'ŏl, *Han'guk kŭndae pŏnyŏk munhaksa yŏngu,* 485.

33. Kim Ŏk, "Isik munje e taehan kwangyŏn."

34. Kim Jin-Sŏp, "Kiihan pip'yŏng hyŏnsang, Yang Ju-Dongssi egye."

35. Kim Yong-Jik, *Han'guk hyŏndae si yŏngu,* 168.

36. Charles Baudelaire, "Pinmin ŭi sa," 54; English translation is mine.

37. Charles Baudelaire, "Pinja ŭi sa," 19; English translation is mine.

38. Charles Baudelaire, *Fleurs,* 147.

39. Oscar Wilde, *Portable,* 569.

40. Oscar Wilde, "Chinhonga," 76.

41. In order to understand nature images in traditional Korean poetry it is helpful to consider *sijo,* a representative poetic form that originated in the fourteenth century and continues to be written today. The basic form, *p'yŏng sijo,* consists of three lines and approximately forty-five syllables; a somewhat longer form, *sasŏl sijo,* was developed later. *Sijo* were first written mostly by upper-class men, but gradually women entertainers became skilled at writing them. While the early *sijo* reflected the Neo-Confucian esthetics of the aristocrats, many of the works of the women entertainers were characterized by wit and refined expression of personal emotions. Since *sijo* originated as songs, they combine both literary and musical elements.

The following are a few examples of nature images frequently found in *sijo.* The peach orchard as a representation of a utopian world inhabited by supernatural beings can be found in both Korean and Chinese poetry and conveys the longing for an earthly paradise (Yi Jong-Ŭn, "*Sijo* munhak e nat'anan ŭnil sasang," 190). Water, stone, pines, bamboo, and the moon are commonly found in the works of traditional Korean poets such as Yun Sŏn-Do, who used the term "five friends" to refer to these elements. Water was taken to represent endless flowing; stone, constancy; pines, fortitude; bamboo, purity; and the moon, silence (Mun Yŏng-O, "Kosan Yun Sŏn-Do ŭi tanga yŏngu," 316). Apricots, orchids, chrysanthemums, and bamboo, known in East Asian countries as the "four gentlemen," frequently appear in the calligraphic works that decorated an aristocrat's study. In many *sijo,* bamboo represents the integrity of the ideal Confucian scholar (Mun Yŏng-O, "Kosan Yun Sŏn-Do ŭi tanga yŏngu," 317). Some *sijo* portray fishermen as leading an idyllic life far removed from the strife and cares of the social world (Chin Tong-Hyŏk, "Yi Hyŏn-Bo yŏngu," 339).

42. Robert Burns, "Pulkŭn changmi," 18.

43. Robert Burns, *Poetical Works,* 435.

44. Ch'oe Jŏng-Rim, "Yŏng munhak sasang ŭi nangmanjuŭi sidae," 27–28.

45. André Lefevere, "Why Waste Our Time," 237.

46. Pak Yong-Ch'ŏl, "Yŏryu sidan ch'ongp'yŏng," 30.

47. *Ewha Paeknyŏnsa* P'yŏnch'an Wiwŏnhoe, *Ewha paeknyŏnsa,* 198.

48. Ibid., 278.

49. Eckert et al., *Korea Old and New,* 282.

50. Song Ji-Hyŏn, *Tasissŭnŭn yŏsŏng kwa munhak,* 96.

Chapter Five: Translation, Gender, and New Forms of Writing in the 1920s and 1930s

1. Song Ji-Hyŏn, *Tasissŭnŭn yŏsŏng kwa munhak,* 94.
2. Kim Bok-Sun, "Chibae wa haebang ŭi munhak, Kim Myŏng-Sun ron," 36–38.
3. Song Ji-Hyŏn, *Tasissŭnŭn yŏsŏng kwa munhak,* 83.
4. Yi Ho-Suk, "Wiakjŏk chagi pangŏgije rosŏ ŭi erot'ijŭm, Na Hye-Sŏk ron," 87.
5. Chŏng Yŏng-Ja, *Han'guk yŏsŏng siin yŏngu,* 96.
6. Song Ji-Hyŏn, *Tasissŭnŭn yŏsŏng kwa munhak,* 90.
7. Ibid., 99–100.
8. Ibid., 106.
9. Ibid., 113.
10. Ibid., 118.
11. Pyŏn Shin-Wŏn, "Tongbanja chakka ka pon pingung kwa yŏsŏng ŭi hyŏnsil," 177.
12. Pak Yŏng-Hye and Sŏ Jŏng-Ja, "Kŭndae yŏsŏng ŭi munhak hwaldong," 233.
13. Chŏng Yŏng-Ja, *Han'guk yŏsŏng siin yŏngu,* 8.
14. Ibid., 102.
15. Han'guk Yŏryu Munhakinhoe, *Yŏkdae Han'guk yŏryu 101 in sisŏnjip,* 15–47.
16. Kim Mun-Jip, "Yŏryu chakka ŭi sŏngjŏk kwihwan ron," 356.
17. Yi Gwang-Su, "Hyŏnsang sosŏl kosŏn yŏŏn," 99. Yi Gwang-Su praised Kim Myŏng-Sun for contributing to the effort to create a new type of writing (ibid.).
18. Song Ji-Hyŏn, *Tasissŭnŭn yŏsŏng kwa munhak,* 70.
19. Chŏng Yŏng-Ja, *Han'guk yŏsŏng siin yŏngu,* 51.
20. Ibid., 55.
21. Ibid., 14.
22. Song Ji-Hyŏn, *Tasissŭnŭn yŏsŏng kwa munhak,* 75.
23. Kim Myŏng-Sun, *T'an-Sil Kim Myŏng-Sun, "Na nŭn saranghanda,"* 219.
24. Ibid., 391.
25. Ch'oe Hye-Sil, *Sin yŏsŏng dŭlŭn muŏs ŭl kkumkkuŏssnŭnga,* 346.
26. Kim Myŏng-Sun, *T'an-Sil Kim Myŏng-Sun, "Na nŭn saranghanda,"* 152.
27. During the Chosŏn period the *yangban,* in an attempt to maintain power, discriminated against the children of secondary wives: "Further, a law banning those of illegitimate birth from important government office made it difficult and, during much of the dynasty, impossible for the sons of *yangban* by secondary wives, and their descendants, to sit for the examinations that would qualify them for civil office appointments" (Lee Ki-Baik, *A New History of Korea,* 174).
28. Ch'oe Hye-Sil, *Sin yŏsŏng dŭlŭn muŏs ŭl kkumkkuŏssnŭnga,* 347.
29. Kim Myŏng-Sun, *T'an-Sil Kim Myŏng-Sun, "Na nŭn saranghanda,"* 194–195.
30. Ch'oe Hye-Sil, *Sin yŏsŏng dŭlŭn muŏs ŭl kkumkkuŏssnŭnga,* 146.
31. Kim Bok-Sun, "Chibae wa haebang ŭi munhak, Kim Myŏng-Sun ron," 58.
32. Kim Myŏng-Sun, *T'an-Sil Kim Myŏng-Sun, "Na nŭn saranghanda,"* 194. My translation.
33. Ibid., 171.
34. Chŏng Yŏng-Ja, *Han'guk yŏsŏng siin yŏngu,* 21.

35. Ibid., 19–20.

36. During the 1930s Pak Hwa-Sŏng was recognized as a socialist writer. In Japan in the 1920s she studied socialism. At this time she placed a higher priority on developing herself as a socialist thinker than as a writer (Pyŏn Shin-Wŏn, "Tongbanja chakka ka pon pingung kwa yŏsŏng ŭi hyŏnsil," 170–172).

37. Sŏ Jŏng-Ja, *Han'guk kŭndae yŏsŏng sosŏl yŏngu*, 66.

38. Yi Jae-Sŏn, *Han'guk hyŏndae sosŏlsa* (1979), 435.

39. Pyŏn Shin-Wŏn, "Tongbanja chakka ka pon pingung kwa yŏsŏng ŭi hyŏnsil," 174.

40. Between 1910 and 1918 the Japanese colonial government undertook a land survey that required all property owners to claim and report their land. Although some large landowners were able to maintain control of their land, many small-scale farmers lost the right to cultivate the land, and in rural areas the numbers of impoverished tenant farmers increased greatly (Eckert et al., *Korea Old and New*, 265–269).

41. Pak Hwa-Sŏng, "Kyegŭp haebang i yŏsŏng haebang," 21.

42. An Yŏn-Sŏn, "Han'guk sikminji chabon chuŭihwa kwajŏng esŏ yŏsŏng nodong ŭi sŏngkyŏk e kwanhan yŏngu: 1930 nyŏndae pangjik kongŏp ŭl chungsim ŭro," 91.

43. Pak Yŏng-Hye and Sŏ Jŏng-Ja, "Kŭndae yŏsŏng ŭi munhak hwaldong," 196.

44. Ibid., 231.

45. Sŏ Jŏng-Ja, *Han'guk kŭndae yŏsŏng sosŏl yŏngu*, 85.

46. In preparation for the March 1 1919 independence demonstrations, women students formed a secret, nationwide network. The active role of women in the Independence Movement marked a new stage in their political participation (Han'guk Yŏsŏng Yŏnguhoe, *Han'guk yŏsŏngsa*, 34–36).

47. Pak Yong-Ch'ŏl, "Yŏryu sidan ch'ongp'yŏng," 24–27.

48. Yi Hŏn-Gu, "Mo Yun-Suk ron," 46–47.

49. Yang Ju-Dong, "1933 nyŏndo sidan nyŏnp'yŏng," 32.

50. Yi Sŏn-Hŭi, "Ren ŭi Aega rŭl ilkko," 224–225.

51. Chŏng Yŏng-Ja, *Han'guk yŏsŏng siin yŏngu*, 139.

52. Kim Yu-Sŏn, "Mo Yun-Suk si yŏngu," 264.

53. Ibid., 251–255.

54. Kim Yŏng-Min, *Han'guk kŭndae sosŏlsa*, 472. Yi Gwang-Su studied in Japan in the 1910s and made his literary debut at this time with fiction works such as *The Heartless*. He participated in the March 1919 Independence Movement as a student in Tokyo and went to Shanghai, where he became involved with the Korean Provisional Government. During the 1920s and 1930s he held administrative positions in the *East Asia Daily* and the *Chosŏn Daily*. After the end of World War II he was accused of collaboration with the Japanese, and he disappeared during the Korean War (Yi Sung-Nyŏng et al., *Kukŏ kukmunhak sajŏn*, 494–495).

55. Mo Yun-Suk, *Yŏngun Mo Yun-Suk munhak chŏnjip*, 15–16. My translation.

56. Mo Yun-Suk, "Ŏttŏhke nan siin i toeŏssna," 94–95.

57. Mo Yun-Suk, "Naega sasukhanŭn naeoe chakka, France wa *Taisŭ*."

58. Kim Yu-Sŏn, "Mo Yun-Suk si yŏngu," 123.

59. Although the first edition of *The Wren's Elegy* bore the inscription "prose volume" *(sanmunjip)*, many discussions on the genre of the work ensued. The 1930s critic Ch'oe Jae-Sŏ pronounced it a work of poetry, and Yi Byŏng-Ki and Paek Ch'ŏl, two scholars of the post–Korean War period, specified that the work should be considered a prose poem. In the 1990s both Song Yŏng-Sun and Ch'oe Tong-Ho agreed that it should be considered a prose poem, while Kim Yu-Sŏn proposed that the work be designated poetic prose (Song Yŏng-Sun, *Mo Yun-Suk yŏngu*, 201–209).

60. Chŏng Yŏng-Ja, *Han'guk yŏsŏng siin yŏngu*, 134–138.

61. Han Yong-Un (1879–1944) was a Buddhist monk who wrote on the revitalization of Korean Buddhism. He was one of the thirty-three signers of the March 1, 1919, Korean Declaration of Independence and was sent to prison for his role in the movement. In 1926 he published a volume of poetry, *The Silence of Love (Nim ŭi ch'immuk)*, which expressed the aspirations for independence in terms of Buddhist thinking (Yi Sung-Nyŏng et al., *Kukŏ kukmunhak sajŏn*, 669).

62. Kim Byŏng-Ch'ŏl, *Han'guk kŭndae pŏnyŏk munhaksa yŏngu*, 455.

63. Rabindranath Tagore, *The Gardner*, 57.

64. Rabindranath Tagore, *Wŏnjŏng*, 61.

65. Sarojini Naidu, "Ecstasy" in *The Golden Threshold*, 54.

66. Sarojini Naidu, "Hwanghol," 43.

67. Mo Yun-Suk, *Ren ŭi aega*, 13. My translation.

68. Kim Ŏk, "Sarojini Naidu ŭi sŏjŏng si," 74.

69. Sarojini Naidu, *Broken Wing*, 91.

70. Sarojini Naidu, "Kŭdae ga chuknŭndamyŏn," 45.

71. Han Yong-Un, "Silence."

72. Mo Yun-Suk, *Ren ŭi aega*, 21. My translation.

73. Mo Yun-Suk, "Ŏttŏhke nan siin i toeŏssna," 95.

74. Kim Yu-Sŏn, "Mo Yun-Suk si yŏngu," 251.

75. Deobrata Prasad, *Sarojini Naidu*, 51.

76. Kim Ki-Rim, "Mo Yun-Suk ŭi ririsijŭm, sijip *Pich'nanŭn Chijŏk* ŭl ilkko."

77. Song Yŏng-Sun, *Mo Yun-Suk yŏngu*, 48.

78. Naidu, *Broken Wing*, 4.

79. Mo Yun-Suk, "Bright Zone," "Daughter of Korea," 110.

80. Sarojini Naidu, *Broken Wing*.

81. Mo Yun-Suk, "Bright Zone," "Daughter of Korea," 112.

82. Kim Ŭn-Jŏng, "Yŏsŏngjŏk chaa ro ŭi chŏpgŭn," 205–207.

83. Hwang Do-Kyŏng, *Uri sidae ŭi yŏsŏng chakka*, 179.

84. Chŏng Yŏng-Ja, *Han'guk yŏsŏng siin yŏngu*, 331.

85. O Se-Ŭn, "Pak Wan-Sŏ sosŏl sok ŭi ŏmŏni wa ttal mot'ipŭ," 220.

86. Chŏng Yŏng-Ja, *Han'guk yŏsŏng siin yŏngu*, 310–311.

87. Ibid., 274–275.

Selected Bibliography

Primary Materials

Baudelaire, Charles. *Les fleurs du mal.* Paris: Éditions 10/18, 1994.
————. "Pinja ŭi sa" (La mort des pauvres). Trans. Yang Ju-Dong. *Kŭmsŏng* 1 (1923): 19–20.
————. "Pinmin ŭi sa" (La mort des pauvres). Trans. Kim Myŏng-Sun. *Kaebyŏk,* October 1922, 54.
Burns, Robert. *The Poetical Works of Robert Burns.* London: Frederick Warne, 1903.
————. "Pulkŭn changmi" (A red, red rose). Trans. Chu Su-Wŏn. *Sin kajŏng,* June 1933, 18–19.
Campbell, Joseph. *The Poems of Joseph Campbell.* Ed. Austin Clarke. Dublin: Allen Figgis, 1963.
Ch'ae Jŏng-Kŭn. "K'aet'ŭlrin Maensup'iltu sojŏn" (A brief biography of Katherine Mansfield). *Sin Kajŏng,* January 1936, 143–152.
Chang Ji-Yŏn. *Aeguk puin chŏn* (The story of a patriotic lady). *Han'guk Kaehwagi munhak ch'ongsŏ 2, Yŏksa chŏngi sosŏl 6* (Collected works of the Korean Kaehwa period 2, Historical and biographical works 6), 335–379. Ed. Kim Yun-Sik et al. Seoul: Asea Munhwasa, 1978.
Chang Kŭm-Sŏn. "Yŏng munhaksang e nat'anan Bairon" (Byron and English literature). *Ewha,* 1931, 112–114.
Ch'ilbosanin. "Wiin ŭi yŏnaegwan" (Famous people's views on love). *Sin yŏsŏng,* January 1926, 26–35.
Cho Hŭi-Sun. "Tokil munhak kwa yŏryu munhak" (German literature and women's literature). *Sin kajŏng,* May 1933, 91–123.
Cho Jae-Ho. "Kŭmil ŭi yŏsŏng" (Today's woman). *Sin yŏsŏng,* March 1933, 7–8.
Ch'oe Jae-Sŏ, ed. and trans. *Haeoe sŏjŏng sijip* (Anthology of foreign lyric poetry). Seoul: Inmunsa, 1938.

Ch'oe Jŏng-Hŭi. "1933 nyŏndo yŏryu mundan ch'ongp'yŏng" (1933 survey of women's literature). *Sin kajŏng*, December 1933, 45–47.

Ch'oe Jŏng-Hŭi, et al. "Yŏryu Chakka Chwadamhoe" (A discussion among women writers). *Samch'ŏlli*, February 1936, 554–575.

———. "Yŏryu Chakka Hoeŭi" (A meeting of women writers). *Samch'ŏlli*, October 1938, 198–211.

Ch'oe Jŏng-Rim. "Yŏng munhak sasang ŭi nangmanjuŭi sidae" (The age of romanticism of English literature). *Ewha*, 22 May 1934, 26–29.

Ch'oe Yŏng-Suk, Hwang Ester, and Pak In-Dŏk. "Oeguk taehak ch'ulsin yŏryu samhaksa chwadamhoe" (Discussion of three women graduates from foreign universities). *Samch'ŏlli*, April 1932, 182–188.

Chŏn Hŭi-Bok. "Che 2 puin munje kŏmt'o" (The problem of the second wife). *Sin yŏsŏng*, February 1933, 2–27.

Chŏng Ch'il-Sŏng. "*Chŏkyŏn* pip'an, K'olont'ai ŭi sŏng todŏk e taehayŏ" (A critique of *Red Love*, Kollontai's sexual ethics). *Samch'ŏlli*, September 1929.

Chŏng In-Sŏp. "P'oo rŭl nonhayŏ oeguk munhak yŏngu ŭi p'ilyo e kŭphago, *Haeoe Munhak* ŭi ch'anggan ham ŭl ch'ukham" (The importance of Poe for foreign literature research, celebrating the inaugural issue of *Foreign Literature*). *Haeoe munhak* 1 (January 1927): 19–31.

Chŏng Rae-Dong. "Chungguk yŏryu chakka" (Chinese women writers). *Sin kajŏng*, October 1933, 148–159.

———. "Chungguk yŏryu chakka ŭi ch'angjakron kwa ch'angjak kyŏnghŏm dam" (Chinese women writers' theories and experiences of literary creation). *Sin kajŏng*, September 1934, 146–153.

Chu In-Suk. "K'olont'ai ŭi *Chŏkyŏn*" (Kollontai's *Red Love*). *Sinhŭng Chosŏn* (Rising Chosŏn), 15 November 1933, 54–57.

Dooling, Amy D., and Kristina M. Torgeson, eds. *Writing Women in Modern China: An Anthology of Women's Literature from the Early Twentieth Century*. New York: Columbia University Press, 1998.

Ha Mun-Ho. "K'olont'ai yŏsa ŭi sasang kwa munhak" (Kollontai's literature and thought). *Sin kajŏng*, December 1934, 112–119.

Ham Tae-Hun. "Chosŏn sin yŏsŏng ron" (Chosŏn's new women). *Yŏsŏng*, February 1937, 124–130.

———. "Hyŏndae Rŏsia yŏryu siin" (Contemporary Russian women poets). *Sin kajŏng*, October 1933, 159–167.

———. "Kŭndae Rŏsia yŏryu munhak e taehae" (Modern Russian women's literature). *Sin kajŏng*, April 1933, 124–130.

Han Yong-Un. *Han Yong-Un chŏngbon sijip Nim ŭi ch'immuk* (The original text of Han Yong-Un's poetry anthology, *The Silence of Love*). Ed. Kim Jae-Hong. Seoul: Si wa Sihaksa, 1996.

———. "The Silence of Love." In *Modern Korean Literature, an Anthology*, 25–26. Ed. Peter H. Lee. Honolulu: University of Hawai'i Press, 1990.

Han'guk taep'yo tanp'yŏn munhak chŏnjip (Anthology of representative Korean short literary works). Vols. 1–3. Seoul: Sinyŏng Ch'ulp'ansa, 1984.

Hong Gu. "Yŏryu chakka ŭi kunsang" (Groups of women writers). *Samch'ŏlli*, January and March 1933, 475–476, 556–559.

Hopkins, Gerard Manley. *The Poetical Works of Gerard Manley Hopkins*. Ed. Norman H. Mackenzie. Oxford: Clarendon Press, 1990.

Hyŏn Ch'ŏl. "Kŭndae munye wa Ibsen" (Modern literature and Ibsen). *Kaebyŏk*, 1 January 1921, 129–138.

Kang Sin-Jae et al., eds. *Chŏngt'ong han'guk munhak taegye* (Selected works of Korean literature). Seoul: Ŏmunkak, 1988.

Kang U. "Ellen K'ei yŏsa ŭi chongkyo kyoyukgwan" (Ellen Key's views on religious education). *Ch'ŏngnyŏn*, 1928, 12–15.

Kim Ha-Sŏng. "Segye yŏryu undongja p'ŭrop'il" (Profiles of members of the international Women's movement). *Sin yŏsŏng*, December 1931, 48–51.

Kim Hwal-Ran. "Yŏhakkyo kyoyuk munje" (Educational problems of women's schools). *Sin yŏsŏng*, March 1933, 10–13.

———. "Yŏja kodŭng kyoyuk e kwanhan ilon" (Higher education for women). *Ewha* 4 (1932): 4–7.

Kim Il-Yŏp. *Mirae se ga tahago namtorok* (Striving toward the future). Seoul: Sŏngmunsa, 1974.

Kim Ja-Hye. "Tenisŭn ŭi *Inakadŭn*" (Tennyson's *Enoch Arden*). *Sin yŏsŏng*, February 1933, 96.

Kim Jin-Sŏp. "Kiihan pip'yŏng hyŏnsang, Yang Ju-Dongssi egye" (The strange condition of criticism, to Yang Ju-Dong). *Tonga ilbo*, 29 March–3 April 1927.

———. "P'yohyŏnjuŭi munhak ron" (Expressionist literature). *Haeoe munhak* 1 (January 1927): 4–13.

Kim Ki-Jin. "Kim Myŏng-Sunssi e taehan konggae chang" (An open letter to Kim Myŏng-Sun). *Sin yŏsŏng*, November 1924, 46–50.

Kim Ki-Rim. "Mo Yun-Suk ŭi ririsijŭm, sijip *Pich'nanŭn Chiyŏk* ŭl ilkko" (Mo Yun-Suk's lyricism: A reading of the poetry volume *The Bright Zone*). *Chosŏn ilbo*, 29 and 31 October 1933.

Kim Mun-Jip. "Yŏryu chakka e taehan konggae chang, Pak Hwa-Sŏngnim kke tŭrinŭn yŏnsŏ" (An open letter to women writers, to Pak Hwa-Sŏng). *Cho kwang*, March 1939, 130–135.

———. "Yŏryu chakka ŭi sŏngjŏk kwihwan ron" (On the return of women writers to gender roles). In *Pip'yŏng munhak* (Literary criticism), 353–365. Seoul: Ch'ŏngsaek Chisa, 1938.

Kim Myŏng-Sun. *T'an-Sil Kim Myŏng-Sun, "Na nŭn saranghanda"* (T'an-Sil Kim Myŏng-Sun, "I Am in Love"). Ed. Kim Sang-Bae. Seoul: Solmoe, 1981.

Kim Nae-Sŏng. "P'ulloberu: *Pobari Puin* ŭi yŏjuinkong, Emma" (Flaubert: the protagonist of *Madame Bovary*, Emma). *Yŏsŏng*, March 1939, 60–61.

Kim Nam-Ch'ŏn. "Chosŏn inki yŏin yesulga kunsang" (The group of popular Chosŏn women artists). *Yŏsŏng*, September 1937, 16–23.

———. "Yŏryu munhak chŏjo ŭi munje" (The problem of the weakness of women's literature). *Yŏsŏng*, June 1939, 42–43.

Kim Ŏk. "Isik munje e taehan kwangyŏn" (A point of view on the problem of transference). *Tonga ilbo*, 28–29 September 1927.

————. "Sarojini Naidu ŭi sŏjŏng si" (Sarojini Naidu's lyric poetry). *Yŏngdae*, December 1924, 70–80.

————. "Sarojini Naidu ŭi sŏjŏng si" (Sarojini Naidu's lyric poetry). *Yŏngdae*, January 1925, 74–83.

————. "T'agoa ŭi si" (Tagore's poetry). *Chosŏn mundan*, November 1924, 58–64.

Kim P'al-Bong. "Kukak esŏ ŭi t'alch'ul" (Break with tradition). *Sin kajŏng*, January 1935, 76–81.

Kim Sŏk-Song. "Sŏngjŏk kwangye ŭi ilgoch'al" (A consideration of sexual relations). *Kyemyŏng*, 1 May 1921.

————. "T'olsŭt'oi ŭi chŏngkyŏl sŏl" (Tolstoy's views on chastity). *Kyemyŏng*, 15 June 1921.

Kim Sŏng-Sil. "Tenisŭn ŭi saenghwal" (Sketch of Tennyson's life). *Ch'ŏngnyŏn*, 1928, 404–405.

Kim U-Jin. *Kim U-Jin chŏnjip* (Kim U-Jin's collected works). Seoul: Chŏnyewŏn, 1984.

Kye Yong-Muk. "Mop'asang chak: *Yŏja ŭi Ilsaeng* ŭi chuinkong Jannŭ" (Maupassant's work: Jeanne, the protagonist of *Une vie*). *Yŏsŏng*, March 1939, 67–68.

Landor, Walter Savage. "Rojŭ Eilmŏ" (Rose Aylmer). Trans. Kim Sang-Yong. *Ch'ŏngnyŏn* 11:1 (February 1931): 99.

Meynell, Alice. "Chŏnyŏk e" (At night). Trans. Ch'oe Jae-Sŏ. *Samch'ŏlli* 10:11 (November 1938): 568.

Michelet, Jules. *Jeanne d'Arc et autres textes*. Paris: Éditions Gallimard, 1974.

Mo Yun-Suk. "The Bright Zone" and "A Daughter of Korea." In *The Immortal Voice: An Anthology of Modern Korean Poetry*, 109–110, 111–112. Trans. Jaihiun Kim. Seoul: Sam Hwa Printing, 1974.

————. "Kasin Naidu yŏsa egye" (To the departed Naidu). *Tonga ilbo*, 5–6 March 1949.

————. "Kŭndae Rŏsia munye sajo" (Modern Russian artistic trends). *Ewha* 3 (1931): 16–21.

————. "Naega sasukhanŭn naeoe chakka, France wa *Taisŭ*" (An international author I admire, France, and *Thais*). *Tonga ilbo*, 19 July 1935.

————. "Ŏttŏhke nan siin i toeŏssna" (How I became a poet). *Sin kajŏng*, March 1936, 92–96.

————. *Ren ŭi aega* (The wren's elegy). Seoul: Ewha Yŏja Taehakkyo Ch'ulp'anbu, 1997.

————. *Yŏngun Mo Yun-Suk munhak chŏnjip* (Collected works of Mo Yun-Suk). Vols. 1, 2, 4, 6, and 8. Seoul: Sŏnghan Ch'ulp'ansa, 1986.

Na Hye-Sŏk. "Isangjŏk puin" (Ideal woman). *Hak ji Kwang*, December 1914.

————. *Pulkkot yŏja Na Hye-Sŏk ŭi kkoch ŭi P'ari haeng* (An ardent woman's journey to Paris). Seoul: Osangsa, 1983.

Na Hye-Sŏk et al. *Han'guk yŏsŏng sosŏlsŏn* (Korean women's fiction). Vol. 1. Ed. Sŏ Jŏng-Ja. Seoul: Kapin Ch'ulp'ansa, 1991.

Naidu, Sarojini. *The Bird of Time: Songs of Life, Death and the Spring*. London: William Heinemann, 1912.

————. *The Broken Wing: Songs of Love, Death and Destiny*. London: William Heinemann, 1917.

————. *The Golden Threshold*. London: William Heinemann, 1906.

————. "Hwanghol" (Ecstasy). Trans. Kim Ŏk. *Yŏngdae*, September 1924, 43.

————. "Kŭdae ga chuknŭndamyŏn" (If you were dead). Trans. Kim Ŏk. *Kaebyŏk*, 10 July 1922, 45.

————. "Kyogun dŭl" (Palanquin bearers). Trans. Kim Ŏk. *Yŏngdae*, October 1924, 53.

————. "Silje" (Caprice). Trans. Kim Ŏk. *Kaebyŏk*, 10 July 1922, 44.

No Ch'ŏn-Myŏng. "Paeknyŏnje ka tolaonŭn siin Ch'alsŭ Laem" (Centennial of the poet Charles Lamb). *Chosŏn chungang ilbo*, 3 August 1934.

No Ja-Yŏng. "Yŏsŏng undong ŭi cheil inja Ellen Key" (Leader of the women's movement, Ellen Key). *Kaebyŏk*, 1921, 46–53.

O Ch'ŏn-Sŏk. "Sera T'ijŭteil ŭi si" (Sara Teasdale's poetry). *Chosŏn mundan* 4 (1925): 101–103.

O Yŏng. "Yŏ siin Sara T'ijŭteil ŭi yesul" (The art of the woman poet Sara Teasdale). *Tonga ilbo*, 6 November 1926.

Oe Kwan Saeng. "Yŏkwŏn undong ŭi ŏmŏni, Ellen K'ei e taehayo" (The mother of the women's rights movement, Ellen Key). *Sin yŏsŏng*, June 1926, 36–37.

Pak Hwa-Sŏng. *Hongsu chŏnhu* (Before and after the flood). Seoul: Paekyangdang, 1948.

————. *Kohyang ŏpnnŭn saram dŭl* (Homeless people). Seoul: Chungang Munhwa Pogŭpsa, 1948.

————. *Kohyang ŏpnnŭn saram dŭl* (Homeless people). Seoul: Ilsin Sŏjŏk Ch'ulp'ansa, 1994.

————. "Kyegŭp haebang i yŏsŏng haebang" (Class emancipation, women's emancipation). *Sin yŏsŏng* 2 (1933): 21–22.

————. *Sungan kwa yŏngwŏn sai* (Between the moment and eternity). Seoul: Chungang Ch'ulp'an Kongsa, 1977.

————. "T'omasŭ Hadi ong kwa Syalot Bŭront'e yŏsa" (Thomas Hardy and Charlotte Brontë). *Tonga ilbo*, 17–18 July 1935.

Pak In-Dŏk. "Miju Kangyŏngi: Hŭkin hakkyo wa widaehan yŏin kyoyukga" (American lecture tour: Black schools and outstanding women educators). *Samch'ŏlli*, August 1938, 59–62.

————. "Na ŭi chasŏjŏn" (My autobiography). *Yŏsŏng*, March 1939, 38–40.

Pak Yong-Ch'ŏl. *Pak Yong-Ch'ŏl sijip* (Pak Yong-Ch'ŏl poetry anthology). Vol. 2. Ed. Munhak Sasangsa Charyo Chosa Yŏngusil. Seoul: Munhak Sasangsa, 1970.

————. "Sara T'ijŭteil ŭi sich'o" (Sara Teasdale's beginning). *Sin kajŏng*, December 1933, 88–91.

————. "Yŏryu sidan ch'ongp'yŏng" (Survey of women's poetry). *Sin kajŏng*, February 1934, 24–30.

Pak Yŏng-Hŭi. "Tarŭn sidae ŭi tu yŏsŏng: *Chŏkyŏn* ŭi Wassirisa wa *Yŏja ŭi Ilsaeng* ŭi Jannŭ" (Two women of different ages: Vassilissa of *Red Love* and Jeanne of *Une vie*). *Chosŏn ilbo*, 6 November 1928.

P'i Ch'ŏn-Dŭk. "Burauning puin ŭi saengae wa yesul" (The life and art of Mrs. Browning). *Sin kajŏng,* January 1933, 66–69.

———. "Yŏngguk yŏryu siin K'ŭrisŭt'ina Roset'i" (The English woman poet Christina Rossetti). *Sin kajŏng,* November 1933, 132–137.

Raran puin chŏn (The story of Madame Roland). *Han'guk Kaehwagi munhak ch'ongsŏ 2, Yŏksa chŏngi sosŏl 6* (Collected literary works of the Korean Kaehwa Period 2, Historical and biographical works 6), 383–425. Ed. Kim Yun-Sik et al. Seoul: Asea Munhwasa, 1978.

So Ch'un. "Yottae ŭi Chosŏn sin yŏja" (Contemporary Chosŏn new women). *Sin yŏsŏng,* November 1923, 58–59.

Sŏ Hang-Sŏk. "Ibsen kwa yŏsŏng munje" (Ibsen and women's issues). *Sin kajŏng,* May 1935, 34–35.

Sŏ Kwang-Je. "Sin yŏnae wa sin puin: K'olont'ai *Chŏkyŏn* ŭl ilkko" (New love and new women: A reading of Kollontai's *Red Love*). *Chosŏn ilbo,* 9–15 November 1928.

Tagore, Rabindranath. *The Gardner.* New York: Macmillan, 1913.

———. *Wŏnjŏng* (The gardner). Trans. Kim Ŏk. Seoul: Hoetong Sŏgwan, 1924.

Tennyson, Alfred Lord. *Tennyson: Representative Poems.* Ed. Samuel Chew. New York: Odyssey Press, 1941.

Whitman, Walt. "Sagong iyŏ uri Sagong iyŏ" (O captain! My captain!). Trans. Chu Yo-Han. *Tonggwang* 2 (June 1925): 88–89.

Wilde, Oscar. "Chinhonga" (Requiescat). Trans. Ch'oe Jŏng-Rim. *Sin kajŏng,* February 1933, 76.

———. *The Portable Oscar Wilde.* Ed. Richard Aldington. New York: Viking, 1953.

Yang Ju-Dong. "Hyŏndae Miguk sidan" (Contemporary American poetry). *Hyŏndae p'yŏngnon,* 1 October 1927.

———. "*Kaebyŏk* 4 wŏl ho ŭi *Kŭmsŏng* p'yŏng ŭl pogo, Kim An-Sŏ Kun ege" (Reading the *Creation* April issue review of *Venus* to Kim An-Sŏ). *Kŭmsong* 3 (1923): 65–72.

———. "1933 nyŏndo sidan nyŏnp'yŏng" (Annual critique of the 1933 poetry world). *Sin tonga,* December 1933, 29–32.

Yi Ch'an-Yong. "Henri Wadŭssŭwodŭ Longp'ello" (Henry Wadsworth Longfellow). *Ch'ŏngnyŏn* 3, 10 (1923): 28–29.

Yi Chun-Suk. "P'ŏl Pŏk chak: *Ŏmŏni* ŭi yŏjuinkong iyagi" (Pearl Buck's work: The female protagonist of *Mother*). *Yŏsŏng,* March 1939, 69–71.

Yi Gwang-Su. "Hyŏnsang sosŏl kosŏn yŏŏn" (Reflections after selecting a prize novel). *Ch'ŏngch'un* 12 (March 1918): 99.

Yi Ha-Yun, trans. "Ch'oegŭn ŭi Miguk sidan" (Recent American poetry). *Chungoe ilbo,* 14–28 November 1929.

———. "Hyŏndae siin yŏngu, Yŏngguk p'yŏn" (Research on contemporary poets, English section). *Tonga ilbo,* 2 November–1 December 1930.

———. *Silhyang ŭi hwawŏn* (Garden of lost fragrance). Seoul: Si Munhaksa, 1933.

Yi Hae-Jo. *Chayu chong* (Freedom bell). In *Sin sosŏl: Pŏnan (yŏk) sosŏl* (New novels: Adaptations and translated fiction), 4: 1–44. Ed. Kim Yun-Sik et al. Seoul: Asea Munhwasa, 1978.

Yi Hŏn-Gu. "Mo Yun-Suk ron" (On Mo Yun-Suk). *Yŏsŏng*, January 1938, 46–47.

———. "Pullansŏ e Pich'nanŭn yŏryu chakka dŭl" (Brilliant French women writers). *Sin kajŏng*, September 1933, 144–148.

Yi Il-Jŏng. "Namnyŏ ŭi tongkwŏn ŭi taerip" (The confrontation over gender equality). *Tonga ilbo*, 3 April 1920.

Yi Jŏng-Ho. "Segye myŏngjak sosŏl haenggak: *Nana* wa *Yuryŏng*" (Famous international fiction works: *Nana* and *Ghosts*). *Sin yŏsŏng*, October 1933, 127–133.

Yi Jong-Hwa. "Hyŏndae yŏnae sajo ŭi pip'an" (Criticism of the trend in contemporary romance). *Sin yŏsŏng*, June 1933, 10–13.

Yi Sŏk-Ch'ŏn. "Sekimal ŭi munhak sajo" (The trend of decadent literature). *Ch'ŏngnyŏn* 3, 4 (1923): 7–11.

Yi Sŏn-Hŭi. "Merime chak: *K'arŭmen* ŭi yojuinkong ŭi saengae" (Merimée's work: The life of the female protagonist of *Carmen*). *Yŏsŏng*, March 1939, 65–66.

———. "*Ren ŭi aega* rŭl ilkko" (On reading *The Wren's Elegy*). *Cho kwang*, May 1937, 224–245.

Yi Tae-Wi. "Hyŏndae Rŏsia munhak chung ŭi yŏmsaejuŭi" (Pessimism in contemporary Russian literature). *Ch'ŏngnyŏn* 3, 4 (1923): 11–16.

Yu Kak-Kyŏng. "Yŏja haebang kwa kyŏngje chayu" (Women's emancipation and economic freedom). *Ch'ŏngnyŏn* 6, 4 (1926): 5–7.

Yu Kyŏng-Sang. "Hyŏndae Miguk mundan yŏryu chakka" (Contemporary American women writers). *Sin kajŏng*, August and September 1933, 58–65, 150–157.

Yu U-Sang. "Yŏsŏng ŭi hyŏksin saenghwal (Ibsen ŭi yŏsŏngjuŭi)" (Innovative women's lifestyle [Ibsen's feminism]). *Sin yŏsŏng*, January 1926, 61.

Yun Kŭn. "Sŏngyok kwa yŏnae" (Sexual desire and romance). *Ch'ŏngnyŏn* 2, 1 (1922): 41–47.

Secondary Materials

An Yŏn-Sŏn. "Han'guk sikminji chabon chuŭihwa kwajŏng esŏ yŏsŏng nodong ŭi sŏngkyŏk e kwanhan yŏngu: 1930 nyŏndae pangjik kongŏp ŭl Chungsim ŭro" (The character of women's labor during the capitalistic phase of the Korean colonial period: Focusing on the textile industry in the 1930s). Master's thesis. Ewha Yŏja Taehakkyo, 1988.

Bassnett, Susan, and Harish Trivedi, eds. *Post-Colonial Translation: Theory and Practice*. New York: Routledge, 1999.

Bhabha, Homi K., ed. *Nation and Narration*. London: Routledge, 1990.

Chai, Alice Yun. "Integrative Feminist Politics in the Republic of Korea." In West, ed., *Feminist Nationalism*.

Chatterjee, Partha. *The Nation and Its Fragments: Colonial and Postcolonial Histories*. Princeton: Princeton University Press, 1993.

Chin Tong-Hyŏk. "Yi Hyŏn-Bo yŏngu" (Research on Yi Hyŏn-Bo). In *Sijo munhak yŏngu* (*Sijo* literature), 325–355. Ed. Kukŏ Kukmunhakhoe. Seoul: Chŏngŭm Munhwasa, 1985.

Cho Dong-Il. *Han'guk munhak t'ongsa* (Complete history of Korean literature). Vol. 1, 2d ed., 1989; vol. 2, 2d ed., 1989; vol. 3, 2d ed., 1989; vol. 4, 3d ed., 1994; vol. 5, 3d ed., 1994. Seoul: Chisik Sanŏpsa.

Ch'oe Hye-Sil. *Sin yŏsŏng dŭlŭn muŏs ŭl kkumkkuŏssnŭnga* (What were the new women dreaming about?) Seoul: Saenggak ŭi Namu, 2000.

Ch'oe Suk-Kyŏng and Ha Hyŏn-Kang. *Han'guk yŏsŏngsa* (History of Korean women). Seoul: Ewha Yŏja Taehakkyo Ch'ulp'anbu, 1993.

Ch'oe Ŭn-Hŭi. *Han'guk Kaehwa yŏsŏng yŏljŏn* (Biographies of Korean women of the *Kaehwa* period). Seoul: Chŏngŭmsa, 1985.

Chŏn Kyu-T'ae. *Han'guk kojŏn munhaksa* (History of traditional Korean literature). Seoul: Yemungwan, 1986.

Chŏng Yŏng-Ja. *Han'guk yŏsŏng siin yŏngu* (Korean women poets). Seoul: P'yŏngminsa, 1996.

Deuchler, Martina. "The Tradition: Women during the Yi Dynasty." In *Virtues in Conflict: Tradition and the Korean Woman Today*, 1–47. Ed. Sandra Mattielli. Seoul: Samhwa Publishing, 1977.

Eckert, Carter J., et al. *Korea Old and New: A History*. Seoul: Ilchokak Publishers, 1990.

Even-Zohar, Itamar. "Laws of Literary Interference." *Poetics Today* 11, 1 (1990): 53–72.

Ewha paeknyŏnsa P'yŏnch'an Wiwŏnhoe. *Ewha paeknyŏnsa* (Ewha one hundred year history). Seoul: Ewha Yŏja Taehakkyo Ch'ulp'anbu, 1994.

Flotow, Luise von. *Translation and Gender: Translating in the "Era of Feminism."* Manchester: St. Jerome Publishing, 1997.

Gilmartin, Christina K. et al, eds. *Engendering China: Women, Culture and the State*. Cambridge, Mass.: Harvard University Press, 1994.

Guillemin, Henri. *The True History of Joan "Of Arc."* Trans. William Oxferry. London: George Allen and Unwin, 1972.

Han'guk Yŏryu Munhakinhoe. *Yŏkdae Han'guk yŏryu 101 in sisŏnjip* (Anthology of 101 Korean women poets). Seoul: Hallim Ch'ulp'ansa, 1986.

Han'guk Yŏsŏng Yŏnguhoe. *Han'guk yŏsŏngsa* (History of Korean women). Volume on modern period. Seoul: P'ulbit, 1992.

Hermans, Theo. *Translation in Systems: Descriptive and System-Oriented Approaches Explained*. Manchester: St. Jerome Publishing, 1999.

———, ed. *The Manipulation of Literature: Studies in Literary Translation*. London: Croom Helm, 1985.

Hŏ Mi-Ja. *Han'guk yŏsŏng munhak yŏngu* (Korean women's literature). Seoul: T'aehaksa, 1996.

Hwang Do-Kyŏng. *Uri sidae ŭi yŏsŏng chakka* (Women writers of our era). Seoul: Munhak Kwa Chisŏngsa, 1999.

Hyun, Theresa. "Byron Lands in Korea: Translation and Literary/Cultural Changes in Early Twentieth-Century Korea." *Traduction, terminologie, rédaction* 10, 1 (1997): 283–299.

Hyun, Theresa, and José Lambert, eds. *Translation and Modernization*. Tokyo: University of Tokyo Press, 1995.

Jayawardena, Kumari. *Feminism and Nationalism in the Third World.* London: Zed Books, 1986.

Kang Yŏng-Ju. "Aeguk kyemonggi ŭi chŏngi munhak" (Biographies in the period of patriotic enlightenment). In *Chŏnhwangi ŭi Tongasia munhak* (East Asian literature in the transitional period), 171–197. Ed. Im Hyŏng-T'aek and Ch'oe Wŏn-Sik. Seoul: Ch'angjak kwa Pip'yŏngsa, 1985.

Kim Bok-Sun. "Chibae wa haebang ŭi munhak, Kim Myŏng-Sun ron" (The literature of domination and liberation, Kim Myŏng-Sun). *P'eminijŭm kwa sosŏl pip'yŏng* (Feminism and fiction criticism), 27–77. Ed. Han'guk Yŏsŏng Sosŏl Yŏnguhoe. Seoul: Hangilsa, 1995.

Kim Byŏng-Ch'ŏl. *Han'guk kŭndae pŏnyŏk munhaksa yŏngu* (History of modern Korean literary translation). Seoul: ŭlyu Munhwasa, 1975 and 1988.

———. *Han'guk kŭndae sŏyang munhak iipsa yŏngu* (Introduction of Western literature in modern Korea). Vol. 2. Seoul: ŭlyu Munhwasa, 1982.

———. *Kŭndae sŏyang munhak iipsa yŏngu* (History of the introduction of modern Western literature). Vol. 1. Seoul: ŭlyu Munhwasa, 1980.

Kim Byŏng-Kuk. *Han'guk kojŏn munhak ŭi pip'yŏngjŏk ihae* (A critical understanding of traditional Korean literature). Seoul: Seoul Taehakkyo Ch'ulp'anbu, 1995.

Kim, Elaine H., and Chungmoo Choi, eds. *Dangerous Women: Gender and Korean Nationalism.* New York: Routledge, 1998.

Kim Hae-Sŏng. *Yŏsŏng kwa munhak* (Women and literature). Seoul: Taegwang Munhwasa, 1985.

Kim Hak-Ju. "Yang Kye-Ch'o ŭi munhak sasang" (The literary thought of Liang Chi-Chao). In *Chŏnhwangi ŭi Tongasia munhak* (East Asian literature in the transitional period), 306–328. Ed. Im Hyŏng-T'aek and Ch'oe Wŏn-Sik. Seoul: Ch'angjak kwa Pip'yŏngsa, 1985.

Kim Hŭng-Kyu. *Han'guk munhak ŭi ihae* (Understanding Korean literature). Seoul: Minŭmsa, 1986.

Kim Hŭng-Su. "Munch'e ŭi pyŏnhwa" (Stylistic change). In *Kukŏsa yŏngu* (History of the Korean language), 955–1021. Ed. Kukŏsa P'yŏnch'an Wiwŏnhoe. Seoul: T'aehaksa, 1997.

Kim Hyŏn and Kim Yun-Sik. *Han'guk munhaksa* (The history of Korean literature). Seoul: Minŭmsa, 1973.

Kim Hyŏn-Sil. "1920 nyŏndae pŏnyŏk Miguk sosŏl yŏngu, kŭ suyongyangsang mit yŏnghyang ŭi ch'ukmyŏn esŏ" (Reception and influence of translated American fiction in the 1920s). Master's thesis. Ewha Yŏja Taehakkyo, 1980.

Kim Ju-Su. "Han'guk kŭndae yŏsŏng ŭi pŏpjesang ŭi chiwi" (The position of modern Korean women in the legal system). In *Han'guk kŭndae yŏsŏng yŏngu* (Modern Korean women), 7–39. Ed. Pak Yŏng-Hye. Seoul: Sukmyŏng Yŏja Taehakkyo Ch'ulp'anbu, 1987.

Kim Mi-Hyŏn. *Han'guk yŏsŏng sosŏl kwa p'eminijŭm* (Korean women's fiction and feminism). Seoul: Singu Munhwasa, 1996.

Kim Tong-Uk, and Hwang P'ae-Kang. *Han'guk kososŏl ipmun* (Introduction to traditional Korean fiction). Seoul: Kaemunsa, 1985.

Kim Ŭn-Jŏng. "Yŏsŏngjŏk chaa ro ŭi chŏpgŭn" (Approaches to feminine identity). In *Han'guk yŏsŏng munhak pip'yŏng ron* (Criticism of Korean women's literature). Ed. An Suk-Wŏn et al. Seoul: Kaemunsa, 1995.

Kim Yong-Jik. *Han'guk hyŏndae si yŏngu* (Modern Korean poetry). Seoul: Iljisa, 1991.

Kim Yŏng-Jŏng. "Han'guk kŭndae ŭi yŏsŏng undong" (Modern Korean women's movement). In *Yŏsŏng Hak* (Women's studies), 205–229. Ed. Chŏng Ŭi-Suk. Seoul: Ewha Yŏja Taehakko Ch'ulp'anbu, 1983.

Kim Yŏng-Min. *Han'guk kŭndae sosŏlsa* (History of modern Korean fiction). Seoul: Sol, 1997.

Kim Yu-Sŏn. "Mo Yun-Suk si yŏngu" (Mo Yun-Suk's poetry). Doctoral dissertation. Sukmyŏng Yŏja Taehakkyo, 1992.

Kim Yung-Hee. "Under the Mandate of Nationalism: Development of Feminist Enterprises in Modern Korea, 1860–1910." *Journal of Women's History* 7, 4 (1995): 120–136.

Kuksa Taesajŏn P'yŏnch'an Wiwŏnhoe. *Han'guksa taesajŏn* (Dictionary of Korean history). Seoul: Koryŏ Ch'ulp'ansa, 1996.

Kwŏn O-Man. *Kaehwagi siga yŏngu* (Kaehwa period poetry). Seoul: Saemunsa, 1989.

Lambert, José, and Hendrik van Gorp. "On Describing Translations." In Hermans, ed., *Manipulation,* 42–53.

Lee Ki-Baik. *Han'guksa sin ron* (A new history of Korea). Seoul: Ilchokak, 1984.

———. *A New History of Korea.* Trans. Edward W. Wagner and Edward J. Shultz. Seoul: Ilchokak, 1984.

Lefevere, André. "Why Waste Our Time on Rewrites? The Trouble with Interpretation and the Role of Rewriting in an Alternative Paradigm." In Hermans, ed., *Manipulation,* 215–243.

McCann, David R. "Formal and Informal Korean Society: A Reading of Kisaeng Songs." In *Korean Women: View from the Inner Room,* 129–137. Ed. Laurel Kendall and Mark Peterson. New Haven: East Rock Press, 1983.

Mun Sŏng-Suk. *Kaehwagi sosŏlron yŏngu* (Kaehwa period fiction). Seoul: Saemunsa, 1994.

Mun Yŏng-O. "Kosan Yun Sŏn-Do ŭi tanga yŏngu" (Tanga of Kosan Yun Sŏn-Do). In *Sijo munhak yŏngu* (Sijo literature), 296–324. Ed. Kukŏ Kukmunhakhoe. Seoul: Chŏngŭm Munhwasa, 1985.

O Se-Ŭn. "Pak Wan-Sŏ sosŏl sok ŭi ŏmŏni wa ttal mot'ipŭ" (The mother and daughter motif in Pak Wan-Sŏ's fiction). In *Han'guk yŏsŏng munhak pip'yŏng ron* (Criticism of Korean women's fiction), 219–241. Ed. An Suk-Wŏn et al. Seoul: Kaemunsa, 1995.

Paik Nak-Chung. "Nations and Literatures in the Age of Globalization." In *The Cultures of Globalization,* 218–229. Ed. Fredric Jameson and Masao Miyoshi. Durham: Duke University Press, 1998.

Pak Byŏng-Ch'ae. "Han'gŭl munhwa hyŏngsŏng kwa minjok chŏngsin" (The formation of Korean culture and the national spirit). In Kim Min-Su et al., eds., *Kukŏ wa minjok munhwa,* 55–62.

Pak On-Ja, "Miguk munhak chakp'um ŭi han'gukŏ pŏnyŏkbon e kwanhan sŏji yŏngu" (Bibliographical research on the translation of American literary works into Korean). Doctoral dissertation. Yŏnse Taehakkyo, 1989.

Pak Yŏng-Hye, and Sŏ Jong-Ja. "Kŭndae yŏsŏng ŭi munhak hwaldong" (Literary activities of modern women). In *Han'guk kŭndae yŏsŏng yŏngu* (Modern Korean women), 185–237. Ed. Sukmyŏng Yŏja Taehakkyo Asea Yŏsŏng Munje Yŏnguso. Seoul: Sukmyŏng Yŏja Taehakkyo, 1987.

Pak Yong-Ok. "1905–10, Sŏgu kŭndae yŏsŏngsang ŭi ihae wa insik, Chang Ji-Yŏn ŭi *Yŏja dokbon* ŭl chungsim ŭro" (The understanding and awareness of images of modern Western women from 1905 to 1910, focusing on Chang Ji-Yŏn's *Women's Reader*). In *Yŏsŏng kwa munhak, kŭndae p'yŏn* (Women and literature, modern times), 197–231. Ed. Sŏngsin Yŏja Taehakkyo Inmun Kwahak Yŏnguso. Seoul: Sŏngsin Yŏja Taehakkyo Ch'ulp'anbu, 1993.

———. "1920 nyŏndae han'guk yŏsŏng tanch'e undong" (The Korean women's movement in the 1920s). In *Han'guk kŭndae yŏsŏng yŏngu* (Modern Korean women), 239–277. Ed. Sukmyŏng Yŏjā Taehakkyo Asea Yŏsŏng Munje Yonguso. Seoul: Sukmyŏng Yŏja Taehakkyo, 1987.

Pak Yŏng-Shin. "Kidokkyo wa Han'gŭl undong" (Christianity and the Han'gŭl movement). In *Kidokkyo wa Han'gŭl yŏksa* (Christianity and Han'gŭl history), 41–69. Ed. Yu Dong-Sik et al. Seoul: Yŏnse Taehakkyo Ch'ulp'anbu, 1997.

Prasad, Deobrata. *Sarojini Naidu and Her Art of Poetry.* Delhi: Capital Publishing, 1988.

Pyŏn Shin-Wŏn. "Tongbanja chakka ka pon pingung kwa yŏsŏng ŭi hyŏnsil" (A socialist author's view of poverty and the situation of women). In *P'eminijŭm kwa sosŏl pip'yŏng* (Feminism and fiction criticism), 165–215. Ed. Han'guk Yŏsŏng Sosŏl Yŏnguhoe. Seoul: Hangilsa, 1995.

Simon, Sherry. *Gender in Translation: Cultural Identity and the Politics of Transmission.* London: Routledge, 1996.

So Jae-Yŏng. *Chosŏnjo munhak ŭi t'amgu* (Chosŏn dynasty literature). Seoul: Asea Munhwasa, 1997.

Sŏ Jŏng-Ja. *Han'guk kŭndae yŏsŏng sosŏl yŏngu* (Modern Korean women's fiction). Seoul: Kukhak Charyowŏn, 1999.

Sŏng Hyŏn-Ja. *Sin sosŏl e mich'in manch'ŏng sosŏl ŭi yŏnghyang* (The influence of late Ching fiction on the new novel). Seoul: Chŏngŭmsa, 1985.

Song Ji-Hyŏn. *Tasissŭnŭn yŏsŏng kwa munhak* (Rewriting women and literature). Seoul: P'yŏngminsa, 1995.

Song Min-Ho. *Han'guk Kaehwagi sosŏl ŭi sajŏk yŏngu* (Historical research on Korean fiction of the Kaehwa period). Seoul: Iljisa, 1975.

Song Myŏng-Hŭi. *Munhak kwa sŏng ŭi ideollogi* (Literature and the ideology of sex). Seoul: Saemi, 1995.

Song Yŏng-Sun. *Mo Yun-Suk yŏngu* (Mo Yun-Suk). Seoul: Kukhak Charyowŏn, 1997.

Spence, Jonathan D. *The Search for Modern China.* New York: Norton, 1990.

Toury, Gideon. *Descriptive Translation Studies and Beyond.* Amsterdam: John Benjamins, 1995.

Wells, Kenneth M. *New God, New Nation: Protestants and Self-Reconstruction Nationalism in Korea 1896–1937.* Honolulu: University of Hawai'i Press, 1990.

West, Lois A., ed. *Feminist Nationalism.* New York: Routledge, 1997.

Yi Ho-Suk. "Wiakjŏk chagi pangŏgije rŏso ŭi erot'ijŭm, Na Hye-Sŏk ron"

(Eroticism as a defense mechanism in Na Hye-Sŏk's works). In *P'eminijŭm kwa sosŏl pip'yŏng* (Feminism and fiction criticism), 79–121. Ed. Han'guk Yŏsŏng Sosŏl Yŏnguhoe. Seoul: Hangilsa, 1995.

Yi Hye-Sun. "Hanjung sosŏl ŭi pigyo munhak" (Comparative literary studies of Korean and Chinese fiction). In *Kojŏn sosŏl yŏngu* (Traditional fiction), 304–339. Ed. Hwakyŏng Kojŏn Munhakhoe. Seoul: Iljisa, 1993.

Yi Hye-Sun and Chŏng Ha-Yŏng. *Han'guk kojŏn yŏsŏng munhak ŭi segye* (The world of traditional Korean women's literature). Seoul: Ewha Yŏja Taehakkyo Ch'ulp'anbu, 1998.

Yi Hye-Sun et al. *Han'guk kojŏn yŏsŏng chakka yŏngu* (Traditional Korean women writers). Seoul: T'aehaksa, 1999.

Yi Hyo-Jae. *Han'guk ŭi yŏsŏng undong* (The women's movement in Korea). Seoul: Chŏngusa, 1989.

Yi Ik-Sŏp, Yi Sang-Ŏk, and Ch'ae Wan. *Han'guk ŭi ŏnŏ* (The language of Korea). Seoul: Singu Munhwasa, 1997.

Yi Jae-Sŏn. *Han'guk hyŏndae sosŏlsa* (The history of modern Korean fiction). Seoul: Hongsŏngsa, 1979.

———. *Han'guk hyŏndae sosŏlsa* (The history of modern Korean fiction). Seoul: Minŭmsa, 1991.

———. *Han'guk Kaehwagi sosŏl yŏngu* (Kaehwa period Korean fiction). Seoul: Ilchokak, 1993.

Yi Jae-Sŏn, Kim Hak-Tong, and Pak Jong-Ch'ŏl. *Kaehwagi munhak ron* (Kaehwa period literature). Seoul: Hyŏngsŏl Ch'ulp'ansa, 1994.

Yi Jong-ŭn. "Sijo munhak e nat'anan ŭnil sasang" (Hermitic thought in Sijo). In *Sijo munhak yŏngu* (Sijo literature), 172–191. Ed. Kukŏ Kukmunhakhoe. Seoul: Chŏngŭm Munhwasa. 1985.

Yi Jong-Wŏn. "Ilje ha Han'guk sin yŏsŏng ŭi yŏkhal kaldŭng e kwanhan yŏngu, 1920 nyŏndae rŭl chungsim ŭro" (Role conflicts and the new women in Korea under Japanese colonialism, focusing on the 1920s). Master's thesis. Han'guk Chŏngsin Munhwa Yŏnguwŏn, 1982.

Yi Kyŏng-Sŏn. *Han'guk munhak kwa chŏnt'ong munhwa* (Korean literature and traditional culture). Seoul: Singu Munhwasa, 1988.

Yi Sung-Nyŏng et al., eds. *Kukŏ kukmunhak sajŏn* (Dictionary of Korean language and literature). Seoul: Singu Munhwasa, 1989.

Yi Yong-Ju. "Hanjaŏ ŭi saengsŏng kwa paldal" (The creation and development of Hanja expressions). In Kim Min-Su, et al., eds., *Kukŏ wa minjok munhwa*, 303–308.

Yi Yong-Nam. *Han'guk kŭndae munhak kwa chakka ŭsik* (The writers' thought and modern Korean literature). Seoul: Kukhak Charyowŏn, 1997.

Yun Hye-Wŏn. "Kaehwagi yŏsŏng kyoyuk" (Women's education in the Kaehwa period). In *Han'guk kŭndae yŏsŏng yŏngu* (Modern Korean women), 113–183. Ed. Pak Yŏng-Hye. Seoul: Sukmyŏng Yŏja Taehakkyo Ch'ulp'anbu, 1987.

Journals and Newspapers

Ch'angjo (Creation)
Changmich'on (Rose village)
Cho kwang (Morning light)
Ch'ŏngch'un (Youth)
Ch'ŏngnyŏn (Youth)
Chosŏn chungang ilbo (Chosŏn central daily), 1934–1935
Chosŏn ilbo (Chosŏn daily), 1924–1933
Chosŏn mundan (Chosŏn literary world)
Chungang (Center)
Chungoe ilbo (Domestic and international daily)
Ewha
Haeoe munhak (Foreign literature)
Hak ji kwang (Light of learning)
Haksaeng (Student)
Hansŏng chubo (Capital weekly)
Honam p'yŏngnon (Honam criticism)
Hwangsŏng sinmun (Capital gazette)
Hyŏndae p'yŏngnon (Contemporary criticism)
Kaebyŏk (Creation)
Kat'ollik ch'ŏngnyŏn (Catholic youth)
Kŭmsŏng (Venus)
Kyemyŏng (Civilization)
Maeil sinbo (Daily news)
Manguk puin (International women)
Pokŭm undong (Evangelical movement)
Samch'ŏlli (Three thousand li)
Sidae ilbo (The times)
Sin Chosŏn (New Chosŏn)
Sin ch'ŏnji (New world)
Sinhŭng Chosŏn (Rising Chosŏn)
Sin kajŏng (New family)
Sin saeng (New life)
Sin sosŏl (New novel)
Sin Tonga (New East Asia)
Sin yŏja (New woman)
Sin yŏsŏng (New woman)
Taehan maeil sinbo (Taehan daily news)
T'aesŏ munye sinbo (Journal of Western literature and art)
Tonga ilbo (East Asia daily), 1926–1949
Tonggwang (Eastern light)

Tongnip sinmun (The independent)
Yŏja kye (Women's world)
Yŏngdae (Spirit ground)
Yŏron (Women's views)
Yŏsŏng (Woman)

Index

102; translation of "A Red, Red Rose," 102
colonialism, 125-127; and women, 86, 114–115. See also Japan.
concubines, 104; and literature, 14; and Yi Ok-Bong, 14
Confucianist values, 9–10, 17

Ding Ling, 53
Dumas *fils'*, Alexandre, 67, 80

educational institutions, 84–85
Expressionist art, 113

feminine ideals (traditional): and Confucianist, 10, 11, 32–33; and *The Song of Ch'unhyang*, 80
feminism: and literature, 86, 115; and nationalism (*see* nationalism). *See* Key, Ellen; Kollantai, Alexandra
Flaubert, Gustave, 58

Gale, James Scarth, 62, 73
Gale, Zona, 51
genre: and Chinese poetry, 4; and fictional works (traditional), 143n. 3; and historical narratives and biographical works (*yŏysachŏn gi sosŏl*), 28; and shamanist narrative songs, 4; and women's writing, 76–77, 83, 98–105
Gibson, Wilfred Wilson, 74
Glasgow, Ellen, 51
Glenn, Isa, 51
Gourmont, Remy de, 68

Ha Mun-Ho, 54
Ha Ran-Sa, 50
Ham Dae-Hun, 52
Han Ch'ung-Hwa, 66, 80
Han Yong-Un, 124, 153n. 61
Henry, O., 63
Hermans, Theo, 63, 143n. 10
Hillmann, Mary, 62, 66

Hood, Thomas, 74. Works: "The Bridge of Sighs," 74, 79, 81; "The Song of the Shirt," 74, 81
Hopkins, Gerard Manley, 64, 66, 81
Horei, Horessŭ, 68
Hwang Ae-Dŏk, 48
Hwang Sin-Dŏk, 104
Hyŏn Ch'ŏl, 57

Ibsen, Henrik, 45, 55, 56

Japan, 24–25; and colonial rule, 42, 85; and translations, 21, 57, 87

Kang Kyŏng-Ae, 86, 115. Works: "The Broken Harp" ("P'akŭm"), 100; "Salt" (Sokŭm"), 100; "The Two Hundred Wŏn Manuscript Fee" ("Wŏngoryo ibaek wŏn"), 100; "The Underground Village" ("Chiha ch'on"), 100
Kasack, Hermann, 68, 76, 113
Key, Ellen, 53–54, 104, 111
Kim Byŏng Ch'ŏl, 62
Kim Han-Suk, 63, 66, 78, 79, 81
Kim Hwal-Ran, 105
Kim Il-Yŏp, 86, 102, 103–104; and women's rights, 44, 45, 47. Works: "The Death of a Young Girl" ("Ŏnŭ sonyŏ ŭi sa"), 99; "Love" ("Sarang"), 99; "My Views on Chastity," 45, 99; "The Need for Women's Education" ("Yŏja kyoyuk ŭi p'ilyo"), 99; "Our Demands and Claims as New Women" (Uri sin yŏja ŭi yogu wa chujang"), 99, 104; "Women's Self-Awakening" (Yŏja ŭi chagak"), 99
Kim Ja-Hye, 54, 66, 79, 80, 81, 104
Kim Jin-Sŏp, 77, 78, 113
Kim Ki-Jin, 82
Kim Ki-Rim, 78
Kim Kŭm-Ju, 67, 80, 81
Kim Kwang-Sŏp, 57
Kim Kyŏn-Sin, 67

About the Author

Theresa Hyun, who holds a doctorate in French literature, has written on the role of translation in bringing about cultural confrontations in Korea in the late nineteenth and early twentieth centuries. She lived for many years in Seoul, where she taught at Kyung Hee University. Currently an associate professor of Korean studies at York University in Toronto, she has organized a number of research projects and international conferences on Korean and cross-cultural studies.